Second Edition

Guided Discovery Activities for Elementary School Science

Arthur A. Carin
Queens College

Robert B. Sund

Merrill Publishing Company
A Bell & Howell Information Company
Columbus   Toronto   London   Melbourne

Cover Art: Michael Linley

Published by Merrill Publishing Company
A Bell & Howell Information Company
Columbus, Ohio 43216

This book was set in Souvenir Light.

Administrative Editor: Jeff Johnston
Production Coordinator: Carol Driver
Art Coordinator: Patrick Welch
Cover Designer: Brian Deep
Text Designer: Cynthia Brunk
Photo Editor: Gail Meese

Photo Credits: Ben Chandler/Merrill, p. 9; Corn's Photo
Service, p. 267; Bruce Johnson/Merrill, p. 123; Merrill, p.
285; Charles Quinlan/Merrill, p. 207; David Strickler, p.1

Library of Congress Catalog Card Number: 88-63748
International Standard Book Number: 0-675-20971-4
Printed in the United States of America
1 2 3 4 5 6 7 8 9—92 91 90 89

PREFACE

This textbook was designed to assist you in presenting to your students the wonder and enjoyment of investigating science. The emphasis presented in this book is for hands-on/minds-on, activity-based science teaching and learning. This approach is called **guided discovery teaching/learning.**

It is vital that you help your students develop an appreciation for the marvels of science while assisting them in learning basic scientific concepts, skills, and processes. You have probably seen that your students are naturally curious about their world, themselves, and how and why things occur. Help them to keep this quality by *actively* involving them in scientific processes.

If you would like additional help in organizing and planning to teach science in the elementary school using a hands-on/minds-on approach, you are urged to see these companion textbooks:

Carin and Sund, *Teaching Science Through Discovery, 6th ed.* (Columbus, Ohio: Merrill Publishing Co., 1989).

——, *Teaching Modern Science, 5th ed.* (Columbus, Ohio: Merrill Publishing Co., 1989).

It is important that you look at these activity lesson plans as resource materials only. Feel free to expand, change, and group them in any way that best meets your individual teaching style, your students' needs, and the type of science program your school requires. I encourage you to be as creative as you can be and hope that you will pass this encouragement along to your students.

You have permission to reproduce those parts of the discovery activities that your students can use directly in your classroom; however, they may *not* be further distributed or sold. Some of the information you will find useful for your own background. In using these activities with primary grades (where a student may not read or read well enough) or in upper grades (where a student may not read well enough), you can read the appropriate sections to the students. Some teachers have even put the directions on cassette audiotapes for students to use by themselves.

The most important element in these discovery activities is for children to discover concepts through actual physical and mental participation in the activities. Do not tell the children beforehand what they should expect to find. This robs them of the joy of discovery.

Keep this text handy on your desk and use the resources in it regularly. It will assist you in making science an exciting, instructive, and enjoyable experience for your wide range of students. In doing so, you will find that teaching science will be less frightening and more rewarding. I wish you much success with your science teaching and in experiencing the joys of seeing your students broadening their scientific knowledge and appreciation of this marvelous world of ours!

ACKNOWLEDGMENTS

First, I must thank my newly acquired computer before it eats all of the materials I put into it over the past months, including this acknowledgment. It is hard to imagine writing the previous edition without this wonderous tool. Of inestimable help with my computer problems was Richard Ohman, my son-in-law. Thanks also to Norman Bodek, President of Productivity, Inc., for supplying the computer, orienting me on its use, and providing the inspiration for me to grow and learn to use it.

The army of people at Merrill Publishing Company deserve meritorious awards for their efforts in putting together this attractive and readable text. Unfortunately, I do not know all their names, but I do wish to recognize those people with whom I worked so closely over the many stages of production: Naura Gillespie, former Editorial Assistant, who was always only a call away; Tim McEwen, former Editor-in-Chief, and Ann Mirels, Administrative Editor—Special Services, for their clear directions on how to successfully negotiate the maze of book production processes; Tanya Tiberi, Electronic Text Buyer, for advice and assistance in my leap to the high-tech world of computers; Jeff Johnston, Administrative Edi-

tor, for his quiet reminders of deadlines and for his encouragement; Patrick Welch, former Art Coordinator, and Cathy Watterson, Cover Designer, for their collaboration in making this book very attractive; and last, Jim Elliott, Copy Editor, and Carol Driver, Production Editor, for their direct involvement in attending to the countless details of edited manuscript, galleys, and page proofs, and of dovetailing the artwork. Their insights substantially contributed to making this edition so readable. Thank you all.

I would be remiss if I did not personally thank the following professors for reviewing my manuscript, sharing their expertise, and providing insightful suggestions that helped to improve this edition: Catherine Cleare, University of Connecticut; Phillip Heath, Ohio State University at Lima; Catherine Kuehn, University of South Carolina; George O'Brien, University of Pittsburgh; Richard Sloop, Frostburg State College; and Dennis Sunal, West Virginia University.

Sincere thanks to Phyllis Marcuccio, Director of National Science Teachers Association Publications, and Marie Barry of NSTA, for their assistance with obtaining permission to use materials from their excellent publications. Thanks, too, to Rita Peterson, Director of Teacher Education at the University of California at Irvine, who gave so freely of her time and materials from her outstanding book, *Science and Society: A Source Book for Elementary and Junior High School Teachers.*

During this revision my mother died, but she left me with a legacy of respect for hard work, of rugged individualism, and for doing the best you can in everything you attempt. This strengthened me constantly during the enormous time and effort required to write and publish this book.

It is vital that Terry, my wife, be given the Carin Medal of Honor for tolerating my daily 5AM forays into my computer room; for missing all the good movies, plays, dinner parties, and walks along the ocean beaches; and especially for her encouragement and assistance in my commitment to this text. I could not have done it without her, or our three children, all of whom continue to teach me so much and refuse to let me stop growing intellectually and personally: Jill for her boundless energy, creative aura, and ability to help me see and put ideas, concepts, and words into visual formats. Amy, and her husband Richard, for stimulating and expanding my horizons to sailing; computers; sampling new wines, foods, and life itself. Jon for introducing me to the fascinating world of electronic music and all the scientific wonders, excitement, and sensory stimulation it offers.

This textbook, therefore, is a product of all my exposures to the positive aspects of what science offers in my quest for understanding and appreciating this fabulous world. May you also partake fully of its riches and help your students to experience them. One purpose of science should be to encourage the affective aspects of life, such as the importance of humanity, respect and reverence for life, and taking time to "smell the flowers" along the way. Remember: Happiness is a way of travel, not a destination.

Arthur A. Carin

CONTENTS

Section 2—Quickie Starters and Guided Discovery Activities for Life Sciences
    123

Section 4—Guided Discovery Science Activities for Special Needs Children   267

Section 5—Piagetian Types of Guided Discovery Activities   285

INTRODUCTION

Seen only as a laundry list of theorems, science can be a bore. But as a "hands-on" adventure guided by a knowledgeable teacher, it can sweep children up in the excitement of discovery. Taught by the regular classroom teacher, it can illustrate the point that science is for everyone—not just scientists.[1]

WHAT IS THE GUIDED DISCOVERY APPROACH?

No one method of teaching science is best for *all* children, *all* of the time, under *all* situations. **Guided discovery teaching/learning,** however, has a number of advantages: students learn how to learn; learning becomes self-rewarding; students are active participants; learning is more transferable; learning builds positive self-concepts; learning by discovery avoids rote memory; and guided discovery learning helps individuals become more responsible for their own learning and as a result, helps them become autonomous persons. In addition, guided discovery science teaching/ learning incorporates the best of what we know about the processes and products of science, how children learn best, the goals and objectives of science, and the relationships among science, humanism, values, and our concerns about the environment.

Discovery teaching is not new. Socrates of ancient Greece, with his questioning style, in a sense used a discovery, nontelling approach of learning. More recently, John Dewey, the main spokesman for progressive education in the 1930s, advocated that children should "learn by doing," rather than be lectured to. Jean Piaget, Swiss psychologist, and Jerome Bruner, former Harvard psychologist, were responsible for a sharply increased interest in learning by discovery in the middle 1960s.

Discovery is the process by which the learner uses the mind in logical and mathematical ways to discover and internalize concepts and principles. For example, students may discover the existence of cells, that is, form a concept of cells; later, they may discover the scientific principle that cells come only from other cells. In addition to learning science concepts, the student learns how to learn. The more students are actively involved in solving problems, the more likely they are to learn to generalize what they have learned into a style of discovery that will serve them well throughout their lives.

To help you "sweep children up in the excitement of discovery" as described in the opening statement, this book contains classroom-tested guided discovery science activities for nursery or preschools, elementary schools (K–6), and middle or junior high schools (6–8). An important advantage of this approach is that teachers and students both are more interested when the learner has a chance to participate, on his or her own level, in physical and mental activities similar to those of scientists. Then your students are actively engaged in scientific processes.

All of the science activities included here have been tested by teachers and children in preschools, elementary schools, and middle or junior high schools. The teachers did not have any special preparation in science. In fact, science had not been part of their preparation for teaching or their curricula until these activities were introduced into their classrooms. Several teachers evaluated each activity; the activities were rewritten to incorporate their suggestions, and then these revised activities were retested. Although the activities were originally

[1]William J. Bennett, *First Lessons. A Report on Elementary Education in America* (Washington, D.C.: U.S. Government Printing Office, 1986), 27.

written for teacher demonstration, in most cases they have been modified to be used as guided discovery activities.

The object of the guided discovery activities is to have students discover the concepts in the course of doing the activity. *Don't tell* your class the purpose of the activity or what can be expected to happen. Before you go into your classroom to present a particular activity, read it thoroughly, however, and go through the steps in the activity. Pay particular attention to the questions. These are meant to be guide questions only. *Remember:* Although these activities have been tested in actual classroom situations, no teacher can be certain that a class will respond according to plan throughout an activity. Nor do you have to follow the activities exactly. The activities are intended only as a resource for ideas. You should modify these activities to meet the needs, interests, and abilities of your individual class.

Guided discovery activities need not be taught in the order presented and are meant as sample activities only. It is best to supplement and integrate discovery activities with many other curricular activities. After you have had experience with the sample activities, you will gain competence and confidence to design your own.

ORGANIZING, PLANNING, AND CONDUCTING HANDS-ON/MINDS-ON GUIDED DISCOVERY SCIENCE ACTIVITIES

Making your science teaching activity-centered means that a major part of it must involve hands-on/minds-on experience for your students. A great deal of thoughtful planning and organization is needed to convert a well-designed plan into enriching first-hand science experiences for children. Here are some guidelines in preparing hands-on/minds-on science experiences.

Planning and Organizing Hands-on/Minds-on Science Activities

1. Decide what you specifically want your students to learn.
2. Select a method by which you will introduce, orient, and structure your science activity.
3. Decide whether you should prepare a science activity sheet for children to use.
4. Work out the details of distribution and collection of science equipment and materials. Generally, it is much safer if children stay at their science activity stations (desks pushed together in a nonlaboratory room). Take supplies and materials to the science activity stations rather than having children come up for them. The same holds true for collection of materials at the conclusion of the lab activity.
5. Will your students work individually or in small groups? If groups are used, set them up so you have your "science leaders" in each group.
6. You should perform the science activity before presenting it to your class.

Preparation for Hands-on/Minds-on Science Activities

1. Make certain you have all necessary science equipment and supplies in sufficient amounts so all your students may participate in the lab activity. Whenever possible, have these at lab stations set up with equipment before the children come into the room.
2. Initial steps like boiling water, heating or cooling of materials, and double checking supplies should also be done before class.
3. If any chemicals are used, even diluted vinegar, make sure washing materials are available.
4. Whenever possible, substitute plastics for glassware. Be careful when using heat that

the plastics are able to withstand the temperatures.

5. Many elementary schools do not allow open flames, or limit their use to teacher-conducted activities only. Be sure to check this out before using open flames. Have a fire extinguisher available.

6. Avoid the use of electrical house current (110 volts) for children's lab activities. Use dry cells wherever possible when children are handling the equipment directly.

7. Assemble glass tubing and stoppers before class. It is convenient to store the assembled stoppers and tubing for later use, rather than to disassemble them after each use. (See following discussion for further suggestions on tubing and stoppers.)

Conducting Hands-on Activities Safely

Hands-on science activities are valuable learning opportunities for students. However, the possibilities for accidents do exist. These possibilities are greatly reduced when students learn and follow laboratory safety procedures. Remember, as a teacher, you are legally responsible for the well-being of your students. It is your duty to instruct students in safe laboratory procedures, to supervise them during these activities, and to maintain the laboratory equipment and environment to be as safe as possible.

The activities in this book are suggested for a range of grade levels. Only you can decide how appropriate each activity is for your own students. Consider the maturity levels and experiences of your students to decide if they can safely carry out each particular activity. Also evaluate your physical facilities to be sure they are adequate for the activity. Modify activities as necessary, or use them as teacher demonstrations if you feel students' safety might be compromised. If you and your students use the following safety guidelines, your laboratory experiences should be educational and accident-free.

1. Help your students see the purpose of the hands-on activity.

2. Check to see if all your students understand the procedures to be followed. Write the steps on the board or have your students refer to their hands-on data collection sheets, or both.

3. Introduce safety precautions before beginning any work. Some general safety precautions to follow are
   a. Stress the serious nature of lab work.
   b. Be sure that you and students use protective eye coverings (safety goggles) whenever hot or dangerous materials are handled, even during teacher demonstrations.
   c. All accidents, regardless of how slight, should be reported to you.
   d. Directions for making chemicals and using heat sources should be followed exactly. If children are not certain about something, they should ask you.
   e. Instruct children always to cut materials away from them, being careful to stay far enough away from other students to avoid cutting them.
   f. Young children in grades K–6 should not be allowed to insert glass tubing into stoppers. Teachers should follow these safety precautions when inserting glass tubing into stoppers.
      1) Use only glass tubing that is fire polished at both ends.
      2) Liberally lubricate the end of the glass tubing and the stopper hole with glycerine before inserting.
      3) After lubricating, start twisting the tubing into the stopper. Hold the tubing close to the end being inserted. This reduces chances of snapping off tubing.

4) Glass thermometers should be inserted in the same way.

5) Wrapping cloth around handles will give greater protection in case the tubing should snap.[2]

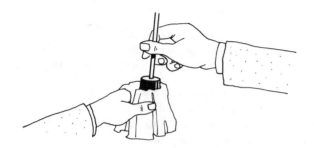

g. Avoid using strong acids. Whenever possible, use a substitute such as vinegar. If acids come in contact with skin, flush liberally with water and then use a baking soda solution to counteract the acid or vinegar.

h. Caution children not to smell or taste *anything* unless they know what it is and that it is safe. Tell them to read all labels carefully.

i. Make provisions for all broken glass, excess chemicals, and other waste materials to be placed in proper containers. Avoid throwing things into sinks.

j. Check to see that there is adequate ventilation in the room.

k. When heating a solution in a test tube, always point the test tube away from any individuals.

l. Tell the children never to mix chemicals unless you tell them to.

4. Move about the room throughout the lab activity to help, answer questions, prevent

discipline problems, and show or demonstrate.

5. Hold a discussion at the conclusion of the lab activity. Review what was learned and apply findings toward tentative conclusions or toward further study. Develop key concepts through artful questioning. Once these are developed, identify them by name. For example, if children doing a Science Curriculum Improvement Study (SCIS) activity observe a chameleon eating crickets, tell them that animals that eat other animals are called predators and those that are eaten are called prey.

FORMAT FOR GUIDED DISCOVERY RESOURCE ACTIVITIES

As used in this book, the ten major parts of the format for guided discovery resource activities are:

1. Age-Level Range or Group
2. Science Topics
3. Statement of Problem
4. What Do I Want Children to Discover?
5. Science Processes
6. What Will I Need?
7. What Will We Discuss?
8. What Will Children Do?
9. How Will Children Use or Apply What They Discover?
10. What Must I Know?/Where Do I Find It?

Here are some suggestions for getting started with guided discovery activities.

☐ Some of the information in items 1 to 10 in the previous list is to be used by you and some by your students. Only you can determine how much the students should receive.

☐ For upper elementary or middle/junior high school grades, you may wish to make copies of some sections for children to use.

---

[2]For specific information, see "Appendix E, Some Safety Suggestions," *Elementary Science Syllabus* (Albany, NY: The State Education Department, 1986), 49; and *Safety in the Elementary Science Classroom* (Washington, D.C.: National Science Teachers Association, 1978).

☐ For primary grades, or where your students may not read well enough (or at all), read the appropriate sections to your students. You can also put directions on audiocassettes for students to use by themselves.

☐ The most important element is for children to discover concepts through actual physical and mental participation in these activities. *Do not tell the children beforehand what will happen.* This robs them of the joy of discovery.

☐ Under item #10 are teaching tips to help you make your students' experiences as meaningful as possible. In addition, you should become as knowledgeable as possible about the science content, so that you can answer your students' questions and guide them to finding answers, but not necessarily to "lecture" them on the content. Some science content is given to you in **What Must I Know?/Where Do I Find It?** Science content is also presented in **What Do I Want Children to Discover?** However, limitations in any textbook mean that you must find science content in your classroom science textbook, children's trade books, and libraries. To assist you, several children's and/or adult science content books are listed in each activity as resources for building your science content background.

Other Less Structured Discovery Activities

In addition to the successful guided discovery hands-on activities of previous editions of this text, this edition includes samples of the following:

☐ Less structured, or "quickie," guided discovery activities for preschool, primary grades, open classrooms, and other classes for enrichment or fun with science.

☐ Guided discovery science activities for special needs children such as the blind or visually impaired, the deaf, and the physically, mentally, and emotionally handicapped.

☐ Piagetian-type guided discovery activities using specific Piagetian operations (i.e., classification, conservation, etc.) and suggestions on how to involve children in these processes.

The less structured, "quickie" starter guided discovery science activities are not meant to be exhaustive, but simply sample activities that

☐ Can be done informally with minimum planning and materials.

☐ Stimulate ideas that can lead to deeper investigations into a problem.

☐ Give children science enrichment opportunities.

☐ Provide fun and success in science.

☐ Supply motivation for "doing more science."

☐ Offer a wide range of individualizing science for your children.

Less structured activities contain fewer lesson plan details than guided discovery activities, using this format:

☐ Materials
☐ Opening Questions
☐ Some Possible Activities

You may want to develop detailed lesson plans yourself for these less structured activities using the guided discovery activity format just described. In doing so, explore other creative ways of using them, or where appropriate, use guided discovery science activities in the less structured format.

As with guided discovery science activities, less structured activities also start with opening questions to raise children's interest and motivation in the activity. Less structured activities are more open-ended and children are freer to wander and explore. For these reasons, less structured, "quickie" activities will be presented before more structured guided discovery activities, so you may use them as motivators and introductions to the more structured scientific investigations.

ORGANIZATION OF GUIDED DISCOVERY SCIENCE RESOURCE ACTIVITIES

It is impossible to know what specific science activities will be useful for all elementary school teachers in extremely varied teaching/learning environments. Therefore, the following guided discovery science activities are presented to you as *possible resources only.* As resources, they are ready for use or to be drawn upon and modified for your particular classroom teaching/learning needs. They are not intended to be a science curriculum. Grade levels are given in a range, as it is impossible to say categorically, "This is a first grade activity," and because different teachers may use all or part of the activity as presented. You are the only one who can determine which activity will fill your teaching needs. To assist you in making these decisions, guided discovery resource activities are organized in this way:

1. Activities are arranged in three general science groups:

Sections	Guided Discovery Activities
1	Physical Sciences
2	Life Sciences
3	Earth and Environmental Sciences

2. Within the three general science groups, activities are clustered around subgroups (i.e., under physical sciences, subgroups are matter and energy, air pressure, etc.).
3. Activities are arranged within subgroups by age range groups (i.e., K–3, 4–6, etc.).
4. Each activity is named with a question, such as "What Are Water Molecules and How Do They Affect Each Other?"
5. Each subgroup of science activities will start with several "quickie" starter activities, followed by the more structured guided discovery activities.
6. Throughout each section, you will follow an overall outline using the following format:

   ☐ General science group
   ☐ Science subgroup
   ☐ Quickie starters
   ☐ Guided discovery activities and age ranges

May you have enjoyable and productive science activities with your students!

SECTION 1

Quickie Starters and Guided Discovery Activities for Physical Sciences

MATTER AND ENERGY

Quickie Starters

Where Did the Water Go?

Materials

Sponges, paint brushes, dish cloths. This should be done on a hot day, outside the classroom

Opening Questions

What will happen to water if you brush it on different things outside? How can you find out?
Where do you think the water will disappear first? Why?

Some Possible Activities

Invite the children to take a paint brush, dip it in water, and brush it over several places to see what happens. Have them play a game to see whose water will disappear first. Have them feel the places where the water disappears rapidly and compare it with places where it doesn't seem to disappear as fast, for example, on hot sidewalks and in the shade. Have them repeat the activity but use sponges and washcloths instead of brushes. Have them place wet sponges on different places and determine which ones dry first.

How Can We Dry Clothes Faster?

Materials

Paper towels, different pieces of cloth (some that are thin and some that are thick like a towel), sponges, twine to hold the cloth, clothespins

Opening Questions

How can we make these wet?
How can we dry them?
How can we use the twine and clothespins to dry them?
Where is the best place to put the clothesline? Why?
Which things do you think will dry first?

Some Possible Activities

Ask the children to make the clothesline. Have them dip various things in water, drain them, and place them on the clothesline with clothespins.

Why Does Water Roll Off Some Things?

Materials

Waxed paper, paper towel, napkins, typing paper, plastic wrap, eye dropper, food coloring

Opening Questions

What will happen when you drop droplets of water on these different kinds of paper and plastic?
How can you find out?
What paper will hold the water the best?
What paper or plastic will water run off of the easiest?

Some Possible Activities

Have the students find which paper and plastic absorbs the water the best and the least. Have them play Water Droplet Chase. Use red food coloring to make some red drops and blue food coloring to

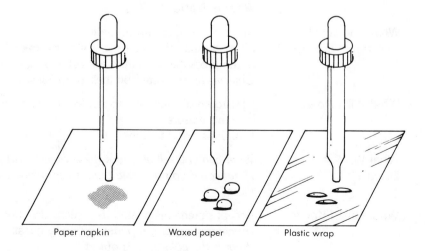

Paper napkin   Waxed paper   Plastic wrap

make some blue drops. Drop the water into separate droplets distant from each other on wax paper or plastic wrap. Place one red drop and several blue drops on the paper. Invite the students to capture all the blue drops, one at a time, with the red drop. Have the students make drop slides of the same lengths and inclinations. They can vary the material they use for the slide. Two students should compete with each other to see which slides the drops will move down the fastest.

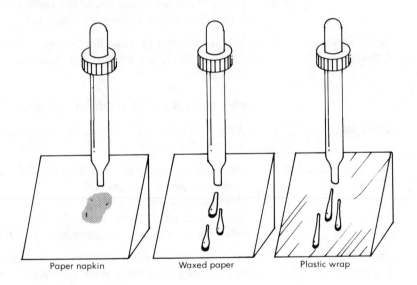

| Paper napkin | Waxed paper | Plastic wrap |

Guided Discovery Activities

What Is Matter? (K–3)

What Do I Want Children to Discover?	An object is made up of matter. All matter has characteristics called **properties.** Some properties of matter are color, size, shape, and texture. Objects can be sorted by their properties.
What Will I Need?	Classroom objects such as books, desks, chairs, pencils, and chalkboard erasers Box of assorted buttons
What Will We Discuss?	*What can you tell us about these objects as I point to them?* *How would you describe them to someone who had never seen them?*
What Must I Know?	Accept statements related to object's *use,* but encourage students to concentrate upon *properties* by using questions such as: *What is the color of this object?*

Is the object smooth or rough?
What is the shape of the object?
Is the object large or small?

After an appropriate amount of discussion, make a chart entitled "Properties of Objects." Encourage children to use the word *property* as they describe their selected object to be added to the properties chart. Reinforce the use of the word *property* by saying things such as, "Red and smooth are *properties* of this apple."

In a few weeks, as the list of property words increases, go over it with the class. Direct students to group property words under headings such as "size words," "color words," "shape words," "texture words."

What Will Children Do?	**PROCESSES***
	PART I
Describing	1. One student is leader and picks an object in the room and whispers it to teacher.
Describing	2. Leader tells the class in which part of the room (near radiator, front, back) the object is located. He or she gives clues about the object using *properties* without giving its name.
Inferring	3. After each clue, the class tries to guess the object picked.
What Must I Know?	Encourage children to concentrate on clues (properties) instead of simply guessing wildly. It works best if you allow only one or two guesses after each clue.
	4. First student to guess the object is the next leader.
	PART II
	1. Obtain a handful of buttons from your teacher.
Observing	*What are some of the properties of the buttons in front of you?*
	2. Group all buttons that have the same properties together.
Summarizing	*What are the properties you used to group your buttons?*
	3. Regroup your buttons using different properties or combinations of properties.
Comparing	*How do these piles of buttons differ from the ones you had first?*
How Will Children Use or Apply What They Discover?	1. Regroup your buttons by using *opposite* properties such as rough-smooth, large-small, shiny-dull.
What Must I Know?	Help children to see that opposite properties are comparative rather than absolute. An object grouped as small in one pile may be large

---

*Note: *Processes* in these activities refer to the italicized words that appear in the left-hand column.

when placed with different objects. As an example, point out that your desk is larger than almost any object in the room, but is smaller than the room itself.

What Are Molecules? (K–8)

What Do I Want Children to Discover?

All matter is composed of tiny particles called **molecules.**
Molecules are too small to be seen with the naked eye.
Sometimes matter is made up of only one kind of molecule and scientists called this matter an **element.**
Sometimes matter is made up of more than one kind of molecule and scientists call this matter **compounds.**
Molecules are almost always in motion.

What Will I Need?

Piece of coal or charcoal
Paper towel
Ether, alcohol, or perfume
Hammer
Shallow dish

What Will We Discuss?

Have you ever heard of molecules?
What do you know about molecules?

What Will Children Do?

PROCESSES

PART I

1. Obtain a piece of coal or charcoal (mostly carbon), a hammer, and a paper towel.
   Place the coal or charcoal on the paper towel and pound it with the hammer until you see fine coal dust.

Observing
Hypothesizing

How does the pounding change the coal?
Do you think you have made a new substance? Why do you think as you do?

Hypothesizing

2. *What would you have to do to change the coal to a new material?*

Hypothesizing

If you keep pounding the dust into smaller and smaller pieces, what will you ultimately end up with?

What Must I Know?

Explain that all elements are composed of tiny invisible particles. These tiny particles are called molecules. *Important:* Do not convey to the children the idea that the dust from the coal is a single molecule. Molecules are too small to be seen by the naked eye and must be seen through a microscope. The dust particles are aggregations or collections of molecules. (See the diagram.)

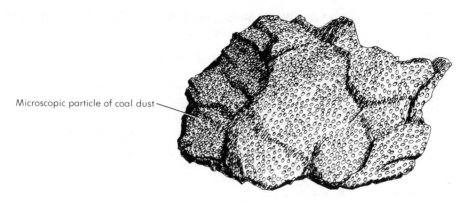

Microscopic particle of coal dust

PART II

1. Your teacher will pour a liquid into a shallow dish at the front of the classroom.
2. Raise your hand when you first notice an odor.

Observing

From the sequence or order in which hands are raised, can you determine the direction in which the smell travelled?

Inferring

Why do you think this happened?

What Must I Know?

A reasonable assumption is that a little of the liquid evaporates and escapes into the air. It may be pointed out that the liquid must have been made up of tiny invisible particles and that the tiny particles called molecules must be in motion.

Designing an investigation

3. *Can you think of some simple experiment to test the idea that molecules in liquids evaporate or go into the air at different rates?*

What Must I Know?

If children cannot come up with an experiment, then suggest they smear ether, alcohol, water, and oil on the chalkboard. Solicit guesses or hypotheses about which liquids will disappear or evaporate at which rates, and possibly why.

4. Test your experiment.

Applying

5. *How can you speed up or slow down the liquid molecules' disappearing or evaporating?*

How Will Children Use or Apply What They Discover?

1. *Why do you think clothes dry faster on sunny days? Windy days?*
2. *Which would you smell first if a small dish were placed in front of your classroom and you were in the back of the room: vinegar, ether, alcohol, or perfume? Why did you pick the one you did? What were you thinking?*

What Are Water Molecules and How Do They Affect Each Other? (K–8)

What Do I Want
Children to Discover?

The deeper the water, the greater the pressure.

Water has cohesive force.

A **force** is defined as push or pull on an object.

Molecules of the same substance tend to stick to each other because they are attracted by an invisible force.

Each molecule of the substance pulls other atoms to it.

The force of attraction between molecules of the same kind is called **cohesive force.**

What Will I Need?

Quart milk carton
Water (enough to fill containers as desired)
Pencil or nail
Ruler
Glass or plastic tumbler
Medicine dropper
Pan or bowl
12-inch squares of wax paper

What Will We
Discuss?

Why does a drop of water hold together as it runs down a window-pane?

Why are beads of water hemispherical, especially on a well-waxed automobile?

Why can some bugs walk on the top of water?

Why do you think drops of water from a medicine dropper are hemispherical?

PROCESSES

PART I

What Will Children
Do?

1. Obtain a 12-inch square of wax paper. Using a medicine dropper, place three or four drops of clean tap water on your wax paper.

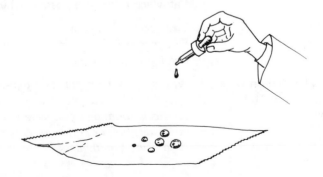

Observing   *How would you describe the shape of the water? What is its color?*

2. Push the drops of water around with a pencil point.,

Observing   *What happens to the water when you push the pencil point into a water droplet?*

Observing   *What happens when you push several droplets near each other?*
Hypothesizing   *Why do you think this happens?*

PART II

1. Obtain a glass or plastic tumbler and place it in a bowl or dish. Fill it completely full of water, until some water overflows.

Hypothesizing   *Do you think you can add any more water to the glass tumbler?*
Designing an   *Can you think of how you might test your hypothesis or guess*
investigation   *what will happen?*

2. Test your hypothesis or try this one.
   Using a medicine dropper, *slowly* drop water into the glass from about ½ inch above the water level of the glass. (See diagram.)

Measuring   *How many drops of water can you add after the glass is "full"?*
Observing   *How would you describe the shape of the water above the rim of the glass?*

Inferring   *Why does the water rise above the rim of the glass?*
Observing   *At what point does the water run over the rim of the glass?*
Inferring   *Why do you think the water finally runs over the rim of the glass?*

PART III

Hypothesizing   *If the side of a milk carton were punctured with holes (one above another) and the carton filled with water, what do you think would happen to the water in it? How would the water pour out of the holes?*

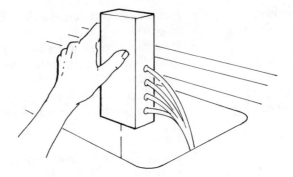

1. Obtain a clean milk carton that has the top cut out of it.
2. Puncture a hole with a pencil or nail from the bottom, about 1½ inches or 4 cm. Puncture three additional holes ½ inch apart above the preceding one. Put masking tape over holes. *Caution:* Do not make holes too large.
3. Over a sink, fill the container with water to within an inch of the top. Remove the masking tape.

Observing   *What do you notice about the way the water comes out of the holes of the carton?*

Inferring   *Why do you think the water comes out of the holes like this?*

Hypothesizing   *If the carton were filled closer to the top with water, do you think there would be a difference in the way the water comes out?*

4. Fill the carton until the water is closer to the top.

Observing   *What do you notice about the way the water comes out of the holes?*

Comparing   *Did you notice any difference in the water coming from the holes of the carton when there was less and when there was more water in it?*

Inferring   *What can you say about how water pressure varies with depth?*

Hypothesizing   *What results do you think you'd get if you used a gallon or half-gallon milk carton?*
     Try it and record your findings.

PART IV

1. Puncture holes in the bottom of the carton about 2–3 cm or 1 inch each apart as shown in the diagram. Put masking tape over holes. *Caution:* Do not make holes too large and make holes very close together.

Hypothesizing   *What do you think will happen when water is poured into this carton and the masking tape is removed?*

Hypothesizing   *How many jets of water will you get coming out of the holes in the bottom of the carton?*

*Observing
Designing an
investigation*

2. Pour water into the carton.
   How many jets of water come out?
   What should you do to the water pouring out of the carton at the bottom so you could only get one jet of water without plugging any holes?
3. Test your hypotheses.
4. Try the above using gallon or half-gallon cartons.

**What Must I Know?/
Where Do I Find It?**

The children should pour water into the carton and pinch the jets of water together with their fingers just as though they were going to pinch someone. The jets will form one stream. If the water comes out in one jet, there must be some kind of force holding the water together. The force that holds similar molecules to each other is called **cohesive force.** Each molecule of water has cohesive force that pulls and holds other molecules of water to it. See the diagram that represents how molecules of water are held together to form a water droplet due to cohesive force. The pinching of the water brings the jets of water in contact, allowing cohesive force to hold together. This is true because the cohesive force between two substances increases as the distance between them decreases.

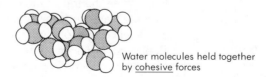

Water molecules held together
by <u>cohesive</u> forces

**How Will Children Use
or Apply What They
Discover?**

1. *Why do you think a dam is built with very thick walls at the bottom and thinner walls at the top?*
2. *Why do your ears sometimes hurt when you dive deep in a swimming pool? What pushes in on your ears as you go deeper?:*
3. *Why are the walls of a submarine so thick and strong?*

4. *What would happen to the water escaping from two of the holes of a can if you stopped one hole?*
5. *What will happen to the water coming out of the bottom hole as the water gets lower in the can?*
6. *Why do many towns have water storage tanks towering high above the city or built on a hill?*

What Causes the Molecules of a Liquid to Move? (4–8)

What Do I Want Children to Discover?

The molecules in liquids are constantly moving in a random pattern, or **Brownian movement.**
This motion is caused by heat.

What Will I Need?

Gallon aquarium or wide-mouthed jar
Water
India ink
Microscope or microprojector
Microscope slide
Pen

What Will We Discuss?

What would happen if you added a drop or two of ink to a bowl of water?
What would you do to find out?

What Will Children Do?

PROCESSES

PART I   MOLECULAR MOTION OF LIQUIDS
1. Fill a gallon aquarium or wide-mouthed jar with water.
2. Dip a piece of glass tubing into a bottle of India ink. (India ink is used because it is an oil-based ink and tends to hold together longer than water-based inks. Place your finger on top of the glass tubing and remove it from the ink bottle so that a column of ink, 2 or 3 inches in length, remains in the lower end of the tube. Wipe off the outside of the tube and, with your finger still in place, lower the tube *carefully* and slowly into the jar or aquarium. When the top of the column of ink inside the tube is level with the water surface, remove your finger for a moment and allow a *few* drops to flow downward without mixing with the water. Replace your finger on the tube and remove the tube carefully.

Observing

Do you see a few drops of ink suspended near the center of the jar?
3. Watch the aquarium or jar for several minutes without moving or shaking it.

Hypothesizing
Observing

Why has the ink gradually moved to all parts of the water?
How long does it take for the color of the ink to be uniformly distributed throughout the aquarium or jar?

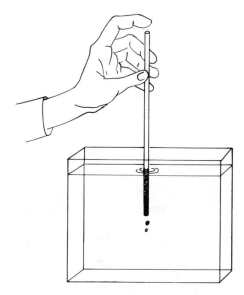

PART II THE MOVEMENT OF WATER MOLECULES

Applying
1. Obtain a microscope or microprojector, a microscope slide, a pen, water, and India ink.
2. Place a drop of water on the microscope slide. Dip only the tip of your pen into the India ink. Place the tip of the pen into the drop of water on the microscope slide. Place as little ink in the water as possible.

Hypothesizing
What do you think is happening to the ink and the water?

What Must I Know?
Caution students about being careful when focusing and handling the microscope. Check to make sure the students are seeing what is expected. If your students are not mature enough or skillful enough with the microscope, you can set the entire activity up on a *microprojector*. In this way, the entire class could view the same activity projected on a screen.

3. Carefully place the slide, with the drop of water and the ink, on the microscope stand. Focus the microscope on the drop. *Caution:* Do not crash the microscope lens into your slide.

Observing
4. Observe the ink in the water.

Observing
What are the particles of ink doing?

Observing
How are they moving?

Inferring
How is this motion caused?

Inferring
What evidence is there that the molecules of water may also be moving?

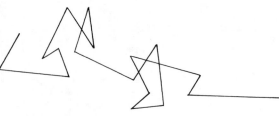

Brownian movement
of a molecule

What Must I Know?

The motion the children see is Brownian movement, which means there is random movement of molecules.

What Are Atoms? (4–8)

What Do I Want Children to Discover?

Changing the size of an object does not change its physical characteristics.

All elements are composed of atoms.

An **atom** is very small.

Atoms are grouped in various ways to make **molecules.**

An atom is made up of electrons, protons, and neutrons.

Negatively charged bodies have more electrons than protons.

Electrons are negatively charged particles.

Protons are positively charged particles.

Neutrons have neither a positive nor a negative charge.

What Will I Need?

Wooden block or lump of clay

2 wire clothes hangers

Picture of solar system

Styrofoam ball about the size of a Ping-Pong ball

6 rubber jack balls or Styrofoam balls that size

Wire cutters

What Will We Discuss?

What do you know about atoms?

What do you think an element is?

What do you think an electron is?

What do you think protons and neutrons are?

How big do you think an atom is?

What do you know about molecules?

What Must I Know?

Atoms are very small. The thickness of a human hair probably contains at least 500,000 atoms. An atom consists of fundamental particles called electrons, protons, and neutrons. Protons and neutrons are found in the center (or nucleus) of the atom and electrons revolve around the nucleus. The revolving electrons are grouped together in shells or orbits around the nucleus. The neutron has nearly the same mass as the proton and, as could be guessed from its name, is electrically neutral and carries no charge. The nucleus contains most of the weight or matter and is the most important part of the atom. Therefore, the nucleus is also the heaviest part of an atom. When an atom is neutral, it has an equal number of electrons and protons. If there are more electrons, the atom is negatively charged. All atoms have a tendency to balance the number of electrons and protons by drawing electrons or giving off extra ones, and in the process become neutral.

What Will Children Do?

PROCESSES

1. Obtain a wire clothes hanger, a block of wood or lump of clay, Styrofoam or Ping-Pong balls, and 6 rubber jack balls. Assemble the materials as shown in the diagram.

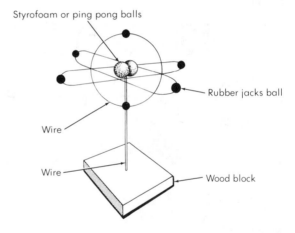

Styrofoam or ping pong balls

Rubber jacks ball

Wire

Wire

Wood block

Inferring

2. *In what ways is your model different from a real atom?*

What Must I Know? Where Do I Find It?

All the particles in the atom would be in motion. The orbits the electrons follow would not be so definite as those formed by the wire in the student model.

Hypothesizing

3. *How could you improve the model shown in the diagram?*
4. Look at a picture of our solar system.

Comparing

What do you notice about the solar system that can be said about an atom?

Comparing

5. *In what ways is the solar system different from an atom?*

Comparing

How is it similar?

Reference Books—Water Franklyn M. Branley, *Water for the World* (New York: Harper and Row, 1982). Alfred Leutscher, *Water* (New York: Dutton, 1983).

THERMAL ENERGY (HEAT)

Quickie Starters

What Does Heat Do to Corn Kernels?

Making different types of foods helps children see how things can be changed and helps them develop a better understanding of how their *actions* can cause an effect.

The children should prepare and mix the ingredients as much as possible. Make a series of experience charts using diagrams to illustrate the steps they need to follow in preparing them. For example, a chart for popcorn is shown in the following diagram:

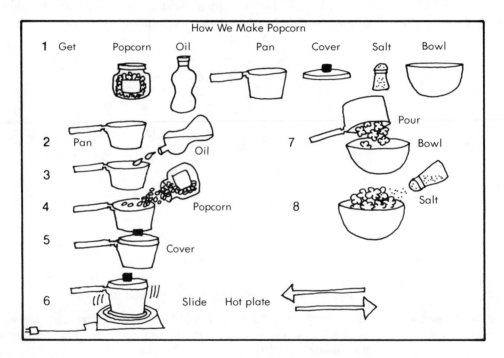

Materials	Popcorn, pan with a cover, cooking oil, heat source. (*Important:* Do NOT use an open-coil electric hotplate.) For safer activity use hot-air popcorn maker.			
Opening Question	*What can we do to make popcorn?*			
Some Possible Activities	Place the popcorn in a pan with a little oil and move it back and forth over the heat source. Invite the children to listen for evidence that the corn is popping; ask them when they think the corn is done and ask how the corn has changed. Have the children draw how the popcorn has changed.			

How Does Heat Change Dough to Bread?

Materials	Things needed to make bread. See recipe book for directions.
Opening Question	*How can we make bread?*
Some Possible Activities	Make bread. Bake some for different lengths of time. Invite children to compare the different effects. (*Hint:* Use an electric slow cooker and breads can be made in the classroom in 1–2 hours.)

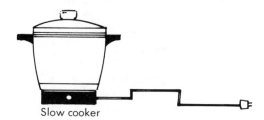

Slow cooker

How Does Taking Heat Away Make Ice Cream and Ice Pops?

Materials	Cookbook, with instructions for making ice cream; fruit juices, straws or popsicle sticks to stick in the ice trays.
Opening Questions	*What is your favorite food?* *How many of you like ice cream?* *How can we make ice cream?* *How many of you like popsicles?* *How can we make some popsicles?*
Some Possible Activities	Invite the children to make different kinds of ice cream. They should mix the different ingredients and note what different things they add. You might give them nuts, pieces of candy, coconut, dried fruit, chocolate, caramel, and so on that they can add as they wish. For ice pops, provide the children with different juices and tell them they can make the popsicles any way they want. Invite them to try to make different shapes and colors, or to add small pieces of fruit, for example, pineapple. Let some of the popsicles melt and ask the children what they think will happen if the melted popsicles are put back in the refrigerator or freezer again.

Guided Discovery Activities

What Is Thermal Energy or Heat? (K–8)

What Do I Want Children to Discover?

When an object is heated, its molecules move faster or vibrate more. When an object is cooled, its molecules move more slowly.

Heat is the total energy an object has because of the motion of its molecules.

What Will I Need?

Small wooden board
12 baby-food jars
Tea bags
Pencils
Sandpaper
Sugar cubes
2 Pyrex or tin pans
Colored cinnamon candies

PROCESSES

What Will Children Do?

Hypothesizing

PART I

What do you think a board will feel like after you rub it very rapidly with sandpaper?

1. Obtain a board and a sheet of sandpaper.
2. Feel the board and the sandpaper.

Observing
   Are they warm?

3. Using the sandpaper, sand the board very rapidly.

Observing
Inferring
Designing an investigation
   Immediately feel the sanded board and the sandpaper.
   Why does the board feel the way it does? The sandpaper?

4. *Can you think of some other things that can be rubbed together to show the same thing?*
   Try rubbing your hands together very rapidly for one half minute.

Observing
   What do you feel?

Hypothesizing
   Why do you think you felt what you did?

What Must I Know?

When the board or hands were rubbed, molecules were agitated and therefore vibrated more, producing heat. The board, when touched, produced the sensation of being warmer, as did the hands when rubbed.

PART II

Hypothesizing
Designing an investigation

What caused the molecules to move?
How could we set up an experiment to test the effect of heat on movement of molecules in a liquid?

1. Fill three baby-food jars or plastic tumblers with water to within ½ inch (1 cm) of the top and let them stand until the water is room temperature.
2. *Slowly* lower a sugar cube, a handful of cinnamon candies, and a tea bag into the baby-food jars or tumblers. (See diagram.)

EXPERIMENT: Substances dissolving without stirring

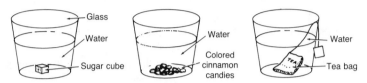

Make certain that the jars are in a spot where they will *not* be moved or jostled.

3. Set up the identical jars and materials as above but this time stir the jars until the materials dissolve, as shown in the diagram.

CONTROL: Substances dissolving with stirring

This is called a **controlled experiment** in science.

Hypothesizing

Why do you think it is called this?

4. Taking one-hour observations, record how long it takes for the experimental jars to look like the control jars.

Hypothesizing
Inferring

Which materials do you think will dissolve first? Why?
Would the results be different if hot water were used? If cold water were used? Why?

Designing an investigation

How could we test this?

PART III

1. Set up two more sets of jars with sugar, cinnamon candies, and tea bags.
2. Place one set in ice-cold water in a pan and the other in a pan of very hot water.

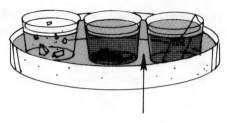 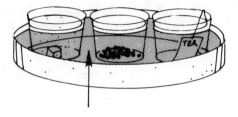

Hot water   Cold water

Hypothesizing	*In which jars—in pans of hot or cold water—will the materials dissolve first?*
Inferring	*What does the hot water in the pan do to the molecules in the baby-food jars?*

What Must I Know?

This is a review of the concept of the continuous movement of particles suspended in a liquid, called **Brownian motion.** It also introduces several new concepts. Children will be helped to see that increasing the motion of molecules generates considerable heat. Conversely, matter that displays greater heat has greater movement of its molecules. In addition, the concept of a control is used as a standard against which scientists check their experimental work. If you think your students are ready, you can introduce the concept of **variables.** For instance, in Part III, the variable being tested is heat and its effect upon dissolving.

How Will Children Use or Apply What They Discover?

1. *Why do you rub a match against the side of a match box?*
2. *Why don't matches catch fire sitting in a match box?*
3. *When you bend a wire back and forth several times, why does it get warm?*
4. *When you put two pencils together and rub them back and forth several times, what happens to your hands?*
5. *A person tried to strike a match against a piece of glass to light it. The match wouldn't light. Why?*
6. *If you feel the tires of your car before you take a trip and then just after you get out of the car, they will not feel the same. How do you think they will differ? How would you explain the difference?*
7. *A person was chopping wood with an axe. After chopping very hard for about 10 minutes, she felt the axe. How do you think the axe felt and why?*

What Happens to Molecules of Solids When They Are Heated or Cooled? (4–8)

What Do I Want Children to Discover?

Heat is a form of energy.
Heat or thermal energy can be transferred.
Matter changes if heat or thermal energy is gained or lost:

When heat or thermal energy is increased, the molecules move faster and farther apart **(expansion).**

When heat or thermal energy is decreased, the molecules move slower and are closer together **(contraction).**

What Will I Need?

Candles	Pair of pliers
Metal pan	Screw eye (The *eye* of this
Matches	should be just *slightly* larger
Nail	than the nail. If it is not,
Forceps or tongs	tighten with pliers.)

What Will We Discuss?

What is heat?
What is energy?
What are molecules?
What do you think heat does to molecules?
What is a nail made of?
How does heat affect metal? What could you do to find out?

What Must I Know?

This activity should be done in groups of two students. *Caution:* For immature or unruly children, the teacher should conduct these activities.

PROCESSES

What Will Children Do?

1. Along with your partner, obtain a candle, matches, a metal pan, forceps, nail, and screw eye.
2. Fix the candle so it stands in the center of the pan. To do this, light the candle wick and permit enough wax to drip onto the center of the pan (about the size of a quarter). Then blow out the candle and place it, wick end up, in the puddle of wax. Hold the candle steadily in the puddle until the wax hardens.
3. Try to fit the nail into the hole of the screw eye.

Observing *Does the nail fit the screw eye?*
Observing *How easily does the nail go into the screw eye?*

Hypothesizing *What do you think will happen if you heat the nail and try to put it through the screw eye again?*

What Must I Know?

The nail will have expanded so it will not fit in the screw eye because the heat has caused the molecules to move faster and farther apart (expansion).

4. Light the candle.
5. With the forceps or tongs, pick up the nail. Hold the head of the nail over the hottest part of the flame. If you do not know where this is, ask the teacher.

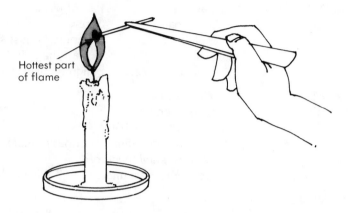

Hottest part
of flame

What Must I Know?

The candle flame is composed of two parts: a lower dark section and an upper bright part. The tip of the darker (inner) part is the hottest point of the flame. (See diagram.) Always have your students hold the object they are heating over the dark tip. Also, be prepared to explain the products of combustion if the children question the black deposit of carbon on the nail.

6. Pick up the screw eye and try to put the nail head through it. After you have done this, put the nail and screw eye in the metal pan—*remember* they are still hot.

Observing | *What happened when you tried to put the nail head through the screw eye?*

Inferring | *Why do you think this happened?*

Inferring | *What happened to the molecules in the nail when you heated them?*

Inferring | *What did the heat do to them?*

Inferring | *Did the molecules move faster or slower?*

Inferring | *Did they gain or lose energy?*

Inferring | *Are the molecules in the heated nail closer together or farther apart than before heat was applied?*

Inferring | *How can you tell?*

Explaining | Using the words *molecules, energy,* and *space between molecules,* try to explain what happens to a metal when it is heated.

How Will Children Use or Apply What They Discover?

Have children try the above using a screw eye that is slightly *smaller* than the nail, so the screw eye does *not* go over the nailhead. Put the nail in a freezer for 24 hours and then try to put the screw eye on.

Does it now go over the nailhead? Why?
Also try heating the *screw eye* and see if it will fit over the nailhead.

What Happens to Molecules of Liquids When They Are Heated or Cooled? (4–8)

What Do I Want Children to Discover?

Convection is the process whereby warm liquids or gases rise and cooler gases fall.

Warm liquids and gases expand and occupy more space. As a result, they have fewer molecules per volume than when they were cold. They are therefore less dense.

Warm liquids and gases rise because they are less dense than they would be if they were cold.

What Will I Need?

Food coloring
Glass container (quart size)
Ink or small paste bottle
2-hole rubber stopper or cork to fit small bottle
2 glass tubes or medicine droppers

Hot water
Cold water
Beaker
Coloring crystals—potassium permanganate crystals or food coloring are suggested

What Will Children Do?

Hypothesizing

PROCESSES

Knowing what you do about warm and cold gases in air, how do you think warm compared to cold bodies of water might behave?

1. Obtain a small ink or paste bottle, two glass tubes, a 2-hole rubber stopper or cork that will fit the bottle, food coloring, and a large glass container in which to put the bottle. Your teacher will insert the glass tubes in the cork stopper so one is higher than the other one as indicated in the diagram.

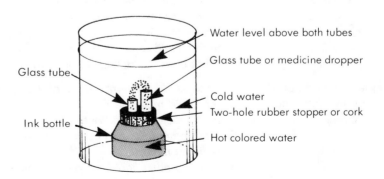

Water level above both tubes
Glass tube or medicine dropper
Glass tube
Cold water
Two-hole rubber stopper or cork
Ink bottle
Hot colored water

2. Put a few drops of food coloring in the small bottle. Fill it with *very hot* water and insert the cork. Fill the larger glass container with *very cold* water.

Hypothesizing
What do you think will happen if you lower the small bottle into the container of cold water?

3. Lower the small bottle into the cold water container.

Observing
What happens when the small bottle is dropped into the large container?

Inferring
Why does it happen?

The process of water and gases moving in this way is called **convection.**

Inferring
Why would it be possible for such currents to occur in the ocean?

4. Obtain a beaker and some colored crystals and fill the beaker with water. Place some of the colored crystals in the beaker in one corner. Place the beaker on the stand over a burner or alcohol lamp and heat the water as shown in the diagram.

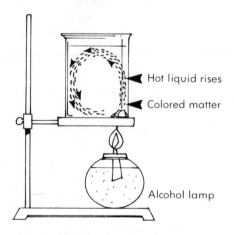

Hot liquid rises

Colored matter

Alcohol lamp

Hypothesizing
What do you think will happen to the crystals?

Observing
Describe what happens as the water is heated.

Inferring
Why does this happen?

5. Convection is defined as the transfer of heat by means of currents in the liquid or gas that is heated.

Summarizing
What does this definition mean to you in your own words?

How Will Children Use or Apply What They Discover?

1. *How would the temperature of the liquid affect the movement of the liquid molecules?*
How would you find out?

2. *What other factors in addition to temperature affect the movement of liquid molecules?*

3. *How do other liquid molecules move?*

What Happens to Molecules of Gases When They Are Heated or Cooled? (K–8)

What Do I Want Children to Discover?

Gases **expand** when heated.

Gases **contract** when cooled.

When gases are heated, the molecules move farther apart and exert greater pressure on the walls of the container.

What Will I Need?

3 balloons (same size)
String (5 feet long)
Measuring tape
Gallon container filled with ice water

Radiator
Infrared lamp or large
  light bulb lamp

What Will We Discuss?

How could you use a balloon to determine if gas will expand or contract when filled with air and heated?

What happens to the molecules in an object when it is heated?

With a given rise in temperature, will gases or liquids expand the most? Why?

What Will Children Do?

PROCESSES

PART I

1. Obtain 3 balloons, a 5-foot piece of string, and a measuring tape. Blow up the balloons so they are about the same size and tie them closed.

Hypothesizing

What do you think will happen to the air in a filled balloon if it is heated?

2. Measure with the measuring tape one of the balloons. Tie this balloon to the upper arm of a chair and place the chair about 2 feet from a heater.

Observing
Measuring

3. Observe the size and shape of the balloon as it is being heated.

4. At the end of 4 minutes, measure and record the balloon's diameter again.

What change has occurred?

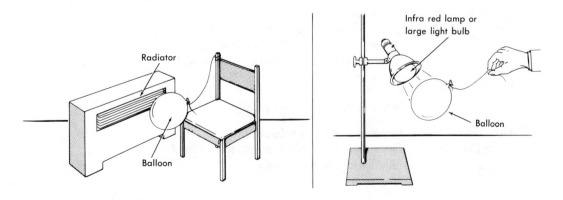

Radiator

Balloon

Infra red lamp or large light bulb

Balloon

PART II

Hypothesizing

What do you think will happen to the shape of a balloon if it is cooled?
What should you do to find out?

Designing an investigation

1. Measure a second balloon. Place it in ice cold water.

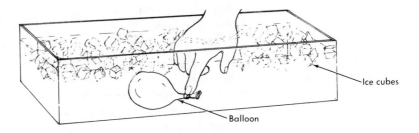

Ice cubes

Balloon

Observing

2. Observe the size and shape of this balloon as it is being cooled.
3. Leave the third balloon at room temperature (control or comparison).

Inferring   *What is the purpose of leaving this balloon at room temperature?*
Observing   *Which of the three balloons expanded?*
Applying   *What do you think happened to the speed of the molecules inside the expanding balloons?*

Observing   *Which balloons contracted?*
Applying   *What do you think happened to the speed of the molecules in the cooled balloon?*

Inferring   *In which of the three balloons do you think the molecules are moving faster and hitting the sides with greater force?*

Summarizing *What evidence do you have that gases expand when heated?*
Summarizing *What evidence do you have that gases contract when cooled?*

How Will Children Use or Apply What They Discover?

1. *What would happen to a balloon if the air inside were overheated?*
2. *What might happen to a tire if the car were driven very fast down the highway on a hot summer day?*
3. *What might happen to a partly filled bottle brought into a warm room from the refrigerator?*

What Is an Insulator? (4–8)

What Do I Want Children to Discover?

Water is a poor **conductor** of heat.
Glass and air are poor conductors of heat.
Heat from a burner rises.

What Will I Need?	Clamp	Matches
	Steel wool	Glass rod
	Test tube	Metal rod (a brass curtain rod or aluminum foil
	Ice	rolled to make a rod can serve for this
	Candle	purpose)
	Candle holder	Wax

What Will We Discuss?

Is water a good conductor of heat?
What could you do to find out?

What Will Children Do?

PROCESSES

PART I

1. Obtain a test tube, clamp, steel wool, ice, candle, candle holder, and matches. Set up the equipment as shown in the diagram.

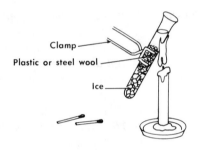

2. Heat the water *above* the ice cubes for several minutes until the water boils.
   What happens to the ice in the test tube?

Inferring   *From this, what can you conclude about water as a conductor of heat?*

Inferring   *Why did you put steel wool in the lower part of the tube?*

What Must I Know?   Steel wool was placed in the tubes to hold the ice cubes down. Plastic wool used to clean pots can be substituted for steel wool.

PART II

1. Obtain a glass rod, a metal rod, a candle, a candle holder, wax, and matches. Place wax on each of the rods as shown in the diagram.

Hypothesizing   *What do you think will happen when you heat these rods as indicated in the diagram on page 36?*

2. Heat the rods gently over the candle.

Observing   *On which rod did the wax melt first?*

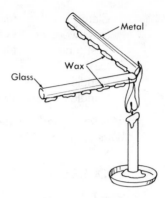

Comparing
Defining

Which is the better conductor of heat: metal or glass?
Define in your own words what a conductor and an insulator of heat are.

How Will Children Use or Apply What They Discover?

1. What are some materials you would use if you wanted to conduct heat from its source to another place?
2. Why can you safely hold your hand below a burning candle but not above its flame?
3. What materials would be good for making cups to hold hot drinks?
4. Where are insulators of heat used in your home?
5. How does house insulation help both heat the house in winter and cool it in the summer? Why is less fuel needed to heat (and cool) well-insulated houses? Why is foil-lined insulation better than paper-lined insulation?

How Is Heat Transmitted by Conduction and Radiation? (4–8)

What Do I Want Children to Discover?

The sun or light bulbs give off **radiant** heat.
Heat can be transmitted from one body to another by conduction and radiation.
Light objects *reflect* radiant energy more than dark objects.
Dark objects *absorb* more radiant energy than light objects.
Some surfaces conduct heat better than others.

What Will I Need?

3 tin cans of same size	Tripod stand
Small can of *dull* black paint	Styrofoam covers for cans
Small can of *shiny* white paint	3 thermometers
Silver or steel knife	4–inch length of copper
Candle	tubing
4x4-inch square of	2 small paint brushes
aluminum foil	Lamp with 150 to 300 watts
9 thumb tacks	

What Must I Know?   These activities may be done in groups. For immature or unruly children, the teacher should conduct these activities.

PROCESSES

PART I RADIATION

What Will Children Do?   *What do you think will happen to the three thermometers in the three different cans after being in the sun or near light bulbs for a while? (See diagram.)*

Hypothesizing   1. Obtain three identical sized cans and remove all labels. Paint one dull black and one shiny white and leave the third can unpainted, shiny metal.
2. Fill each can with regular tap water.
3. Put a styrofoam cover on each can and insert a thermometer through each cover.
4. Set the cans in the direct sunlight or at equal distances from a 150 to 300 watt light bulb.

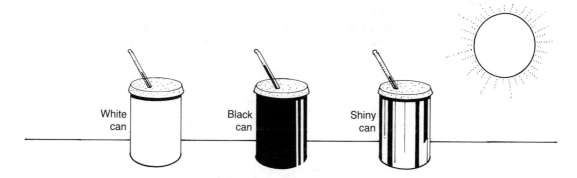

White can   Black can   Shiny can

Measuring
Observing
Hypothesizing   5. Prepare a table for data collection and record the temperature of the water in each can at one-minute intervals.
What do you think will happen to the temperature of water in the different cans?
If there are different temperatures, how would you explain that?
Inferring   *How would you relate the results of the unequal absorption of heat in the tin cans to different land and water surfaces of the earth?*
Inferring   *Knowing what you do about how radiant (light) energy reacts on different surfaces, how would you explain the differences in the three thermometers?*
Hypothesizing   *How might this be related to microclimates of certain geographic areas?*

What Must I Know?/
Where Do I Find It?

The shiny aluminum of the unpainted can and the shiny white paint of the second can reflect radiant energy, whereas dull black paint absorbs most of the radiant energy. Dark patches of ground absorb more radiant energy faster than shiny water surfaces or lighter colored land surfaces.

PART II CONDUCTION

Hypothesizing

What do you think will happen to tacks that have been attached with wax to a strip of aluminum foil, a silver or steel knife, and a copper tube, when the tips of these metals are heated? (See diagram.)

1. Obtain a 4 x 4-inch square of aluminum foil, a candle, a match, and nine tacks.
2. Roll the aluminum foil tightly.
3. Light the candle. Drip some wax onto three tacks and the aluminum foil rod so the tacks stick to the foil.
4. Obtain a tripod stand, silver knife, and a 4-inch length of copper tubing.
5. Stick three tacks each to the knife and the tube as you did with the foil.
6. Place foil, knife, and copper tubing on a tripod stand as indicated in the diagram. Heat the tips of each of these with a flame from a candle.

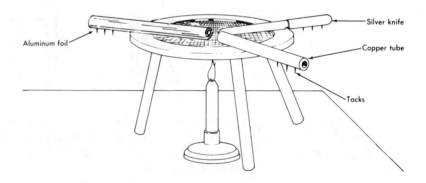

Aluminum foil

Silver knife

Copper tube

Tacks

Observing
Inferring
Inferring

Observe and record what happens.
Why didn't the tacks all fall at the same time?
From observing this activity, how do you think the heat affected the three metals?

How Will Children Use
or Apply What They
Discover?

1. *When you stand in front of a fireplace and the front of you is warmed by the fire, how is the heat transferred?*
2. *How does heat or thermal energy come from the sun?*
3. *What colors are more likely to absorb heat?*

4. *Why do people generally wear lighter colored clothes in the summer?*
5. *In the can experiment, what kind of energy did the black surface absorb?*
6. *How was the heat transferred from the black surface to the thermometer?*
7. *Why is it desirable to have a copper-bottomed tea kettle?*
8. *Why wouldn't you want a copper handle on a frying pan?*
9. *What metals conduct heat well?*
10. *What advantage would there be in ordering a car with a white rather than a black top?*
11. *Why do many people in warmer climates paint their houses white?*
12. *Why would you prefer to put a hot dog on a stick rather than a wire to hold the hot dog above a camp fire?*
13. *Why do astronauts wear shiny space suits?*

Reference Books—Thermal Energy (Heat) Barbara R. Fogel, *Energy Changes for the Future* (New York, 1985). Kathryn Whyman, *Science Today: Heat and Energy* (Gloucester Press, 1986).

CHANGES IN STATES OF MATTER

Guided Discovery Activities

How May Matter Be Changed? (K–8)

What Do I Want Children to Discover?	Matter may be changed **chemically** or **physically.** If matter is changed chemically, its chemical makeup is altered. Matter changed physically may be altered in its form, but its chemical makeup remains the same.
What Will I Need?	Prepared gelatin dessert Butter Water Hot plate Candle Matches Quart container (pan)
What Must I Know?	Assemble the items you will need in the classroom. *Caution:* In the interest of safety, only *you* should handle the hot plate. Place all these materials on your demonstration area.
What Will We Discuss?	*What kinds of things are there on the desk?* *How do they vary?* *In what ways could you cause these things to change?*

What changes do you think would occur in these items?
What would change other than the form?
How can you find out?

What Must I Know?

The terms for matter should have been introduced in previous lessons.

What Will Children Do?

PROCESSES

1. Obtain a candle, some prepared gelatin dessert, and a match.
2. Light a candle.

Observing

Observe and record the changes you see.
3. Observe the gelatin dessert.

Observing
Hypothesizing and designing an investigation

What is its form?
How could you change its form?

4. Try to change the gelatin dessert's form.
5. Obtain some butter.

Observing
Hypothesizing

What is the form of the butter?
How can you change its form?
6. Try to change its form.

What Must I Know?

Set butter and gelatin dessert in a warm place or in a pan over the candle. Students should suggest that, after melting, the butter's form can be restored by cooling it.

Summarizing

What have you learned about how matter can be changed in this activity?

How Will Children Use or Apply What They Discover?

1. *Which of the things above could easily be restored to the form they were originally?*
2. *What is the difference between a physical and a chemical change?*
3. *Observe the raw materials of gelatin dessert (powder and water) and butter (heavy cream) and describe the changes that went on from raw materials to end product.*

What Effect Does Heat Have on the States of Matter? (K–6)

PART I SOLIDS

What Do I Want Children to Discover?

There are many forms of sugar.
It is possible to obtain carbon from burning sugar.
Sugar may be broken down chemically.

What Will I Need?

Bunsen or alcohol burner or hot plate
Aluminum pie pan
Ring stand and ring
Teaspoon of sugar or cube sugar

Empty glass cup (tall)
Pot holder

What Will We Discuss?

Hold up a piece of sugar, and ask:
What are some of the properties or characteristics of this piece of sugar?

What Must I Know?

They might say it is white, cubical in shape, small, made up of crystalline material, sweet, and so on. In its present form, sugar is a white solid. There are, however, ways of changing its appearance. One of the easiest ways is simply to crush the cube, producing sugar in smaller crystal form. These crystals can be crushed further to make a powdered sugar. Another way to change this cube's appearance is to dissolve it in a cup of water. No sugar can be seen, yet the solution will taste sweet. It is, nevertheless, sugar because some of its characteristics are identifiable.
In what ways can sugar be changed so it cannot be identified?

PROCESSES

What Will Children Do?

1. Obtain an aluminum pie pan and place it on top of an electric hot plate or ring stand. Regulate the burner so the pan is heated *slowly.*

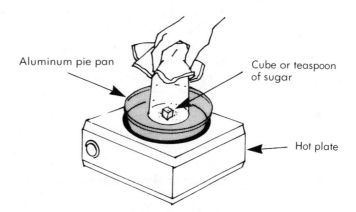

Aluminum pie pan

Cube or teaspoon of sugar

Hot plate

2. Obtain one teaspoon of sugar and place it in the middle of the pan.

Hypothesizing *What do you think will happen when the sugar is heated?*
Observing 3. Watch what happens to the sugar.
Observing *What happens as the sugar begins to melt?*
4. Obtain a tall, empty glass cup and hold it upside down over the bubbling sugar. Use a pot holder to do this.

Hypothesizing	*What do you think will appear on the inside* of the glass?
Observing	5. Observe the inside of the glass.
	6. Touch the inside of the glass with your fingers.
Observing	*What do you feel?*
Inferring	*What do you think it is?* (water vapor)
	7. After the sugar stops bubbling, describe what you see in the pan.
Inferring	*What do you think this material could be?*
Comparing	*What does it look like?*
	Taste this material.
Observing	*How does it taste?*
	Does it have the properties of sugar?

What Must I Know?   It is probably **carbon.** Sugar has carbon combined in its molecular structure.

How Will Children Use or Apply What They Discover?

1. *From what you have learned about sugar, can you explain why a marshmallow turns black when roasted over a fire?*
2. *Why does sugar turn brown as it slowly heats up and melts?* (This brown liquid is caramel flavor.)

PART II LIQUIDS

What Do I Want Children to Discover?

The temperature of water rises to the boiling point proportional to the amount of heat it absorbs.

At the boiling point, the temperature of water remains constant.

The heat added to water at the boiling point works to change the state of water to water vapor.

Whenever a state of matter is changed, for example, a liquid to a gas or a gas to a liquid, a considerable amount of energy must be added or given off in the process.

What Will I Need?

Beaker (500 ml.)	Graduated cylinder
Thermometer (centigrade)	Ring stand
Stirring rod	Ring clamp
Crushed ice	Wire gauze
Bunsen or alcohol burner	Stopwatch or wristwatch

PROCESSES

What Will Children Do?

1. Obtain a 500 ml. beaker, ring stand, ring clamp, wire gauze, thermometer, stirring rod, crushed ice to fill the beaker, a watch, and a Bunsen or alcohol burner.

Carrying out experiment

2. Arrange the ring stand, ring clamp, and wire gauze according to the diagram. Using the graduated cylinder, measure out 50 ml. of water and pour it in the beaker.

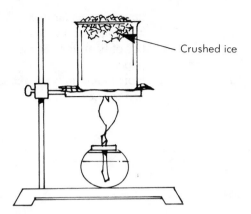

Crushed ice

3. Fill the rest of the beaker to the top with crushed ice.
4. Light and adjust the burner.
5. Adjust the height of the ring on the ring stand so the tip of the flame will just touch the wire gauze.
6. Place the burner under the beaker and time it with the stopwatch for 30 seconds.

Measuring

7. At the end of the 30-second interval, remove the burner. This will constitute one unit of heat. Stir continuously while heating, and as soon as the burner is removed, take the water temperature as quickly as possible. The data should be recorded in a manner similar to the sample data table.

No. of Heat Units	Temperature
0	(initial)
1	
2	
3	
etc.	

8. As soon as the temperature has been read and recorded, replace the burner and add another unit of heat, quickly taking the temperature again. Continue doing this, working as rapidly as possible, until all of the ice has melted and the temperature seems to

have risen as far as it will go (until it becomes constant). Make a line graph of the data from the table. Use temperature and number of heat units as the coordinates. (Make the graph on graph paper.)

Inferring

How many units of heat were added before the temperature began to rise?

Graphing

(diagram of graph)

Temperature

No. of heat units added

Inferring

What is the significance of the point at which the temperature begins to rise?

Inferring

What is the significance of the point at which the temperature seems to reach a maximum?

Inferring

What happens to the heat supplied when no temperature change takes place?

How Will Children Use or Apply What They Discover?

1. *How do you think your results would have varied if you had used sugar or salt water?*
2. *What would you think would be the results if you continue heating the water until it boils?*
3. *Why do you think you were asked to stir continuously while heating the water? What differences (if any) would you expect in the results if you did not stir continuously? Why?*

What Must I Know? Where Do I Find It?

Reference Books—Thermal Energy (Heat) Changes in Matter
Sheila Kaplan, *Solar Energy* (Milwaukee, WI: Raintree, 1983). Lisa Yount, *Too Hot, Too Cold, or Just Right* (New York: Walker, 1981).

AIR PRESSURE

Quickie Starters

What Makes Balloons Grow Bigger and Move Farther?

Materials

Balloons, metric tape or meter stick

Opening Question

Which team can get their balloons to go the farthest?

Some Possible Activities

Go outside and divide the class into groups of five. Students should blow their balloons up as much as they dare. One student in each group releases his or her balloon. The second student then goes to where that balloon landed and releases his or her balloon. This continues until all the children in the team have had a turn. The distance is then measured metrically to determine how far their balloons went from the starting point. The team whose balloons went the greatest distance wins.

How Can You Make a Paper Airplane Fly?

Materials

Different kinds of paper, for example, typing paper, construction paper, poster board, plastic backed paper, and so on

Opening Questions

How can you make a paper airplane out of these things?
Which kind of paper will make the best airplane?
What will an airplane have to do to be good?
After they have made their airplanes, ask: *How do you feel about your airplanes?*
State: *If someone is having trouble with an airplane, would you please help him or her?*
Discuss some things they might try to make their airplanes go farther.
Later ask: *What have you discovered about your plane? What seems to affect how the plane flies?*

Some Possible Activities

Invite students to set a distance goal and try to reach it by modifying their planes or making new ones until they reach it. Discuss how the size of the wings and shape of the nose and tail affect how the plane flies. Have them time how long their plane stays up and determine what they can do to increase the time.

Observe some birds or films of them and discuss how the birds differ and which ones soar the best and why.

Invite the children to see how good their spatial relations are by having each student sail his or her plane, one at a time, while another student tries to hit it in midair with his or her plane. After this, discuss what can be done to prevent air collisions. Ask:

What can you learn from birds that might help you make better airplanes? What factors seem to affect how your airplane flies?

How do you think your airplanes would fly with the wind or against the wind? Why?

What could you do to find out?

What could we do to make our planes more attractive?

How could we display them?

Invite students to make gliders and test how they fly.

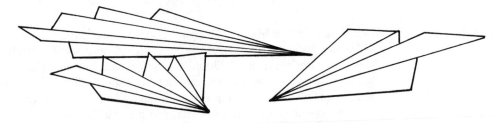

How Can You Make a Toy Helicopter Fly?

Materials

Small thin pieces of wood, candy sticks, and wood glue

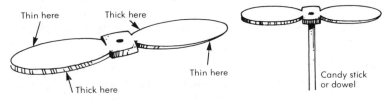

Opening Questions

Who can make a helicopter to stay up the longest?
Who can make a helicopter go the farthest?

Some Possible
Activities

Invite students to make a helicopter. Have them make a propeller from a small piece of wood about 14 cm long, 1.5 cm wide, and 1 cm or less thick. It is suggested that the propeller initially be made of wood and be cut with a knife or prepared in advance in a wood shop. It should be sandpapered and the tips rounded to make a good propeller. Make a small hole in the center of the propeller with a point of a knife or a small drill so it will just fit over a candy stick or a small dowel as shown in the figure. Place some wood glue around this hole and allow it to dry for 24 hours or more.

When it is dry, pick up the helicopter and roll it rapidly several times between the palms of the hands. When the propeller is spinning rapidly, let it spin away from the hands. If this is done correctly, it should spin in the air for several meters. It may be caught by other students or allowed to fall, preferably on a surface that will cushion its fall, like a lawn.

Invite students to study what factors influence how well the helicopter flies, what they need to do to make a better helicopter, and how they can make it more appealing to the eye. For example, ask how they would make one from plastic and cardboard, how the weight of the materials they use affects the flying of the helicopter, and so on.

Challenge them to try to construct a super helicopter from several kinds of materials.

How Can You Make a Kite and Get It to Fly?

Materials

Plastic such as that used by dry cleaners and paper to cover the kite, small pieces of wood to form the supports, string, transparent tape or glue, cloth for the tail

Opening Questions

How can we make some kites?
What will we need?
How should they be constructed?
What shape should they be?

Some Possible Activities

Encourage the children to plan in small groups how they are going to make their kites and then construct them. After they have done this, you might bring in some books on kites. Discuss the role of the tail and how it helps to stabilize the kite. Have them experiment with how long the tail should be by flying their kites on windy and calm days. If there is a local kite store, invite the children to visit it. Discuss some of the dangers of flying kites near power lines. *Caution:* Point out that they should *never use thin wire instead of string to fly a kite because of the danger involved if it hits a power line.* Invite them to make several kinds of kites and find out how different cultures use them, for example, how the Japanese use them to celebrate certain holidays.

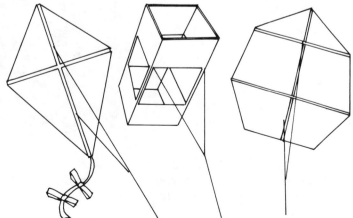

Guided Discovery Activities

What Is Air? (K–3)

What Do I Want
Children to Discover?

Air is real.
Air is around us all the time.
Air is found inside solids and liquids.
Air takes up space and has weight.

What Will I Need?

Piece of cardboard
Commercial-sized mayonnaise jar or aquarium
Drinking glass
Food coloring

What Will We
Discuss?

How do you know something is real?
What could you do to find out whether air is real?

PROCESSES

What Will Children
Do?

1. Swing your hands back and forth.

Observing

    What can you feel?

2. Swing a piece of cardboard.

Observing
Inferring
Observing

    What do you feel now?
    What is the cardboard pushing against?
    *What do you feel pushing against you when you ride your bicycle
    down a hill?*

Hypothesizing

    *What do you think will happen to a glass if it is turned upside
    down and placed under water?*

3. Obtain a drinking glass. Turn the glass upside down and hold it in
   a large jar of water or an aquarium as shown (use food coloring
   to make water more visible).

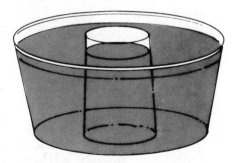

4. Turn the glass sideways.

Observing

    What happens to the inside of the glass?
    What are the bubbles that escape from the glass?

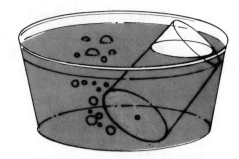

How Will Children Use or Apply What They Discover?

1. *How can you keep water in a straw by holding it with your finger on the end like this?*

2. *If you fill a paper bag with air and then crush it, what happens and why?*
3. *Why does juice flow better from a tin can if you punch two holes instead of one?*

What Shapes and Volumes May Air Occupy? (K–6)

What Do I Want Children to Discover?

A gas has no fixed shape.
A gas has no distinct surface of itw own.
A change in shape or state is a **physical change.**
Air or gas is elastic in that it can expand or contract to fill a space.
Air can exert a force.

What Will I Need?

Plastic bag (quart size)
Balloon (oblong shape)
Beach ball
Tire pump

What Will We Discuss?

What helps a kite to fly?
Why does your hair blow in the wind?
What do you breathe?

Where do you find air?
How do you know air is around you?
What form or shape does air have? How can you find out?

What Must I Know?

The materials described above are for a group of two or three children.

What Will Children Do?

PROCESSES

PART I

1. Obtain a balloon, a plastic bag, a beach ball, and a tire pump.
2. Inflate the balloon by blowing into it.

Observing
Inferring or interpreting

   What is the shape of the balloon?
   What made it that shape?

3. Squeeze the balloon.

Observing
Inferring

   What shape is it?
   Why does it take on different shapes when you squeeze it?

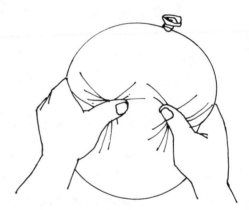

Observing
Inferring

4. Open the balloon.
   What happens to the air?
   What is the shape of the air now?

PART II

1. Obtain a plastic bag and blow into it.

Comparing

2. *Is the shape of it the same or different from the shape of the balloon?*
3. Release the bag.

Inferring
Inferring

   What happens to the shape of the bag?
   Why is the shape of the balloon similar to the shape of the plastic bag even though they are different?

PART III

1. Obtain and inflate a beach ball.

Comparing
Is the shape of it the same or different from its shape before inflating?

Inferring
Why do you think the ball changed its shape?

Summarizing
What can you say about the shape of the air in all these things?

Designing an investigation
How do you think you could use a tire pump to show that air will fill any container?

2. Obtain a tire pump. Have your partner put his finger over the end of the pump.

3. Push the plunger of the pump down.

Observing
Was it easy or hard to push it down?

4. *Keep the finger over the end, push the plunger down, and then let go of the plunger.*

Observing
What happens to it?

Inferring
What causes it to bounce back?

5. Now remove the finger and push the plunger down again.

Comparing
Is it easy or hard to push?

Inferring
Why does it push differently now?

Comparing
How does this compare with the stretching of a rubber band or a balloon?

Inferring
How is it possible for the air to cause a balloon to become larger?

What Must I Know?
Explain that a **force** is a push or pull and then ask the children to determine if air can exert a force and to explain how they know that it can or cannot.

How Will Children Use or Apply What They Discover?	*How can you use an inflated ball and an uninflated ball to show that air can fill a big space?*

How Can Air Pressure Move Objects? (K–8)

What Do I Want Children to Discover?	Air pressure may be strong enough to crush a strong can. A **partial vacuum** is a space in which the atmospheric pressure has been lessened; in other words, the space contains fewer molecules of air than the air surrounding it.
What Will I Need?	Empty ditto fluid can with screw cap Water Marking ink Bunsen or alcohol burner or hot plate Cork
What Will We Discuss?	*What are some things you know about air?* *What ways can you think of to crush a can?* *What would happen to the can if you took out some air?* *How could you remove some of the air from a can?*
What Will Children Do?	PROCESSES
What Must I Know?	This activity should be done as a demonstration in the lower grades and may be done in groups in the upper grades. *Caution:* If children do the activity, it is best to use an alcohol burner instead of the Bunsen burner.

1. Obtain an empty ditto fluid can with its screw cap. *Rinse thoroughly.*
2. Add ¼ inch water to it.
3. Place it over a Bunsen or alcohol burner or hot plate for several minutes.
4. When the steam starts to rise from the can, cork it or screw on the top and *take it off the burner immediately. Use mittens to protect hands.*
5. Mark the cork where it enters the can.

Inferring	*Why did you put water in the can before heating it?*
Inferring	*What is happening to the air inside the can as it cools?*
Hypothesizing	*Now that the can is cooling, what do you think will happen to it?*
Observing	*What changes do you observe taking place beside the can?*
Inferring	*What is causing the sides of the can to be changed?*
Observing	*What happens to the cork?*
Hypothesizing	*How can you prove your answer?*
Inferring	*Why did this happen to the cork?*
Inferring	*What is now inside the can?*

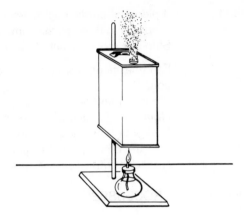

Hypothesizing   *Why didn't the can cave in immediately?*
Inferring   *Why did you put the cork in the can?*
Hypothesizing   *What would have happened to the can if you had not put the*
                     cork in it?

What Must I Know?

Two variables affecting the outcome of this activity are (1) rapid boiling of water as seen by steam bellowing out of the opening and (2) tight fit of the cork or screw top to make airtight seal of the can.

How Will Children Use or Apply What They Discover?

1. *How could you have made the can cave in faster?*
2. *How do some people use the ideas involved in this activity when they can fruit?*
3. *Why should you open a can of food before heating it?*

What Must I Know?

When the can is heated, the water in the can changes from water to water vapor. This warm water vapor expands into the can exerting a pressure causing some of the air in the can to escape. This process is fairly complete by the time the water has boiled for a few minutes. When the burner is removed and the can corked, the air inside the can begins to cool. As the air cools, some of the water vapor condenses back into water resulting in reduced pressure. The remaining air also contracts. Actually, a partial vacuum is formed by this process inside the can. Since there is less pressure pushing outward than there is pushing inward, the can caves in.

How Big Should You Make a Parachute? (K–8)

What Do I Want Children to Discover?

Air exerts pressure.
A larger surface will collect more air beneath it.
The more air beneath the surface of a parachute, the slower it will fall to the earth.
Large weights need larger parachutes.

What Will I Need?

3 pieces of plastic bag material
3 objects that weigh the same (something light like corks)
String or monofilament line

What Will We Discuss?

Fan your hand from one side of your body to the other in front of you.
What can you feel?
How does fanning affect the movement of air?
Cup your hands together and fan them from one side of your body to the other in front of you.
How does this affect the movement of air?

What Will Children Do?

Carrying out experiment

PROCESSES

1. Obtain three pieces of plastic bag material and a weight for each.
2. Make three parachutes of different sizes but attach equal weights to each parachute as shown in the diagram. Make the string or monofilament line at least 1 foot long.

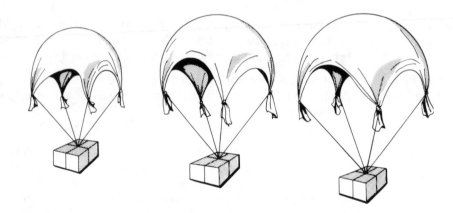

3. Throw the parachutes as high into the air as possible and let them fall. If possible drop from second-floor window.

Observing
Comparing
Inferring
Applying
Inferring
Hypothesizing

4. Record what happens.
   Which parachute falls the fastest?
   Why do you think one parachute falls faster than another?
   What are the parachutes catching as they fall?
   From this activity, what can you tell about the air?
   What do you think would happen if you used lighter weights on your parachute?
5. Obtain some heavier weights and repeat the activity.
6. Record your observations.

Summarizing
Applying

   What general rule could you make about the size of a parachute?
   Could anything besides the size of the parachutes be a factor?

How Will Children Use or Apply What They Discover?

1. Do the activity again and change other factors.
2. *How would you improve the observations and data you recorded to make them more accurate?*

How Do the Effects of Moving Air Differ from the Effects of Nonmoving Air? (4–8)

What Do I Want Children to Discover?

The pressure of liquids or gases will be low if they are moving fast and will be high if they are moving slowly. This principle is called **Bernoulli's principle.**

What Will I Need?

3 pieces of notebook paper
Pop bottle
Thread spool
Small card (3 x 3 inches)
Pin with a head
Ping-Pong ball
Thistle tube or funnel

What Must I Know?

Before doing this student inquiry activity, **potential energy** and **kinetic energy** should be explained.

PROCESSES

What Will Children Do?

PART I
1. Obtain a piece of notebook paper.
2. Make a fold 1 inch wide along the long end of the paper. Make another fold at the other end as indicated in the diagram.
3. Place the paper on a flat surface.

Hypothesizing
What do you think will happen if you blow under this folded paper?

4. Blow a stream of air *under* the paper.

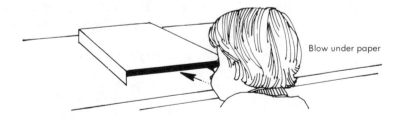

Blow under paper

Observing
What do you notice about the way the paper moves?
Describe how the air was circulating under the paper before you blew under it.

Comparing
What do you know about the air pressure under the paper (when you blow under the paper) as compared with the air pressure exerted on top of the paper?

PART II

Hypothesizing

What do you think will happen to a wad of paper placed in the opening of a pop bottle if you blow across the bottle opening?

1. Obtain a small piece of paper and a pop bottle.
2. Wad the paper so it is about the size of a pea (¼-inch or ½-cm) diameter).
3. Lay the pop bottle on its side.
4. Place a small wad of paper in the opening of the bottle, next to the edge of the opening. (See diagram.)
5. Blow across the opening in front of the bottle.

Blow across opening of bottle

Observing
Inferring
Comparing

Hypothesizing

What happens to the wad of paper?
Why does the wad of paper do this?
What do you know about the air pressure in the bottle and the air pressure at the opening of the bottle when you blow across it?
What do you think will happen if you place a wad of paper in the opening of a pop bottle (as before) and blow directly into the bottle?

6. Blow directly into the bottle.

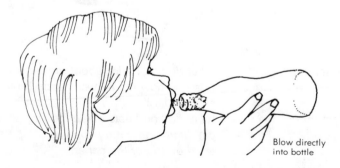

Blow directly into bottle

Observing   7. Record your observations.
Inferring   8. *What do you conclude from your observations?*

PART III

Hypothesizing   *If a pin with a head is inserted through the center of a card and into a spool, what happens when you blow through the other end of the spool?*

1. Obtain a spool, a small card (3 x 5 inches), and a pin with a head.
2. Place the pin in the center of the card so that the head is under the card. (See diagram.)
3. Hold the card, with your hand, against the bottom of the spool.
4. While blowing, let go of the card. *Warning:* Instruct children never to suck in on the spool.

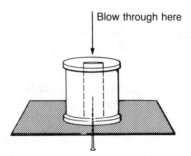

Blow through here

Observing   *What did you see the card do?*
Inferring   *Why does the card do this?*
Inferring   *What is holding the card?*
Inferring   *Why doesn't the air you blow through the hole make the card fall?*
Inferring   *Why do you need the pin in the middle of the card?*

What Must I Know?   Two variables affecting the outcome are (1) bottom of spool must be *very* smooth (sandpaper it if necessary) and (2) the student must get a deep breath and sustain a *long*, steady air column down the spool.

PART IV

Hypothesizing   *What will happen to a Ping-Pong ball if it is placed in the large end of a thistle tube and you blow through the small end of the thistle tube?*

1. Obtain a Ping-Pong ball and a thistle tube or funnel.
2. Place the Ping-Pong ball in the wide, larger opening of the thistle tube and blow through the other end with a *long*, steady breath.

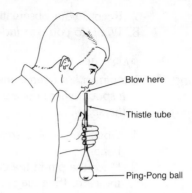

Observing   Record your observations.

Inferring   *Why does the ball do what it does?*

                 Why does the ball rotate?

PART V

Hypothesizing   *If you were to hold a piece of paper by each corner and blow across the top of the paper, what would happen to the paper?*

1. Obtain a piece of paper.
2. Hold the lower left corner with your left hand and the lower right corner with your right hand. (See diagram.)

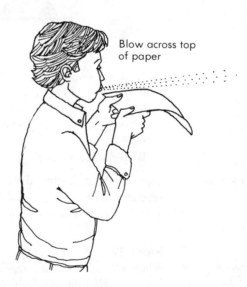

Blow across top of paper

3. Blow across the top of the paper.

Observing   *What happens to the paper?*

Inferring   *Why does the paper move in this direction?*

Applying   *Why wouldn't it be wise to stand close to a moving train?*

How Will Children Use or Apply What They Discover?

1. *When you rapidly pass by another pupil's desk with a sheet of paper on it, what happens to the paper?*
2. *How would this principle of air pressure work when you fly a kite?*
3. *What happens to a girl's skirt if a car speeds close by her?*
4. *What would happen if a plane stopped moving in the air? Why would this happen?*

What Must I Know?/ Where Do I Find It?

If a plane is moving fast enough, the upward pressure on the wings is enough to overcome gravity. It must keep moving to stay aloft. If it stopped in midair, it would glide down immediately.

5. *In the drawing of the airplane wing below, is the air moving faster at A or B?*
6. *How do wing slopes vary and why?*

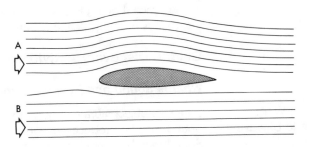

Reference Books—Air Pressure Franklyn M. Branley, *Air Is All Around You* (New York: Harper and Row, 1982). Henry Smith, *Amazing Air* (New York: Lothrop, 1983).

SOUND ENERGY

Quickie Starters

What Makes a Drum Louder?

Materials

Cylindrical oatmeal container, puffed rice or wheat cereal, large balloon or sheet rubber, strong rubber band

Opening Question

How can you make a drum sound louder?

Some Possible Activities

Stretch the large balloon or sheet rubber over the open end of the oatmeal container and place a strong rubber band over the rubber to hold it securely. This makes a simple drum. Sprinkle puffed rice or wheat cereal on drum head. Tap the drum head and observe what happens. Now hit it harder. Ask:
What differences did you notice?

Help children to see the patterns formed in the puffed rice or wheat when the drum head is struck, and how the pattern changes when it is struck harder. Also notice how much higher the cereal moves above the drum head when hit harder. Relate more energy (hitting the drum harder) with louder sound from drum.

How Can You Make Sounds Less Noisy?

Materials

A small radio; several different-size boxes, each of which can fit over one or more of the others and over the radio; cloth; paper; insulating material; cotton balls

Opening Question

How can we deaden the sound of this radio using these materials?

Some Possible Activities

If possible, have two radios with the same volume and invite two groups of students, in a stipulated time, to have a "deadening the sound" race. Later, discuss how sound can go through objects and what kinds of things deaden sound well.

Guided Discovery Activities

What Is Sound and How Is It Produced and Conducted? (K–6)

What Do I Want Children to Discover?

When an object vibrates, sound may be produced.
Sound may be produced by vibrating a number of different objects.
Sound may be conducted by a number of different objects.

What Will I Need?

As many of the following things as possible should be placed on the desks of groups of four or more children:

Rubber band	4 feet of string	Aluminum foil
Alarm clock	Aluminum foil pie pan	Toothpicks
Bell	6 empty pop bottles	Cotton
Fork and spoon		

What Will We Discuss?

How could you make a sound with a rubber band?

What Will Children Do?

Designing an investigation

PROCESSES

1. *How could you make a rubber band produce a sound? How is the sound produced?*

What Must I Know?

The children should stretch a rubber band and vibrate it. They should get the idea that the vibration causes the sound.

Hypothesizing

How many ways can you hear sound by placing your ear to the objects you have and causing a sound to occur?

2. *Try these different ways.*

Hypothesizing

What can you do to stop the noise once the sound is started?

Observing

3. Test your ideas.
4. Determine what materials are better than others to produce sound.

Comparing

   In what ways are these materials the same or different?

How Will Children Use or Apply What They Discover?

1. *How would you produce a loud sound?*
2. *What would you do to make a room less noisy?*
3. *Why do drapes in a room make sounds softer?*

How Does the Length of the Vibrating Body Affect Sound? (3–6)

What Do I Want Children to Discover?

Bodies in vibration make a sound.
The longer the vibrating body, the lower the tone.

What Will I Need?

Balsa wood strip 12 inches long
10 straight pins
Piece of wood approximately 6 × 6 inches × 1 inch
3 tacks or nails
Rubber band
Hammer

What Will We Discuss?

What do you think would happen if you vibrated pins set to different depths in a strip of balsa wood?
Would you get the same sound from each of the pins?
If you think that different pins will give off different tones, which one would give off the highest tone?

PROCESSES

PART I

What Will Children Do?

1. Obtain a balsa strip and set pins in it to varying depths. (See the diagram.)

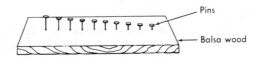

Pins
Balsa wood

Observing
Inferring
Hypothesizing

2. Determine if each vibrating pin gives off the same tone.
   What relationship is there between pin length and tone?
   Would nails stuck in balsa wood give the same results as the pins?

PART II

1. Look at the diagram.

Hypothesizing

   Where would you pluck the rubber band to get the highest note?

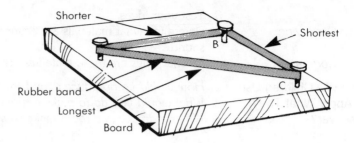

Hypothesizing

Where would you pluck the rubber band to get the lowest note?

2. Obtain three tacks or nails, a rubber band, and a piece of wood. Pound the tacks or nails into the wood block as shown in the diagram. Place the rubber band around the tacks or nails.
3. Pluck the rubber band to see if your hypothesis was correct.

Comparing

4. *How do the results of Part I compare with the results of Part II?*

How Will Children Use or Apply What They Discover?

1. *What would happen if you plucked rubber bands having the same length but different thicknesses?*
2. *What would happen to a tone if the vibrating length of the rubber band were kept the same, but different amounts of tension were applied?*
3. *How does sound travel from the rubber band to your ears?*

How Does a Violin or Cello Work? (4–6)

What Do I Want Children to Discover?

Tension of string determines pitch.
If the tension is increased, the pitch is raised.
The length of the string determines the pitch.
A thick string will give a lower tone than a thin string if both are the same length.
The longer the string, the lower the tone.

What Will I Need?

Cigar box
Strings of equal and varying thicknesses—about 18 inches long (nylon fishing line may be used)
3 thumb tacks
Weights of equal and varying weight—small metal film containers filled with sand can serve this purpose
Small board to serve as a bridge—8 inches long

What Will We Discuss?

What are some things you know about sound?
If you were to stretch three strings of varying thicknesses across a cigar box and vibrate them by plucking, how would the pitch and tone of the sound vary?

What Will Children Do?

Carrying out experiment

Hypothesizing

PROCESSES

1. Obtain a cigar box, thumb tacks, weights, and strings of varying thicknesses. Insert the thumb tacks at one end of the box. Tie strings around these tacks.
    Tie the weight to the other end of the strings. Place the strings over the box.

What do you think will happen when you vibrate each string by plucking it?

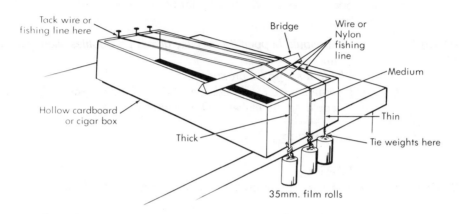

Comparing and inferring

2. *Which string gives the highest tone. Why?*

Comparing and inferring

3. *Which string gives the lowest tone? Why?*

Hypothesizing

What do you think would happen to the tone of the string if you were to take a weight off one of the thin strings and add a heavier weight to it?

4. Replace one of the weights with a heavier one.

Inferring

What does increased tension on the string do to the sound?

Hypothesizing

What other ways do you think you could arrange the strings to get different sounds?

5. Place a small triangular ruler under the strings and move it back and forth as you pluck them.

Classifying

What happened to the sound made by the strings?

How Will Children Use or Apply What They Discover?

1. *What other things could you do to show how sounds can be changed from lower to higher pitch?*
2. *List some of the different sounds you hear every day and classify them from high to low. Why do you think they are high or low?*
3. *When you listen to a violin or cello, what can you say about how the sounds are produced in these instruments?*

How Does the Length of an Air Column Affect Sound? (K–6)

What Do I Want Children to Discover?

The higher the pitch of a note, the more rapid the vibrations of the producing body.

Pitch can be varied by adjusting the depth of an air column.

The higher the water level, the shorter the air column, and the higher the pitch.

What Will I Need?

8 identical pop bottles
Medium-sized beaker
Soda straws (waxed paper, not plastic, work best)
Scissors

What Will We Discuss?

What would happen if you blew across pop bottles filled with varying amounts of water?

Would a sound be produced?

If sounds were produced, would they all be the same? If not, which would be the highest? The lowest?

PROCESSES

PART I

What Will Children Do?

1. Fill eight pop bottles with varying amounts of water.

Hypothesizing

What will happen if you blow across the lips of the bottles?

2. Blow across the bottles.

Observing

Do all bottles give off the same sound?

Observing

Which bottle gives off the highest note? the lowest note?

Hypothesizing

How could you make a musical scale out of the pop bottles?

3. Arrange the bottles to make a musical scale.

4. After you have made the musical scale, try to make a harmonizing chord.

If you number the lowest note "1" and the highest note "8," what are the numbers of chords?

Inferring

5. *What conclusions can you draw concerning the length of an air column and the sound produced?*

Hypothesizing

What is the relationship between the length of an air column and a note produced in an open tube?

PART II
1. Give each child a soda straw and a pair of scissors.
2. Have children cut and pinch the straw to form a reed like this:

Pinch here

Side view

Cut a V

Top view

Hypothesizing

Why do we cut and pinch the straw?

3. Have children blow on the "V" cut into straw. (*Note:* They will need to experiment to get the proper lip vibration.)
4. Now cut soda straws into different lengths to get different pitches.

Inferring

What is the relationship between the length of the straws and the sound produced?

Hypothesizing

How can the soda straws be used to play songs?

How Will Children Use or Apply What They Discover?

1. *How would the results vary if you put the same amount of water in bottles of varying sizes?*
2. *Does the thickness of the glass in the pop bottle affect the tone produced?*
3. *Could you produce the same results using test tubes? How can the soda straws be used to play songs?*
4. Experiment to get straws calibrated in lengths in relation to octave. Then have the children play simple songs like "Mary Had a Little Lamb."

What Must I Know?/ Where Do I Find It?	Once a scale is achieved, drop oil from a medicine dropper on top of the water in each bottle just enough to cover the top. This will prevent evaporation and change of pitch.

What Causes Sound to Be Louder? (K–6)

What Do I Want Children to Discover?	Sound is made when an object vibrates. **Loudness** of a sound is caused by an object's vibrating with increased energy, but not an increased number of times per second. The pitch is not changed by increased vibration.
What Will I Need?	Tin can with plastic lid Piece of rubber large enough to fit over the can Stick Cork
What Will We Discuss?	*What is pitch?* *Is pitch affected by the loudness of sound?*
What Will Children Do?	PROCESSES 1. Make a drum by fitting a piece of rubber over the opening of the can. An alternative is a plastic cover for sealing a coffee can. Place the cork on top of the drum.

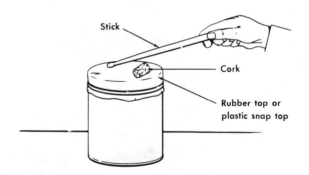

Hypothesizing	*What will happen to the cork if you hit the drum lightly?*
	2. Hit the drum hard.
Observing	*What happens to the cork?*
Hypothesizing *Inferring*	3. *What do you think will happen if the drum is hit much harder?* 4. *How does the pitch of the drum change by hitting it harder? Does a change in loudness occur? Why?*
How Will Children Use or Apply What They Discover?	1. *How would you use a piano to show what was demonstrated on the drum about pitch and loudness?* 2. *How can musicians play loud and soft music and still retain the pitch?* 3. *Explain how you make sound louder with your voice.*

How Do Solids and Liquids Conduct Sounds? (4–6)

What Do I Want Children to Discover?	Sound can travel through solid substances. Sound can travel through liquid substances.

What Will I Need?

2 paper cups
20 feet of strong cord or nylon fishing line
20 feet of steel wire
20 feet of copper wire
1 thick board about 12 × 4 inches × 1 inch

Wooden ruler
Bucket
Water
2 rocks
Buttons

What Will We Discuss?

Have you ever heard people talking when you were in one room and they were in the room next to yours?
How do you suppose you could hear them through the wall?
You know that sound travels, but what substances will sound travel through?

PROCESSES

PART I

What Will Children Do?

1. Obtain two paper cups and 20 feet of string or nylon fishing line.
2 With a pencil, punch a very small hole in the bottom of the paper cups just large enough to stick the string through.
3. Stick the ends of the string through each one of the paper cups. Tie a button to the ends of the string so the string will not be easily pulled from the cups.

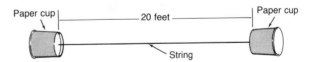

Paper cup | —— 20 feet —— | Paper cup
String

Hypothesizing

When you talk into one end of the cups, what will happen to the other cup? Why?

4. Talk into one cup while a student holds the other cup to his or her ear and listens.

Designing an investigation

Determine how sound can best be transferred from one cup to the other.

Observing

Record what you did to transmit the sound the best.

Hypothesizing

5. *How will the sound be conducted if you use copper or steel wire? Try it.*

Observing

What happens when you use copper wire?

Inferring and comparing

Is the sound carried better through copper wire than through string?
Why or why not?

Hypothesizing   6. *Why is it important for the string to be tight and not touching anything?*

PART II
1. Obtain a small board and a pencil.

Observing   2. Hold a board to your ear. Scratch the other end with a pencil. *What happens?*
3. Hold the board away from your ear and repeat the activity.

Applying   *Does sound travel better through a solid or through air?*

PART III
1. Obtain a wooden ruler. Hold it firmly with one hand against a desk. With the other hand pluck the overhanging part of the ruler, causing it to vibrate.

Hypothesizing   2. *What causes the sound to be produced?*
Designing an   Produce a high-pitched sound by vibrating the stick.
investigation   Produce a low-pitched sound by vibrating the stick.

PART IV

Hypothesizing
Designing an
*   investigation*

How is sound carried in liquids?
How would you find out?

1. Obtain a large bucket full of water. Obtain two pieces of metal or two rocks and hit them together under water.

Inferring

2. *Did you hear a sound when you hit them together? Why? What is your conclusion about the ability of a liquid to carry sound?*

How Will Children Use or Apply What They Discover?

1. *How far do you think sounds would travel between phones using copper wire, string, and steel wire?*
   Design an experiment to see which conducts sound farther.
2. *How would you use eight rulers to make a musical scale?*
   Think about what you did to get a low pitch and a high pitch.
3. *What is the purpose of making musical instruments out of wood?*
4. *How do you think liquids other than water conduct sounds?*

How Can the Reflection of Sound Be Changed (3–6)

What Do I Want Children to Discover?

When sound waves hit a hard surface, they may be thrown back.
Sound waves may be taken in and held in much the way a sponge holds water.
Some things **absorb** sound waves better than others.

What Will I Need?

2 large tin cans (about the size of a 2-pound coffee can)	Aluminum foil
	Sheet of newspaper
Nail	Shoebox with its lid
Hammer	Alarm clock or small transistor radio
About 1 square foot of cotton cloth	
About 1 square foot of wool cloth	Coat
About 1 square foot of silk	Sweater
About 1 square foot of paper	

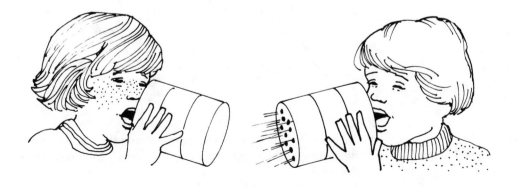

What Will We Discuss?

What would happen to the sound of your voice if you yelled into a large can?

What would happen to the sound of your voice if you put holes in the end of the can and yelled into it?

What do you think would happen if you put something into the can before yelling into it, for example, a wool cloth?

What would you do to find answers to these questions?

What Will Children Do?

PROCESSES

PART I

1. Obtain two large tin cans about the size of a two-pound coffee can (the larger cans are better), a nail, hammer, several pieces of cloth, newspaper, an alarm clock or small transistor radio, and aluminum foil.

Hypothesizing   *What do you think will happen if you yell into one of these cans?*

Observing   2. Yell into one can and note what happens.

Inferring   *What do you hear?*

Inferring   *What do you think happens to the sound waves when they hit the end of the can?*

3. Take the other can and make six nail holes in the end of it.

Hypothesizing   *What do you think will happen to the sound now if you yell into it?*

Comparing   4. Yell into the unpunctured can and then into the punctured can and note any differences.

Inferring   *Why do you think the sounds coming from each can are not the same?*

Hypothesizing   *What happens to some of the sound waves in the punctured can?*

Pieces of cotton cloth

PART II

1. Take a piece of cotton cloth and put it into the can without holes.

Hypothesizing   *What do you think will happen to the sound when you yell into this can?*

2. Yell into the can and note what happens.

Inferring	*Why does the sound seem different?*
Hypothesizing	*What do you think will happen to the sound when you use other substances such as newspaper, wool, or aluminum foil?*

3. Repeat steps 1 and 2 in Part II using a different substance each time, such as newspaper or wool, and note any differences in the sounds produced.

Comparing	*What do you notice about the sounds produced when you use each of these substances?*

4. Obtain an alarm clock or transistor radio and some wool cloth.

Hypothesizing	*What do you think will happen to the sound of the alarm clock if it is wrapped in the wool cloth?*

5. Turn the alarm clock on with the alarm ringing and wrap it in the wool cloth.

Observing	*What happens to the sound of the alarm when the cloth is wrapped around the clock?*

6. Repeat steps 4 and 5 in Part II using a different material to wrap the clock in each time, such as cotton, silk, newspaper, a coat, and a sweater.
   Record your observations.

Inferring	*Why are the sounds different for each of the articles?*

7. Turn on the alarm and place the clock in the shoebox and cover the box with its top.

Inferring	*Why doesn't the sound seem as loud?*
Hypothesizing	*What happens to the sound?*

How Will Children Use or Apply What They Discover?	1. *What kind of surface do you need for sound to reflect well?*
	2. *What suggestions would you make for building an auditorium so there would be no reflected sound or echoes?*
	3. *What things do you have in your classroom to help reduce noise or reflection of sound?*

Reference Books—Sound Energy Calvin R. Graf, *Exploring Light, Radio and Sound Energy* (New York: Tab Books, 1985). Frederick R. Newman, *Zounds! The Kid's Guide to Sound Making* (New York: Random House, 1983).

SIMPLE MACHINES (MECHANICS)

Quickie Starters

How Can You Make Balls Roll Faster?

Materials	Balls of different sizes including Ping-Pong, golf, tennis, and larger ones; straws; boards to make inclined planes
Opening Question	*What things can you do with these balls?*
Some Possible Activities	Find out which balls roll the easiest across the floor, what happens when they are kicked, and which ones will roll down an inclined plane the farthest. Find out which balls balance best. Throw the balls

against the wall at different angles and find out how they bounce off the wall. For example, how should the children throw the ball so it will come back to them? Float the balls in water and find out which ones float and which do not. Also, notice how deep they sink in the water. Line up the balls and roll a ball down an inclined plane so it hits the end of the line. Then roll two balls down so they hit the line one after another. Place all but one of the balls in a close group. Roll another ball into the group and see how the balls scatter. Play croquet with different balls. Construct a tetherball.

How Do Wheels Help Toys Move?

Materials

Rollers, small round wheels, buttons, toy cars, small round rocks, oranges, apples, thimbles, boards to make inclined planes, milk bottle paper caps or some cut from poster board, thumb tacks, match boxes

Opening Questions

What can you do with these things?
What kind of game can you play?
How can you make a toy car using the match boxes and other things?
Which of the things you see are wheels? Which are not wheels?
How are wheels different from the other things?

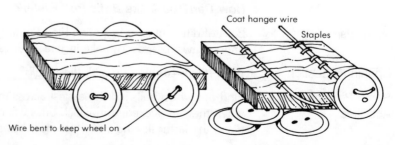

Coat hanger wire
Staples
Wire bent to keep wheel on

Some Possible Activities

The children could try seeing how far different things would roll on the floor, down an inclined plane. They could also make toy cars with the match boxes with the bottle caps or buttons tacked to the sides. The children may also be invited to make toy cars out of a square, small board where axles are made from clothes hangers. These are nailed to the board and bent at the ends after the button or bottle cap wheels are attached.

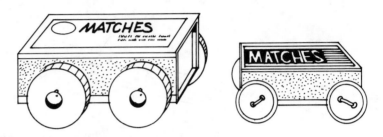

Guided Discovery Activities

What Is an Inclined Plane and How Can You Use It? (K–8)

What Do I Want Children to Discover?

Inclined planes are used for moving objects that are too heavy to lift directly. The work done by moving an object up an inclined plane is equal to the weight of the object times the height of the plane.

Resistance × the Height of the plane = Effort × the Length of the plane

An **inclined plane** is one example of a **simple machine.**

What Will I Need?

Smooth board 4 feet x 6 inches
Support block 4 × 8 inches
Spring scale
Block with screw eye in one end or a rubber band wrapped around it to be pulled by a scale

What Will We Discuss?

What is an inclined plane?
Why use an inclined plane?
Where are there inclined planes on the school grounds?

What Will Children Do?

Carrying out experiment

PROCESSES

1. Obtain a smooth board 4 feet × 6 inches, support block 4 × 8 inches, spring balance, and a block with a screw eye.
2. Take the 4-foot board and place the 4 × 8-inch block under one end so the end of the board is raised 4 inches. Place the block with the screw eye in it on the inclined board as shown in the

diagram. Slip the hook of the spring scale through the eye of the block.

Hypothesizing

What force do you think will be required to pull the block?
Will it be greater or less than the weight of the block?
Why?

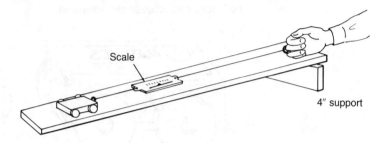

3. Slowly and evenly, pull the scale and block up the board.

Measuring

4. Record the amount of force needed to pull the weight up the board.
   Do this several times, and record your observations.
   Using the data obtained, determine the average force required to pull the weight.

5. Repeat the activity, but this time make the inclined plane steeper by changing the support block so its 8-inch dimension is under the end of the board.

Measuring

6. Again, find the average force needed to pull the weight up the board.

Comparing

How do the two forces compare?

Applying

7. Lift the weight straight up, as shown in the diagram. Repeat this several times and find the average of the readings.

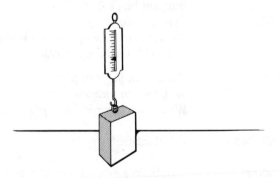

8. The following formula is used to calculate the force needed to move a weight up an **inclined plane:**

Resistance × Resistance distance = Effort × Effort distance

Inferring	Use this formula to calculate the force that should have been necessary to move the weight up the inclined plane.
Inferring	*Why don't the experimental results and the calculated results agree exactly?*
Hypothesizing	*What can you say about the amount of force required as an inclined plane becomes steeper?*
Hypothesizing	*What is the advantage of having a long inclined plane rather than a short inclined plane if both planes are the same height?*

How Will Children Use or Apply What They Discover?

1. *Why don't roads go straight up and down mountains?*
2. *Which of the following examples is an inclined plane?*
   a. ramp
   b. hill
   c. gangplank
   d. stairway
   e. wedge
   f. head of an axe
3. A person moved a 100-pound safe up an inclined plane 20 feet long and 2 feet high.

   How much effort did the person have to use to move the safe?

What Is the Advantage of Using a Wheel and Axle? (K–8)

What Do I Want Children to Discover?

A **wheel** is a simple machine that aids in moving an object.
Every wheel has an axle. The wheel is used to turn the axle or the axle is used to turn the wheel.
The work obtained from a simple machine is equal to the work put into it less the work used in overcoming friction.
A small effort applied to a large wheel can be used to overcome a large resistance on a small wheel.
A **wheel and axle** usually consist of a large wheel to which a small axle is firmly attached.
The mechanical advantage is equal to the radius of the wheel divided by the radius of the axle.

What Will I Need?

1 bicycle per class
Board
Hammer
Screw hook
Nail
Rubber bands
Balance weight
4 spools
5 or 6 round pencils
1 of the following: can opener, egg beater, or meat grinder

What Will Children Do?

PROCESSES

PART I

Hypothesizing

1. *In what way does the wheel help to move objects?*
2. Obtain a screw hook. Turn the hook into the end of a block of wood. Attach a rubber band to the hook (spring balance can be used) and measure the stretch of the rubber band as you drag the block on the floor. Use a wooden ruler and make a measurement just before and after the block begins to move.

Measuring

Record all of your measurements.

Observing

3. With the rubber band on your finger, lift the block into the air and measure the stretch.

Observing

4. *What change is made in the stretch of the rubber band?*
5. Now place two round pencils underneath the block and measure the stretch of the rubber band just before and after the block begins to move.

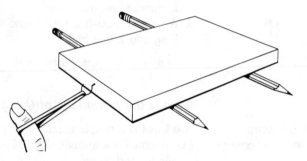

Observing

6. *What happens to the stretch of the rubber band this time?*

Comparing

7. *What difference do the pencils make underneath the wood when you are moving it?*

Comparing

8. *How does your measurement change?*

Inferring

9. *What do you suppose is the purpose of measuring the movement of the block of wood?*

Observing

10. Try the experiment again, only this time use four spools for the wheels and round pencils for the axles. Place the wood on the axle.

Observe what happens as you push the block of wood very gently.

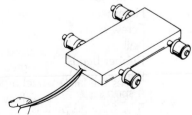

Measuring   Measure the stretch of the rubber band as you pull the block of wood.

Comparing   11. *What difference is there in the stretch of the rubber band this time compared to moving the board without wheels?*

PART II
1. Obtain a small wheel and axle or use a pencil sharpener, meat grinder, or can opener.

Hypothesizing   *What is the advantage of using a wheel and an axle?*
2. Hook a weight to the axle as shown in the diagram.

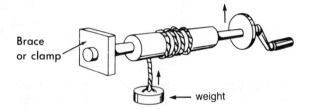

Brace or clamp

weight

Hypothesizing   *What do you think will be gained if a large wheel is turned to move a small axle?*
3. Turn the large wheel.
4. Count the number of turns you make to raise the weight 2 inches.

What Must I Know?   A small force applied to a large wheel can be used to move a large resistance attached to the axle. This is done, however, at the expense of distance, since the large wheel has to be moved a great distance to raise the resistance a short way.

PART III
1. Observe a bicycle.

Inferring   *Where on a bicycle is friction used to advantage?*
      How is the bicycle wheel constructed to help reduce friction?

What Must I Know?   The wheel produces less friction because there is less of its surface coming in contact with pavement than if a weight such as a person were pulled along a surface.

Observing   2. *Where are the wheels and axles on a bicycle?*
       When you ride a bicycle, where do you apply the force?

Inferring   *Why do you apply the force to the small wheel?*

What Must I Know?   The effort is applied to the small wheel to gain speed. You move the small sprocket with a great force a short distance, and it, in turn, moves the large wheel a greater distance but with less force. Look at the diagrams of the following objects and decide whether they increase the ability to move heavier objects or increase the speed.

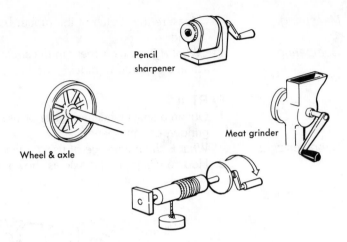

Pencil sharpener

Wheel & axle

Meat grinder

How Will Children Use or Apply What They Discover?	1. Pulling an object across the table produced a force. *How can you tell whether you applied a greater amount of force by pulling the board without pencils under it or by using the pencils as axles?*
What Must I Know?	A spring scale can be substituted for the rubber band. If you have a balance, you can determine how many pounds of force you need to pull the board across the table. If you use a rubber band you must calculate how far the rubber band stretches. The rubber band will not stretch as much the first time.
	2. *How are roller bearings and ball bearings used?* 3. A girl wants to move a heavy desk drawer across her room to another shelf. *How will she go about doing this with the least amount of effort and the greatest amount of speed?*

What Is a Jack and How Is It Used? (4–8)

What Do I Want Children to Discover?	A **screw** is an inclined plane wrapped around a rod. As with an inclined plane, force is gained at the expense of distance. A large weight can be moved by a small force if the smaller force is applied over a greater distance.
What Will I Need?	Triangular pieces of paper Pencil Ring clamp Hammer Screwdriver Tape measure Model of a hill Board Nail Several screws Colored pencil or crayon

What Will We Discuss?

Show the class several examples of screws and ask the following questions:
What are these called?
What purpose do they serve?
Where are they in the classroom?
What advantage do they have over nails?
What type of machine studied thus far resembles a screw?

What Must I Know?

A screw is a circular, inclined plane.

PROCESSES

What Will Children Do?

1. Obtain a small piece of paper and cut it in the shape of a triangle as shown in the diagram. The paper will wind around the pencil. Color the edge of the paper so you can see it.

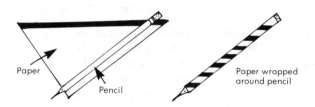

Observing

What kind of machine did the paper represent before you rolled it around the pencil?

Observing

What kind of machine did the paper represent after you rolled it around the pencil?

Comparing

How are the screw and the inclined plane related?

2. Obtain a ring stand clamp and insert a pencil as shown in the following diagram.

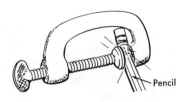

Hypothesizing

What do you think will happen to the pencil when you move the screw inward?

Hypothesizing

How much effort will have to be applied to break the pencil?

Jack

Communicating
Comparing
Inferring
Inferring

3. Look at the diagram of the jack.
   Describe how the jack works.
   How is the jack similar to a screw?
   What is the purpose of using a jack on a car?
   How is it possible for a person who weighs 150 pounds to lift a car weighing 3,000 pounds with a jack?

How Will Children Use or Apply What They Discover?

1. *When were jacks used in old barber shops?*
2. *Where else are jacks used?*
3. *How many seconds would a person have to exert a force to raise a car a small distance?*
4. *What machine is involved in a spiral notebook?*
5. *If you were asked to push a heavy rock to the top of a hill, how would you move it up the hill?*

What Is a Lever and How Can You Use It? (4–8)

What Do I Want Children to Discover?

A **lever** is a simple machine.
A lever cannot work alone.
A lever consists of a bar that is free to turn on a pivot called the **fulcrum.**
By using a first-class lever, it is possible to increase a person's ability to lift heavier objects. This is called the **mechanical advantage.**
The mechanical advantage of a lever is determined by the formula:

$$\text{M.A.} = \frac{\text{Effort Arm}}{\text{Resistance Arm}}$$

The weight times the distance on one side of the fulcrum must equal the weight times the distance on the other side if the lever is balanced.
A first-class lever has the fulcrum between the resistance and the effort.

What Will I Need?

Ruler
100-gram weight
20-gram weight

Roll of heavy string or nylon fishing line
Assorted weights of various sizes
Platform with an arm for suspending objects

What Must I Know?   Define *resistance, force,* and *fulcrum* before beginning the activity.

PROCESSES

What Will Children Do?

1. Obtain some heavy string, a ruler, a 100-gram weight, a 20-gram weight, a ring stand, and a ring clamp.

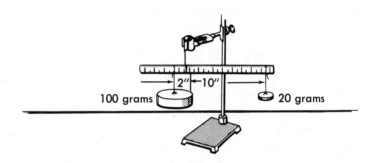

2. Assemble the apparatus as shown in the diagram.

Hypothesizing   *Where do you think you should attach the 100-gram weight and the 20-gram weight so the ruler will balance?*

3. Attach the weights so the ruler is balanced.

Observing   *How far is the 100-gram weight from the end of the ruler?*
Observing   *How far is the 20-gram weight from the end of the ruler?*

4. Look at these three things: the string, which is suspending the ruler, the 20-gram weight, and the 100-gram weight.

Inferring   *What is the relationship between the weight and distance on each side of the fulcrum?*

Inferring   *What are the advantages of using a first-class lever of this type?*

5. Use the following formula to calculate the mechanical advantage (M.A.) of the lever.

$$\text{M.A.} = \frac{\text{Effort Arm}}{\text{Resistance Arm}}$$

What Must I Know?/ Where Do I Find It?   At the completion of the activity, explain to the class that a **first-class lever** consists of a bar that is free to turn on a pivot point called the **fulcrum.** The weight moved is called the **resistance.** The force exerted on the other end of the lever is called the **effort.** Draw the diagram (see p. 82) on the board to illustrate this point. State that in a first-class lever, the fulcrum is always between the resistance and the effort. Have the children do some different problems as suggested by the following formula:

$$\text{M.A.} = \frac{\text{Effort Arm}}{\text{Resistance Arm}}$$

Use metric measurements, if possible.

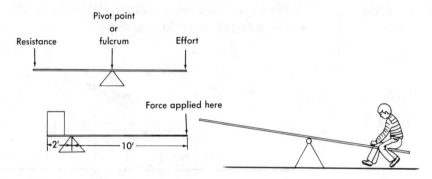

| How Will Children Use or Apply What They Discover? | 1. *How is the M.A. affected when different weights are used?*
2. *What does an M.A. of 4 mean?*
3. *Where are first-class levers used?* |

How Does a Second-Class Lever Work? (4–6)

What Do I Want Children to Discover?	In a **second-class lever,** the weight is located between the effort and the fulcrum. The closer the resistance is to the fulcrum, the less the effort required to move the lever.
What Will I Need?	Board for a lever—a ruler will do Triangular block of wood Rock Pull-type scale Yard or metric stick
What Will We Discuss?	*How is the lever in the following diagram different from a first-class lever?*

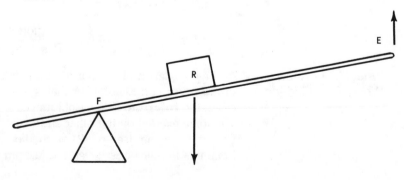

Where do you think the effort and the resistance are in the diagram?

You used a formula when working with the first-class lever in the last
activity.

*What do you think the mechanical advantage will be with this type of
lever?*

What Must I Know?

This lesson should follow the first-class lever activity.

**What Will Children
Do?**

PROCESSES

1. Obtain a lever, a block of wood, and a rock.

   Assemble your equipment as indicated in the next diagram.

   Hypothesizing

   *What would you do to determine the effort needed to move the
   rock?*

2. Obtain a pull-type scale and attach it to the end of the lever farthest from the fulcrum and raise the rock by lifting the scale.

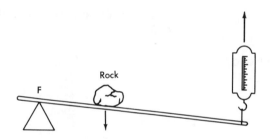

Rock

F

Observing
Hypothesizing

*Designing an
investigation*

Hypothesizing

How is the scale affected when you raise the rock?

*What do you think the distance of the rock from the fulcrum has
to do with how much effort is needed to raise the rock?*

What should you do to find out?

3. Test your ideas.

   What do you think would happen if a lighter rock were used?

   How would the amount of effort needed change?

**How Will Children Use
or Apply What They
Discover?**

1. *How could a yardstick be used to obtain additional information in
   the above activity?*

2. *What are some examples of second-class levers?*

3. *How are second-class levers useful?*

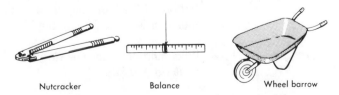

Nutcracker   Balance   Wheel barrow

4. *Which of the following are second-class levers and why?*
   a. *Crowbar*
   b. *Nutcracker*
   c. *Ice tongs*
   d. *Bottle opener*
   e. *Balance*
   f. *Teeter-totter*
5. *What advantage is there to having long rather than short handles on a wheelbarrow?*
6. *Where is it easiest to crack a nut with a nutcracker and why?*

How Does a Third-Class Lever Work? (4–8)

What Do I Want Children to Discover?

In a **third-class lever,** the effort is always between the resistance and the fulcrum.

Third-class levers make it possible to multiply distance at the expense of force.

The mechanical advantage of a third-class lever is always less than one.

What Will I Need?

Ring stand	200-gram weight
Ring clamp	Scissors
Meter stick	Ice tongs
Spring scale	Ice cubes
String	

What Will We Discuss?

How many types of levers have you learned about?
What are some examples of each type?
How many types of levers are there?

What Must I Know?

This activity should be done in groups of two.

What Will Children Do?

PROCESSES

1. Obtain a ring stand, ring clamp, meter stick, spring scale, 2 feet of string, 200-gram weight, and a pair of scissors.

Carrying out experiment

2. Assemble the equipment as shown in the next diagram by fastening the end of the meter stick to the ring clamp. With the string at 10 cm., tie a loop of string around the meter stick at the 95-cm. mark. Slip the hook of the 200-gram weight over the bottom of the loop. Slip the hook of the spring scale under the meter stick at the 50-cm. mark.

Inferring

What kind of a machine do you have?
How do you know?

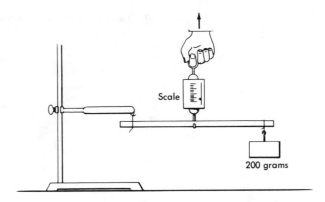

Comparing

What is different about this machine compared to others you have studied?

Refer to the diagram next for help.

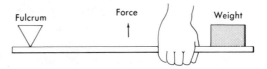

Hypothesizing

What effect will the arrangement have on the force necessary to lift a weight?

3. Using this arrangement and the scale, determine the effort necessary to support the weight as shown in the diagram.

4. Do this two or three times by moving the position of the 200-gram weight. Note the lengths of the effort resistance arms in each case. (Be sure the spring balance remains between the fulcrum and the load.)

Inferring

What do you conclude about the effort required to lift a load with a lever of this type?

Inferring

What can you say about the mechanical advantage of this kind of lever?

5. Calculate the force that should be necessary to support the weight in each case you tested by using the lengths of resistance and the effort arms. To do this, use the following formula:

Resistance × Resistance Arm = Effort × Effort Arm

6. Obtain some ice tongs and a piece of ice.

7. Pick up the piece of ice.

Observing
Inferring

8. What type of lever are the ice tongs, and why?

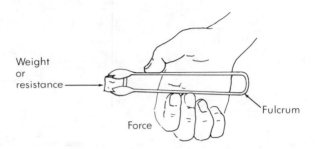

Weight or resistance

Force

Fulcrum

How Will Children Use or Apply What They Discover?

1. *For what purpose is a third-class lever used?*
2. *Mark in front of each of the following what class lever each represents:*
   a. _____ *sugar tongs*
   b. _____ *tweezers*
   c. _____ *scissors*
   d. _____ *human forearm*
   e. _____ *crowbar*
   f. _____ *nutcracker*
   g. _____ *wheelbarrow*
3. *What examples of first-class levers do you find in school yards?*
4. *What machines may consist of two levers?*
5. *What advantage is there in using pliers?*
6. *What advantage is there in using a rake?*
7. *What kind of lever would you have had if, in your experimental procedure, you had placed the spring scale beyond the weight?*
8. *A shovel is often used in two ways: to dig and to throw material. What class lever does the shovel represent when used to dig?*
9. *What class lever is represented in the action of throwing with your arm?*
10. *How could you change the experimental procedure and find the answers to the same questions? (Remember not to change it so you would no longer have a third-class lever.)*

Why Use a Single Fixed Pulley? (4–8)

What Do I Want Children to Discover?

A single fixed pulley has no positive mechanical advantage, but it can be used to move an object in one direction while pulling in the opposite direction.

If a pulley is attached to a beam and does not move, it is called a **fixed pulley.**

The **mechanical advantage** (M.A.) of a pulley is computed by using the formula:

$$\text{M.A.} = \frac{\text{Resistance}}{\text{Effort}} \text{ or}$$

$$\text{M.A.} = \frac{\text{Number of strands holding up the resistance}}{\text{Number of strands holding up the effort}}$$

What Will I Need?

Single fixed pulley
Thin cord or nylon fishing line
Pull-type scale
50-gram weight
100-gram weight

What Will We Discuss?

What do you think will happen if you attach a weight and a scale to the ends of a pulley and attempt to move the weight?
How will the scale be affectd when you raise the weight?

What Will Children Do?

Carrying out experiment

PROCESSES

1. Obtain a single fixed pulley, a piece of cord, a pull-type scale, and a 50-gram weight. When assembled, your equipment should be similar to the diagram.
2. Pull the scale, lift the weight, and record your observations.

Inferring

Why does the scale measure more force than the weight being lifted?

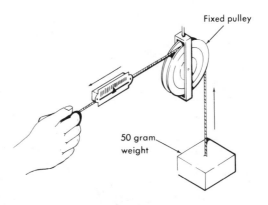

Fixed pulley

50 gram weight

Hypothesizing
Inferring
Measuring

What do you think happens to the extra force?
Why should the activity be done more than once?
3. Complete the activity several times and record each measurement.
4. Compute the average measurement.
   The following formula is used to compute mechanical advantage:

$$\text{Mechanical Advantage (M.A.)} = \frac{\text{Resistance weight}}{\text{Effort weight}}$$

Inferring

Where in the formula will you use the measurement recorded from the scale?

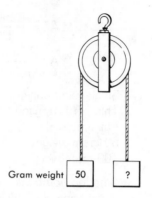

Gram weight | 50 | ?

Applying
: *Where in the formula will you use the gram weight used in the activity?*

5. Compute the mechanical advantage of a single fixed pulley as used in your activity.

Applying
: *What can you tell about the M.A. of the pulley in the preceding diagram?*

Hypothesizing
: *What would you have to do in the situation shown in the following diagram to keep the weight in place?*

100 gram weight

Summarizing
: *What are the advantages in using the single fixed pulley?*

How Will Children Use or Apply What They Discover?
: 1. *How would you make a single fixed pulley so it produced very little friction?*
2. *Why is there an advantage to pulling down instead of up with a pulley arrangement?*

What Is a Movable Pulley and How Can You Use It? (4–8)

What Do I Want Children to Discover?
: Pulleys that move with the resistance are called **movable pulleys.** Movable pulley systems have a mechanical advantage greater than one.

The mechanical advantage of a movable pulley system is equal to the number of stands holding up the resistance.

What Will I Need?

Ring stand for attaching pulleys
2 single pulleys
Pull-type scale
100-gram weight

50-gram weight
Yard or metric stick
String or nylon fishing line

What Will Children Do?

Carrying out experiment

PROCESSES

1. Obtain a ring stand and a clamp for attaching a pulley, a single pulley, a pull-type scale, and a 100-gram weight. Assemble your equipment as shown in the diagram.

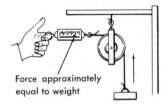 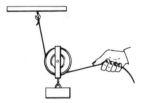

Force approximately equal to weight

Hypothesizing

How much do you think you will have to pull on the scale to raise the 100-gram weight?

2. Pull on the scale and raise the weight.

Observing
Measuring
Hypothesizing

How is the scale affected when you raise the weight?

3. Repeat this activity several times and record each measurement. *What do you think will happen when you use two pulleys to raise the 100-gram weight as shown in the diagram?*

4. In addition to the equipment you have, obtain a single fixed pulley and a 50-gram weight. Assemble your equipment as shown in the diagram.

Observing

5. Pull the 50-gram weight and record your observations.

6. Remove the 50-gram weight and attach the scale.

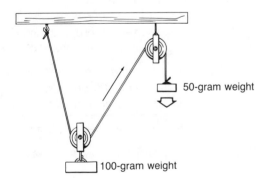

50-gram weight

100-gram weight

Your equipment should be constructed as shown in the diagram below.

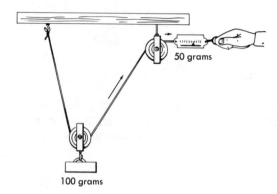

Hypothesizing

How will the scale be affected when you raise the 100-gram weight?

7. Raise the weight by pulling on the scale.

Observing
Measuring

What happens to the scale when you raise the weight?

8. Repeat the activity several times and record each measurement.
   Why is there an advantage in using this type of pulley system?

9. Remove the scale and once again attach the 50-gram weight.

Hypothesizing

How far do you think the 50-gram weight will move when it raises the 100-gram weight?

Hypothesizing

How far do you think the 100-gram weight will move when it is raised by the 50-gram weight?

10. Obtain a yard or metric stick.

Observing

11. Move the 50-gram weight and measure how far both the weights move.

Measuring

12. Repeat this part of the activity several times and record your measurements.

Summarizing

What can you say about pulleys from the measurements you just recorded?

13. Look at the measurements you recorded when one pulley was used and those you recorded when two pulleys were used.
    What does the information tell you about pulleys?

How Will Children Use or Apply What They Discover?

1. *What kind of pulley system would be needed to raise a piano weighing 300 pounds?*
2. Draw a sketch of that pulley system.

Reference Books—Simple Machines (Mechanics) Jan Adkins, *Moving Heavy Things* (New York: Houghton, 1980). Harvey Weiss, *Machines and How They Work* (New York: Harper and Row, 1983).

MAGNETIC AND ELECTRICAL ENERGIES AND INTERACTIONS

Quickie Starters

What Can Magnets Do?

Materials
Several strong magnets, steel ball

Opening Questions
What might happen if you bring a magnet next to the steel ball or another magnet?

Some Possible Activities
Put a magnet on a table and hold a steel ball 1 inch (2-3 cm) away from the magnet's end.
What happens when you let go of the steel ball?
Try it again.
Why do you think this happens?

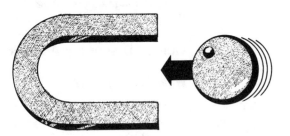

Now try the same thing using two magnets instead of one magnet and a steel ball.
What happens to the magnets?

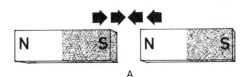

A

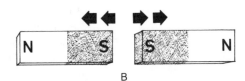

B

Try the same thing but reverse one end of one magnet.
What happens now? Why do you think that happened that way?
What other things might you be able to move with magnets?
How could you find out?

What Are the Shapes and Names of Magnets?

Materials
Large assortment of magnets of different sizes, shapes, colors, and materials—i.e., lodestone, bar, U-shaped, horseshoe, cylindrical, disk,

doughnut-shaped, etc.; variety of items attracted to magnets—i.e., paper clips, iron or steel washers and nails, etc.

Opening Questions

How are all these things the same?
What are they called?

Some Possible Activities

Touch one object at a time to the piles of paper clips, iron or steel washers or nails, etc.
What happens to the paper clips and other things?
Try the same thing with the other objects.
What happens? Why do you think the paper clips, the iron or steel washers and nails were pulled to and stuck to these objects?
Objects that pull and hold iron and steel things are called **magnets,** and their exact names are descriptive of their shapes, such as lodestone, bar magnet, U-shaped magnet, cylindrical magnet, and doughnut-shaped magnet.
What other shapes might magnets have?
Bring in magnets you have at home.
Where are the magnets used?

Guided Discovery Activities

What Is a Magnet? (K–6)

What Do I Want Children to Discover?

A magnet has two **poles.** One end is called the **north,** and the other is called the **south.**
Like poles repel.
Unlike poles attract.
Around every magnet is an area called the **magnetic field** made up of magnetic lines of force.

What Will I Need?

2 round bar magnets
String
Steel needle
⅛" slice of cork
Glass or plastic pan
Water
2 rectangular bar magnets

What Must I Know?

The materials listed are for a group of two or three children. Set up stations and equip each as previously indicated.

What Will We Discuss?

Display a round bar magnet to the class.
What is this called?
What is it made of?
How can it be used?
What are the properties or characteristics of a magnet?
What things can a magnet do?

What do you think will happen if two magnets are placed side by side?

How could you find out?

PROCESSES

PART I

What Will Children Do?

Observing

Observing

1. Obtain two round magnets. Place one magnet on the table. Place the second magnet near it.
   Observe what happens.
2. Reverse one of the magnets.
   Observe what happens.

What happens when you put the second magnet beside the first one?

What happens when you turn one magnet around?

Why do you think one magnet rolls when the other comes near it?

What did you notice when the magnets pulled together?

What did you notice when the magnets pushed apart?

Inferring

How do you know from this that both ends of the magnet are not the same?

Inferring

What did you do to make the magnets push apart?

Inferring

What did you do to make the magnets pull together?

PART II

1. Obtain two rectangular or round bar magnets.
2. Tie a string around the middle of one of the magnets.

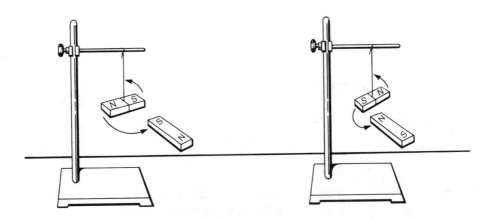

3. By holding the string, suspend the magnet in air.

Hypothesizing

What do you think will happen when another magnet is brought near the suspended one?

4. Bring another magnet near the suspended one.

Inferring   *Why do you think the magnet moves?*

Hypothesizing   *What do you think will happen when you reverse the magnet in your hand?*

Observing   5. Reverse the magnet and bring it near the suspended one.

Inferring   *Why does the suspended magnet react differently when you approach it with the other end of the magnet in your hand?*

Inferring   *What causes the magnet to react in different ways?*

Inferring   *How do you know there is a force present when it cannot be seen?*

Explaining   *What is a force?*

What Must I Know?   Point out that a **force** is a push or pull. This can be shown by pushing or pulling a child in a chair.

PART III

1. Obtain a steel needle, a magnet, and a pan with an inch or two of water in it.

Hypothesizing   *What can you find out about the needle and the magnet?*

2. Magnetize a needle by holding a magnet in one hand and stroking a needle downward several times. Lay the needle on the cork so the needle is in a horizontal position. Float it in the water you have placed in a pan.

3. Bring a magnet near the cork and needle.

Inferring   *Why do the cork and the needle move when you bring a magnet near them?*

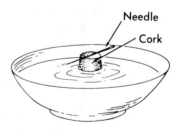

Inferring   *What happens to the needle when it is stroked with the magnet?*

Summarizing   *What causes the cork and needle to move?*

How Will Children Use or Apply What They Discover?

1. *How does a compass work?*
2. *How could you use a magnet to make a compass?*

What Is a Magnetic Field? (K–3)

What Do I Want Children to Discover?	Around *every* magnet there is an area where the magnet can change the direction of iron filings. This is called the **magnetic field.** Not *every* part of the magnetic field around a magnet is the same.

What Will I Need?

Bar magnet
Paper clip
String
3 books

What Will We Discuss?

What happens when a magnet is brought near a steel object?
Why doesn't the magnet have to touch the object to move it?
What causes the object to move when a magnet comes near?
What part of the magnet has the most pull?
How can you show there is a force around a magnet?

What Will Children Do?

PROCESSES

1. Obtain a paper clip, some string, heavy books, and a magnet.
2. Tie the string around one end of the paper clip.
3. Put the other end of the string on the table and put a heavy book or two on it.
4. Hold up the string and paper clip. Place the magnet just above the paper clip and place another book on it. Be sure the clip and magnet do not touch as indicated in the diagram.

Observing
Inferring
Inferring
Inferring

5. *What happens to the clip when you let go of it?*
   Why does the paper clip stay suspended?
   Why doesn't gravity pull the clip down again?
   What force overcame gravity?

Observing
Inferring
Inferring

6. Bring another magnet close to the clip.
   What happens to the clip?
   Why do you think this happens?
   How did the second magnet affect the pull of the first magnet?

What Must I Know?

The children should discover that around *every* magnet there is an area capable of attracting or repelling objects. This area is called the **magnetic field.**

How Will Children Use or Apply What They Discover?	1. *Where is the field of force of a magnet?* 2. *How can you find out where the field is?*

What Would a Magnetic Field Look Like? (3–8)

What Do I Want Children to Discover?	In a magnetic field there are magnetic lines of force. The earth has a magnetic field. The concentration of the lines of force around any part of the magnet determines the strength of the field at that point. Magnetism will pass through most solid objects.

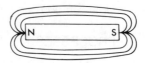

What Will I Need?	Bar magnet Piece of cardboard or thick paper Iron filings Colored pencil or crayon

What Will We Discuss?	*What do you call the areas of force around a magnet?* *What parts of the magnet attract objects with the greatest pull?* *Why doesn't a magnet need to touch a magnetic object to attract it?* *What part of a magnet do you think has the greatest field of force around it?* *What can you do to show where most of the force is located around a magnet?*

What Must I Know?	Make a study sheet for the children to use in showing lines of force and the magnetic field similar to the preceding diagram. Have them label the poles, magnetic lines of force, and magnetic field.

What Will Children Do?	PROCESSES PART I 1. Obtain some cardboard or thick paper, some iron filings, a colored pencil or crayon, and a bar magnet. 2. Place the magnet on the table and put the paper or cardboard over it.

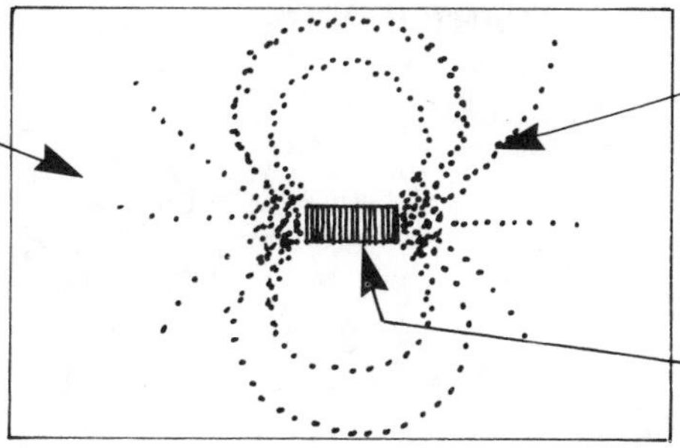

Paper

Iron filings

Bar magnet

3. Sprinkle some iron filings on the cardboard.

Observing   *How are the filings scattered around the cardboard?*

Inferring   *How far out are the filings affected by the magnet?*

What do you notice about the way the filings arrange themselves?

Observing   *Are the filings in lines or are they solidly grouped?*

Observing   *Where is the greatest concentration of filings?*

These lines are called **magnetic lines of force.**

Comparing   *In what way is the pattern that these lines make similar to a map?*

Inferring   *Where is the greatest force located around a magnet and why?*

What Must I Know?

The iron filings have become magnetized by induction. They organize themselves into little magnets that point north and south and that are arranged in lines. These are called magnetic lines of force. They run from the north to the south poles without crossing. The more lines of force there are in an area, the stronger the magnetic field. Since the ends of the magnet have the most lines, they have the greatest force.

How is the earth's magnetic field distributed?
What similarities can you think of concerning a magnet and the earth?

What Must I Know?

Make mimeographed lab sheets showing lines of earth's field of force and magnetic field similar to the following diagram and hand it out to the children to discuss.

In what direction does a compass point?

Inferring   *Why does a compass point north?*

Designing an investigation   *How can you show the lines of force of the earth's field?*

Hypothesizing   *How do you think the lines should be placed around the earth?*

Assuming   *How do you know that the earth has a magnetic pole?*

Hypothesizing   *Where should the magnetic poles be placed?*

How can you show this?

PART II

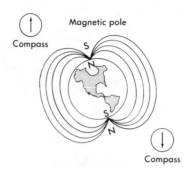

1. Obtain a lab sheet showing the earth.
2. Label the poles of the earth.
3. Color the magnetic field.
4. Label the magnetic lines of force.
5. Show the direction a compass will point on the lab sheet.

Summarizing
Inferring or
*   interpreting*

What pole of the magnet of a compass will really point north?
Why does that end of the compass needle point north?

Summarizing

What can you say will always happen to the needle of a compass in reference to the poles of the earth?

Summarizing
Inferring

What other things can you say about the magnetic field?
How do you know that magnetism can pass through solid substances?

Summarizing

6. Draw on a piece of paper the lines of force and the magnetic field of a bar or round magnet.

How Will Children Use or Apply What They Discover?

1. *How does the magnetism of other planets vary from the earth's?*
2. *What else do you know of that has a north and a south pole?*

What Is Static Electricity? (4–8)

What Do I Want Children to Discover?

All bodies are capable of producing electrical charges.
Conductors allow electrons to move, but **insulators** do not allow electrons to move easily.
Like charges repel; unlike charges attract.

What Will I Need?

Lucite or resin rod or a hard rubber comb
Wool cloth
Flour
Glass rod
Small pieces of paper
Large piece of paper

Balloon
Tap water
Piece of silk about the size of a small handkerchief

**What Will We
Discuss?**

*What can you state about the reactions of poles of magnets toward
   one another?*
*What is the energy that we use to produce light and to operate many
   machines and household equipment?*
What things can produce electricity?
How can you find out if all charges of electricity are the same?

PROCESSES

PART I

**What Will Children
Do?**

1. Obtain the following materials: a lucite or resin rod or a hard
   rubber comb, wool, flour, a glass rod, small pieces of paper, a
   large piece of paper, a balloon, tap water, and a piece of silk.
2. Take the resin rod (or hard rubber comb) and rub it with the
   wool cloth.

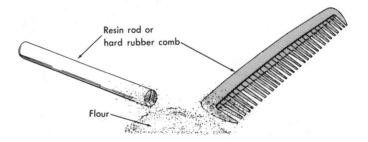

Hypothesizing

*What do you think will happen when the rod is touched to the
flour?*
3. Touch the rod to some flour.

Observing
Hypothesizing

What happens to the flour?
Why do you think the flour is affected by the rod?
4. Clean the rod, rub it again, and touch it to small pieces of paper.

Observing

What does the rod do to the paper?

PART II

5. Rub the rod briskly with the wool cloth.
6. Turn on a water tap so a very slow stream of water comes out.

Hypothesizing

*What do you think will happen to the stream with the rod is
moved close to it?*
7. Move the rod close to the stream.

Observing

What happens as the rod comes near?

Inferring   *Why does the water react as it does?*
Inferring   *Why do you think it reacts as it does without being touched?*

What Must I Know? The students should note how close they have to bring the rod before it affects the stream of water. Develop the concept that there is
an invisible field of electrical force around the rod that either pushes
or attracts the water. This force cannot be seen, but it must be there
because it affects the stream of water. Define **force** as a push or
pull. In this case, the water is pushed or pulled without being
touched by moving the rod toward and away from the water.

Designing an   *How can you find out if the rubbing of the cloth on the rod*
investigation   *causes the electrical force?*

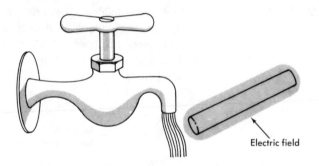

Electric field

8. Rub the rod again with the cloth.
9. Now rub your hand over the rod.

Hypothesizing   *What do you think will happen to the stream of water?*

10. Repeat the procedure by approaching the slow stream of water
with the rod.

Observing   *What effect does the rod have on the water this time?*
Inferring   *Why doesn't the rod have the same effect?*
Inferring   *What happens to the charge that the wool cloth induces in the*
                       rod?
Inferring   *Why do you think the charge fails to last?*

What Must I Know? When the resin rod is rubbed with wool or fur, **electrons** are
rubbed off these materials onto the rod. The rod, however, is an insulator, so the electron movement is slight. The rod becomes negatively charged since each electron produces a small amount of negative charge. When a hand is rubbed over the rod, the rod becomes
discharged because the electrons leave the rod and enter the hand.
The rod is then neutral. Explain the difference between a *conductor*
and an *insulator.*

PART III

Summarizing

1. *After your discussion concerning conductors and insulators, would you say the rod is a conductor or an insulator?*

Inferring

Why do you think so?

2. Obtain two balloons.

3. Inflate the balloons.

4. Tie a string to each balloon and suspend it from a bar as shown in the next diagram.

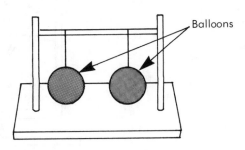

Balloons

5. Rub each balloon with the wool cloth.

Observing

What do the balloons do?

Inferring

Why do they repel each other?

Summarizing

Do you think the balloons are conductors or insulators?

Hypothesizing

What do you think will happen if a charged resin rod is brought near the balloons?

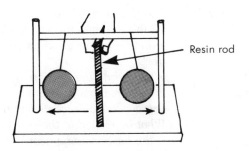

Resin rod

6. Rub the resin rod with wool and place it near the balloons.

Observing

In which direction do the balloons move?

Inferring

Why do you think they were repelled by the rod?

Assuming

Do you think the balloons have a like or unlike charge? Why?

Hypothesizing

What do you think will happen to the balloons if you touch them with a glass rod?

What Must I Know?

These balloons were charged in the same way; therefore, each must have the same charge. When they do have the same charge, they repel each other because like charges repel.

7. Rub the glass rod with the piece of silk.
8. Place it near the balloons.

Observing
Comparing

What happens as it comes near the balloons?
How does the glass rod affect the balloons in comparison to the resin rod?

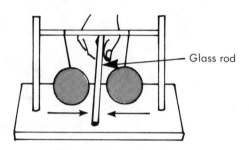

Glass rod

Comparing

What can you say about the charge on the resin rod compared to the glass rod?

PART IV
1. Rub one of the inflated balloons against the piece of wool.
2. Place it next to a wall. (See next diagram.)

Hypothesizing

What do you think will happen to the balloon?

What Must I Know?

The glass rod will have a positive charge since electrons were rubbed off the rod onto the silk. It will attract the balloon because the balloon was negatively charged by the resin rod, and unlike charges attract.

Inferring
Inferring

Why doesn't the balloon fall?
Is the force that pulls the balloon to the wall greater or less than the gravitational force pulling the balloon down to earth?

Inferring

What happened to the negatively charged particles in the wall when the balloon came near?

Summarizing

What can you say about charging matter after following the previous steps?

Summarizing
Summarizing

What is a conductor?
What is an insulator?

What Must I Know?

When you rub the balloon, it becomes negatively charged. When it is placed next to the wall, its negative charge forces the electrons in the wall away from the surface, leaving the surface positively charged. The balloon sticks because the unlike charges attract. The balloon is negative and the wall surface is positive, as is indicated in the diagram.

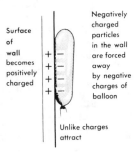

| | How Will Children Use or Apply What They Discover? | 1. *What is electricity?*
2. *How can you use a magnet to make electricity?* |

How Can You Make Electricity by Using Magnetism? (4–8)

What Do I Want Children to Discover?

Around a magnet there are magnetic lines of force.
If you break the magnetic lines of force, you can make electricity.
A **force** is defined as a push or a pull.

What Will I Need?

Copper wire (about 3 yards)
Compass
Bar magnet

What Will We Discuss?

How is electricity used?
How does electricity get to your home for you to use?
What happens when you slide your feet across a wool rug?
What can you produce when you rub a glass rod with wool?
What is the area of force around a magnet called?
What is a force?
How can you use a magnet to produce electricity?

PROCESSES

What Will Children Do?

1. With a partner, obtain a length of wire (about 3 yards), a bar magnet, and a compass.
2. Take the wire and wrap it 20 to 30 turns around the compass as indicated in the diagram.
3. Loop the other end of the wire several times as shown in the diagram.

Inferring

What happens when electricity goes through a wire?

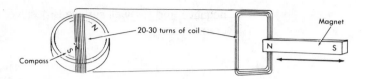

Inferring	*What do you think the area around the wire could be called?*
Inferring	*What has the electricity produced?*
Designing an investigation	*How do you think magnetism could be used to produce electricity?*
Observing	4. Take the bar magnet and plunge it back and forth inside the loops of wire. Instruct your partner to watch what happens to the compass.
Observing	*What happens to the compass?*
Inferring	*Why do you think the compass needle does what it does?*
Applying	*What attracts the compass needle?*
Hypothesizing	*What do you think causes the needle to be deflected?*
Hypothesizing	*Where do you think the magnetism was produced to cause the compass needle to move?*
Inferring or interpreting	*If there is magnetism produced in the wire around the compass, what do you think the plunging of the magnet through the loops of wire has to do with it?*
Inferring or interpreting	*When is electricity produced in the wire?*
Summarizing	*What is the force of a magnet called?*
Summarizing	*What does a magnet do to a magnetizable object?*
Summarizing	*What does a magnet do to a nonmagnetizable object?*
Summarizing	*Explain how magnetism can be used to produce an electrical current.*

What Must I Know?

Around every magnet there is an area that can push or pull objects such as iron filings. This area is thought to consist of lines of force. When these lines of force are broken by plunging the magnet back and forth through a coil of wire, electricity is made in the wire. **Electricity** is defined as a flow of electrons along the wire, making an electrical current. Whenever there is an electrical current produced, there will be a magnetic field around the wire. This magnetic field causes the magnet (compass) in this activity to move. Using magnets to produce electricity is the principle involved in making electricity in a dynamo. Make certain that the compass is far enough away from the magnet to avoid direct magnetic influence.

How Will Children Use or Apply What They Discover?

How can you use electricity to make a magnet?

How Can You Make a Temporary (Electro) Magnet? (4–8)

What Do I Want Children to Discover?

When electricity passes along a wire, it produces a magnetic field around the wire that acts like a magnet.

A magnetic field can make iron temporarily magnetic.

The more current flows through a wire in a unit of time, the more magnetism is generated around the wire.

If a circuit is broken, electricity will not flow.

What Will I Need?

Insulated copper wire
Steel nail
Dry cell battery
Teaspoon of iron filings
Paper clips

What Will We Discuss?

How is magnetism made by electricity?

By using a wire that is carrying a current, how could you make a large magnetic field?

If you wanted to magnetize a nail, how would you do it?

What Must I Know?

The supplies listed above are for two or three students.

PROCESSES

What Will Children Do?

1. Obtain a dry cell battery, a steel nail, a piece of copper insulated wire, some iron filings, and a paper clip.
2. Wrap the wire around the nail several times as shown in the diagram.

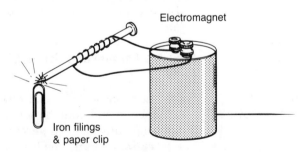

Electromagnet

Iron filings
& paper clip

3. Scrape the insulation off two ends of the wire. Connect one end of it to one terminal of the dry cell and the other end to the other terminal of the dry cell. *Caution:* Avoid leaving both terminals attached for more than a few seconds as intense heat builds up.

Hypothesizing

What do you think will happen to some iron filings if you place them near the nail?

4. Place them near a nail.

5. Place a paper clip on the nail.

Observing   *What happens to the filings and paper clip?*

Inferring   *Why do the iron filings stay on the nail?*

Inferring   *What has been produced around the wire?*

Inferring   *What has the nail become?*

Hypothesizing   *What do you think will happen if you disconnect one of the terminals?*

6. Disconnect one of the terminals.

Observing   *What happens to the iron filings?*

Inferring   *Why do they fall when you disconnect the wire?*

Applying   *What must you do with the circuit to produce electricity?*

Summarizing   *What can you say about the production of magnetism around a wire when electricity goes through it?*

Summarizing   *What would you call the magnet you made by passing electricity through a conductor?*

Designing an investigation   *How do you think you could increase the magnetism in the nail?*

Hypothesizing   *What do you think would happen if you wrapped more wire around the nail?*

Hypothesizing   *Will the magnetism increase or decrease? Why?*

Assuming   *Is the magnet you produced a temporary or a permanent magnet? Why?*

Inferring   *How do you know?*

How Will Children Use or Apply What They Discover?

1. *In what other ways can you use a battery and wire to make a circuit?*
2. *How could you make a parallel or series circuit?*
3. *By what other means could the magnetic field around the nail be increased?*

How Are Parallel and Series Circuits the Same and Different? (4–8)

What Do I Want Children to Discover?

For the electrons to move in a **circuit,** there must be a path that is unbroken to and from the source of electrical energy.

If one lamp burns out in a **series circuit,** the circuit is broken.

In a **parallel circuit,** one lamp can burn out, but the rest of the circuit will still function.

What Will I Need?

2 batteries
4 small lamps
4 sockets
Connecting wires
2 switches

What Will We Discuss?

What would happen if one light on a string of Christmas tree lights were unscrewed?

What would you do to find out?
Why don't all strings of Christmas tree lights behave the same?

PROCESSES

What Will Children Do?

1. Obtain a battery, two small lamps, a switch, two sockets, and connecting wires.
2. Connect these things so that the lights work.
   What do you need to make the lights work?

Hypothesizing

What Must I Know?

The diagram of the series circuit is for your information. It should not be shown to the children until they have done the activity.

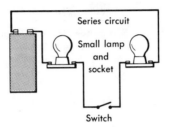

Hypothesizing
Hypothesizing

What purpose does the switch serve?
What do you think will happen when you unscrew one of the lights?
3. Unscrew one of the lights.

Inferring
Hypothesizing

Why did the other light go out?
What can you do to make the lights go on again?
4. Using the same equipment, rearrange it so if one light goes out, the other will burn.

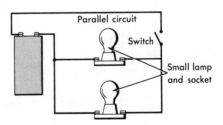

What Must I Know?

The diagram of a parallel circuit is available for your information. It should not be shown to the children until after they finish this activity.

5. Unscrew one of the lights. If you wired it differently than the first time, one of the lights should still burn even though you unscrewed the other.

Inferring *Comparing*	*Why?* *What is the difference between the two types of circuits you have constructed?*
What Must I Know?/ Where Do I Find It?	In a **parallel circuit,** there may be more than two paths for the current to take to complete its circuit. If one of the circuits is broken, the current can still use the other circuit as indicated in the preceding diagram.
How Will Children Use or Apply What They Discover?	1. *What kind of circuits do you have in your home?* 2. *How could you find out what kind of circuit a string of Christmas tree lights is?* 3. Examine a flashlight. *What kind of a circuit does it have?*

Reference Books—Magnetic and Electrical Energies and Interactions
David Adler, *Amazing Magnets* (New York: Troll Associates, 1983). Martin J. Gutnik, *Electricity from Faraday to Solar Generators* (New York: Franklin Watts, 1986).

LIGHT ENERGY AND COLOR

Quickie Starters

What Makes Things Have Color?

Materials	Several different colored objects
Opening Questions	*What do you notice about these things?* *What colors are they?* *How can you group these things?*
Some Possible Activities	Give the children several objects with different colors and ask them to identify and name the colors. After doing this, have them find things around the room that have the same colors. Give the children several objects and ask them to group them by color. Ask them to find other objects in the room that they could place in the same color groups.

What Do Things Look Like under Sun Lamps?

Materials	White cloth, any kind of rocks that will give off a fluorescence under ultraviolet light
Opening Question	*What do things look like under ultraviolet lamps?*
Some Possible Activities	Have the children look at white cloth in normal light and then under ultraviolet light. Invite them to look at all kinds of things. If you can get some fluorescent paints or rocks, have them look at these as well. *Caution:* Students should not look into these lamps as they might

burn the retina of the eye. They should also be warned not to have the light shining on their skin as they could get sunburned in only a few minutes.

Guided Discovery Activities

What Does a Prism Do to White Light? (K–8)

What Do I Want Children to Discover?	White light, when passed through a prism, disperses to form a continuous **spectrum,** or a rainbow. White light is a mixture of many colors of light. Each color in the spectrum has a different wavelength.
What Will I Need?	A prism
What Will We Discuss?	*What is a prism?* *What does a prism do?*
What Must I Know?	This activity should be done in groups of two or more children.

PROCESSES

PART I

What Will Children Do?

1. Obtain a prism.

Hypothesizing

What do you think will happen to the light rays after they pass through the prism?

2. Place the prism in the path of a strong beam of light as indicated in the diagram.

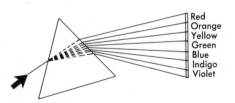

Observing — *What does the prism do to the light rays when they pass through it?*

Observing — *What colors do you see?*

Observing — *Which color seems to have bent the most?*

Observing — *Which color seems to have bent the least?*

Inferring — *What do you know about the way the different colors of lights are refracted (bent) by the prism?*

Inferring — *What is white light made of?*

What Must I Know?   The children should see that white light is produced by the combination of several wavelengths of light. Draw a prism on the board and have the children show how the spectrum is formed. Their drawing should be something like the previous diagram.

PART II

Hypothesizing   *What do you think will happen if you look through the prism at your partner?*

Experimenting   1. Look through the AB side of the prism at your partner.

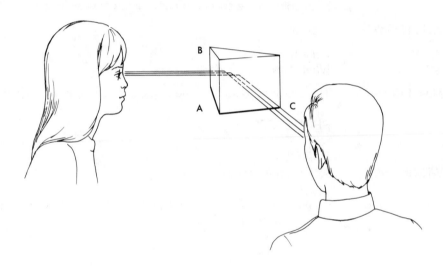

2. Record your observations.

Inferring   *Why is it possible to see what your partner is doing without looking directly at him or her?*

Inferring   *What happens to the light entering the prism that makes it possible for you to see your partner?*

Inferring   *What does the prism do to the light rays?*

Comparing   *What is the difference between a prism and a mirror in the way that each affects light?*

What Must I Know?   A prism is used in expensive optical equipment instead of mirrors because prisms absorb less light. At the conclusion of this activity, place a diagram of a prism on the board and have the children draw how light passes through it. If they do not understand how a prism can be used in a periscope, draw and discuss the following diagram.

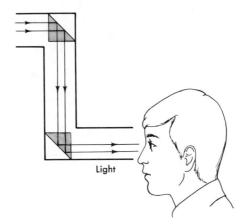

Light

How Will Children Use or Apply What They Discover?	1. *What happens to X-rays when they pass through a prism?* 2. *What would happen if you passed light through two prisms?* 3. *Why are prisms used in expensive optical equipment instead of mirrors?*

How Is Light Changed When It Passes from Air to Water? (3–8)

What Do I Want Children to Discover?	A substance that is curved and transparent can be used as a **lens.** Light may be refracted (bent) when it passes through water or glass.
What Will I Need?	Quart jar filled with 16 ounces of water and 8 ounces of cooking oil Coin Pint jar or small aquarium (only 1 is needed for a class) Shallow pan Water Flashlight Ruler Black paper Milk
What Will We Discuss?	*What is a lens?* *How are lenses used?* *How do light rays affect the appearance of an object in water?* *How can the direction of light rays be changed?* *How can light rays be bent?*
What Must I Know?	This activity should be done in groups of two.
What Will Children Do?	PROCESSES
	PART I
Hypothesizing *Hypothesizing*	*How may water serve as a lens?* *How do you think a ruler would look if you placed it in a jar of water?*

1. Obtain a jar of water and a ruler.
2. Place the ruler in the jar.

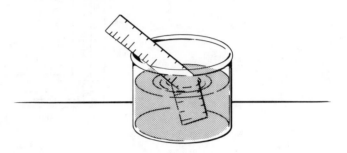

Observing

3. Observe the ruler.
   How has the ruler changed in appearance?

PART II

1. Obtain a pan, a small coin, and a jar of water.
   Put the coin in the bottom of a pan. Have a student back away from the pan until the coin disappears out of his or her line of sight.

Hypothesizing

   How could it be possible for the student to see the coin again without moving?

Designing an experiment
Hypothesizing
Applying

2. Another pupil should gradually fill the pan with water until the pupil observing the pan sees the coin.
   Why is it easier to see the coin after water is added than before?
   What must the water do to the light rays coming from the coin to your eyes?

Inferring

   How is the light bent?

Inferring

   What conclusions may be drawn from the activity with the coin and ruler?

What Must I Know?

After the activity you might insert the following diagram and discuss it.

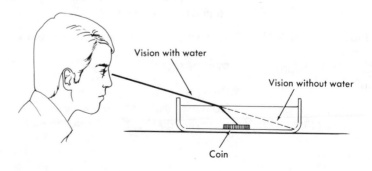

PART III

1. Obtain a glass jar or square aquarium filled with water, a flashlight, a piece of black paper, and a teaspoon of milk.
2. Add just enough milk to the jar or aquarium so a light beam from a flashlight is visible when passing through the milk.
3. Make a small hole in a piece of black paper.
4. Turn the flashlight on and shine a beam of light through the hole in the black paper into the milky water as shown in the diagram.

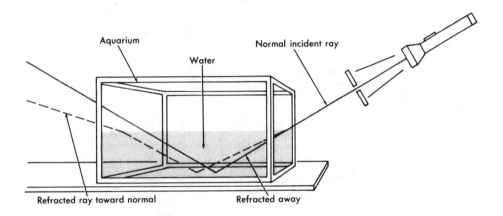

Observing

How is the beam of light refracted (bent) when it enters the water?

5. Have another pupil hold the jar or aquarium off the desk and shine the light through the hole in the paper onto the solution from above as before.

Observing

How does the light beam leaving the bottom of the aquarium or jar look?

Comparing

How does this differ from the way the light behaved when entering the solution?

What Must I Know?

Air is said to be less optically dense than water. This means that when a light beam goes from one less optically dense medium into something more optically dense, it will bend. Oil is optically more dense than water. Do not confuse optical density with the density of a substance. Remember oil is really less physically dense than water because it will float on water.

Hypothesizing

Draw how you think light rays would look when passed through a jar of water containing a layer of oil.

6. Obtain from your teacher a jar of water with oil and determine whether your ideas are correct.

What Must I Know?   When the activity is completed, ask the class to draw on the chalk-board what happens as the light passes through plain water with milk. They should make a diagram something like the one below.

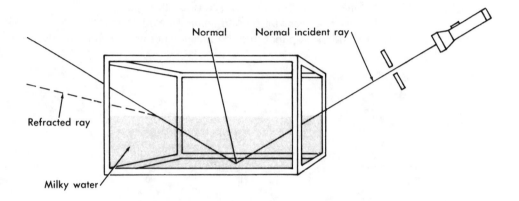

Normal   Normal incident ray

Refracted ray

Milky water

Discuss how light bends.

Observing   *How is the light refracted when it leaves the solution?*

What Must I Know?   Draw the last two diagrams on the board after the lesson and explain that when a light ray passes obliquely from one medium into another of greater optical density, it is refracted toward the normal. The normal is defined as a perpendicular line to the plane at a given point.

How Will Children Use or Apply What They Discover?

1. *Would colored water change the way light rays are reflected from the ruler?*
   What would you do to find out?
2. *What other substances could you use to show that light rays may be altered?*
3. *What would happen if you used a clear plastic glass and rubbing alcohol or vinegar instead of water?*

How Is Light Reflected? (4–8)

What Do I Want Children to Discover?   When light is reflected from a mirror, it is reflected at the same angle as the angle of light hitting the mirror. A physicist would say that the angle of incidence equals the angle of reflection.

What Will I Need?   Rubber ball
Mirror

What Will We Discuss?   *How is light refracted?*
How is light reflected?
What are some ways that light is reflected?

What Will Children Do?

PROCESSES

Observing

1. Obtain a rubber ball and bounce it at an angle against the wall.
   How does the ball bounce away from the wall?
2. Continue to bounce the ball against the wall, hitting the wall at various angles.

Observing
Hypothesizing

At what angles does the ball bounce back from the wall?
What do you think will happen to light if you shine it onto a reflecting surface in a manner similar to the way you threw the ball?

Comparing

How does the way light reflects off a wall resemble the way a ball bounces off a wall?

3. Hold a mirror so you can see yourself.
   Where did you have to hold the mirror?
4. *How did the light coming from your face reflect so you could see your face?*
   Hint: Remember how a ball bounces when you throw it straight against a wall?

Hypothesizing

What will happen if you hold the mirror at an angle?

5. Hold the mirror in front of yourself.
   Move the mirror so you can see another person or another part of the room.
6. Diagram on a piece of paper your location compared to the mirror. Indicate with arrows how the light comes from the mirror to you.
7. Now hold the mirror at different angles.

Observing and inferring

How is light reflected when you hold the mirror at different angles?

How Will Children Use or Apply What They Discover?

1. *What things besides mirrors may be used to change the direction of light?*
2. *How would you make a periscope from mirrors? Tell how it would work.*

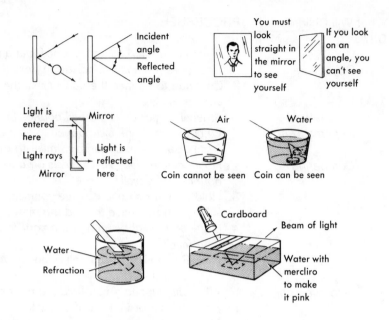

What Must I Know?   To summarize what the children have discovered about light, draw the preceding diagram on posterboard by using a felt pen. Hold the charts up and ask the children to explain what is taking place.

How Does Light Appear to Travel? (3–8)

What Do I Want Children to Discover?   Light appears to our eyes to travel in a straight line.

What Will I Need?

4 index cards (5 × 8 inches)	Rubber band
Modeling clay	Matches
Hole puncher or pointed object (pencil)	Waxed paper
Round (oatmeal) box	Candle
Flashlight or projector	Pie tin

What Will We Discuss?   *How does light appear to your eyes to travel?*

What Must I Know?   You may conduct these simple activities, or students may do them by themselves, to assist them in seeing that light appears to our eyes to travel in a straight line. In a camera, due to light appearing to travel in a straight line, images appear upside down (inverted). **Focusing**—moving objects back and forth—is also a result of light appearing to travel in a straight line.

PROCESSES

PART I

What Will Children Do?

1. Holding all the index cards together, punch a ¼-inch (7mm) hole in the center of each with a hole puncher or pointed object. Push each card into a lump of modeling clay and space the cards about 1 foot (30 cm) apart, making sure to line up the center holes as below.

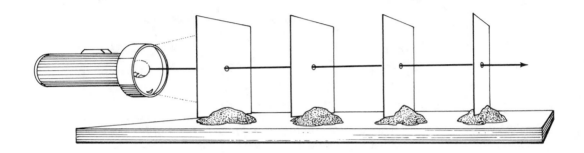

Hypothesizing

What do you think will happen if you shine the light through the first hole in the cards?

2. Shine a light with the flashlight or projector in the first card's hole.

Observing *What do you notice about the path of the light?*

Hypothesizing

3. *What will happen if you move the first card 1 inch (25mm) to one side?*

Observing

4. Move the first card 1 inch over.
   What happens now?

Comparing *How is this different from what you observed in step 2?*

Inferring *What does this tell you about how light appears to our eyes to travel?*

PART II

What Must I Know?

You should demonstrate this for immature or unruly children. For older children, this activity should be done in groups of two. One child will perform the activity for the other to observe and vice versa.

What Will We Discuss?

How does a camera use light?
What does it mean to focus a camera?

PROCESSES

What Will Children Do?

1. Obtain a round oatmeal box, waxed paper, rubber band, candle, and matches. Puncture a very small hole in the end of the box

with your pencil. Cover the open end of the box with waxed paper and secure the paper with a rubber band.
2. Place the candle (attached to the pie tin with melted wax) in front of the box and light the candle. Darken the room.
3. Move the small-holed end back and forth in front of the candle while your partner watches the waxed papered end.

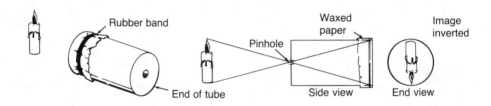

Observing	*What appears on the waxed papered end of the box?*
Observing	*What is different about the image on the waxed paper?*
Inferring	*Why do you think the image appears this way?*
Hypothesizing	*Why did you move the punctured end of the box back and forth?*
Inferring	*From this activity, what would you conclude about how light appears to our eyes to travel?*
Inferring	*How do you think a picture of an object appears on the film in back of a camera?*

How Will Children Use or Apply What They Discover?

1. *What would happen to the image on the waxed paper if you moved the box 3 feet (or a meter) from the candle?*
2. *What would happen to the image if you blew the candle flame out? Why?*

What Must I Know?/ Where Do I Find It?

After the children have completed the previous activity, place the diagrams on the board and have the children draw the image of the candle. They should draw something like the one that appears in the first diagram. Discuss how the light travels through the hole, as indicated by the second diagram, and results in an inverted candle flame on the wax papered end.

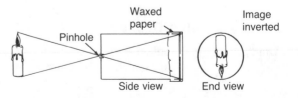

How Do Convex and Concave Lenses Affect Light Passing Through Them? (4–8)

What Do I Want Children to Discover?

When light is passed from a dense to a less dense medium, or vice versa, it may be **refracted** (bent).

A convex lens may magnify close objects and invert objects far from the lens.

The thicker the lens, the more the light rays will be bent.

Convex lenses converge light rays.

Concave lenses diverge light rays.

Concave lenses make objects look smaller.

What Will I Need?

Convex lens
Concave lens
Piece of plain glass
Paper and pencil
Cardboard box and scissors
Flashlight (or slide projector)

What Will Children Do?

PROCESSES

Hypothesizing

In what ways could you find out if a lens can change the direction of light?

1. Obtain a convex lens, a concave lens, a piece of plain glass, a cardboard box, a pair of scissors, paper and pencil, and a strong light source such as a flashlight or slide projector. Cut the top and one end of the cardboard box as shown in the diagram. Cut a slit for the light to pass through as indicated in the diagram. Place a projector or strong light source in front of the slit. (A good flashlight may be substituted for the projector.) This apparatus will be used with the lenses and glass to find out how they work.

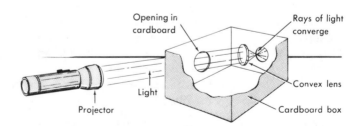

Opening in cardboard   Rays of light converge   Light   Projector   Convex lens   Cardboard box

Observing

2. Before using the cardboard box, examine the two lenses and the piece of glass very carefully. Hold them to your eye. Look at the glass through them. Have someone look through the other side.

3. Compare what you see through each of the three lenses.

Comparing

How do the objects differ?

Observing
Inferring
Hypothesizing

4. Take the convex lens and move it slowly away from your eye.
   What happens as you move the lens away?
   Why do you think this happens?
   What could you do to find out the reason for what happens?

What Must I Know?

The image becomes **inverted.** This happens because as the lens is moved away from the eye, it reaches a point where the distance is greater than the focal length of the lens, and the image becomes inverted as a result. (The **focal length** is the distance from a lens or a mirror to the point where rays of light are brought together to form an image.) When a student first looks at another student through a convex lens, the student appears right-side up. As the student moves the lens away from his eye so that it is at a greater distance than the focal length of the lens, the student he is looking at becomes inverted as shown in the diagram.

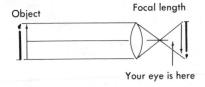

Object   Focal length

Your eye is here

Observing

Comparing

Hypothesizing

Observing
Observing
Collecting data

5. Take the concave lens now and place it near your eye and move it slowly away like you did the convex lens.
   What happens as you move the lens back and forth in front of your eye?
   What do you see in the two lenses that differs from what you saw with the plain glass?
   What do you think will happen when you shine light through the lenses and flat piece of glass onto a surface?
6. Hold the plain piece of glass inside your box as indicated by the diagram.
   What happens to the light?
   What effect, if any, does the box have on the lens?
7. Draw a side view of the lens light when it passes through the glass onto the cardboard.
8. Repeat this step but substitute the concave and convex lenses for the plain glass.

What Must I Know?

In a convex lens the edges are always thinner than the center. When light passes through a convex lens, it converges as shown in the diagram.

Concave diverges light

The edges of a concave lens are always thicker than the center, and light is diverged by this type of lens as shown in the diagram.

Convex converges light

9. Observe your lenses again.

Comparing

How does the shape of the concave lens differ from that of the convex lens?

Comparing

In what ways does the shape of the plain lens differ from the convex and concave lenses?

Comparing

In what ways does the light passing through the convex lens differ from the light passing through the concave lens?

Inferring

What evidence do you have to support the statement that a converging lens may cause light to approach a single point?

What Must I Know?

Draw the two previous diagrams on the board and discuss them.

How Will Children Use or Apply What They Discover?

1. *What proof is there that light can be refracted (bent) by lenses?*
2. *If you wanted to start a fire and had no matches, which lens could you use and why?*
3. *How might fires be started by old bottles lying in dry grass?*
4. *What kind of lenses do you have in your eyes?*
5. *Why do some people have to wear glasses?*

Why Do You See Better with Two Eyes? (2–6)

What Do I Want Children to Discover?

To judge the third dimension adequately (depth and distance), you need two eyes.

Two eyes are needed to see well, especially to see how far away things are and how high or low they are.

What Will I Need?

Table or desk lower than waist high

Pop bottle

Nickel or object similar in size and thickness

What Will Children Do?

PROCESSES

Hypothesizing

What do you suppose will happen if, using only one eye, you try to flip a coin standing on end out of a bottle?

Organizing

1. Obtain the following materials: a pop bottle and a nickel from the teacher (or your own). Be sure to work on a table or desk that you have to look *down* upon so it is below your eye level.

Observing

2. Place the coin in the pop bottle on the desk; walk 10 to 15 feet away from the table in any direction. Facing the table, cover one eye with your right hand. With the left hand held waist high, walk toward the table at a normal pace. When you reach the bottle, flip the coin without hesitation with your free hand. Do not just push the coin off the pop bottle, but flip it with your finger. (See diagram.)

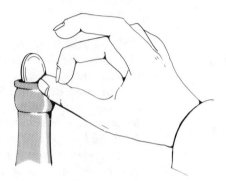

Observing

What happened to the coin?

What Must I Know?

Most people will not flip the coin out of the bottle because they cannot locate it easily. One cannot judge depth and distance well with only one eye.

3. Repeat the activity again. Follow step 2 very carefully, only this time cover your eye with your left hand and use your right hand to flip the coin.

Observing   *What happens to the coin this time?*
Inferring   *Does changing hands make any difference?*
Comparing   *How does this differ from the first time?*
Hypothesizing   *What would happen if you repeated the activity again, only this time using both eyes?*

4. Repeat it and use both eyes.

Observing   *What happens to the coin this time?*
Inferring   *Why do you think using both eyes is better? Explain your answer.*
Inferring
5. *What effect does repeating this activity have on how accurately you can flip the coin?*

Reference Books—Light Energy and Color
Dorothy Collins, *My Big Fun Thinker Book of Colors and Shapes* (Education Insights, 1983). Kathryn Whyman, *Light and Lasers* (Gloucester Press, 1986).

SECTION 2

Quickie Starters and Guided Discovery Activities for Life Sciences

HUMAN ANATOMY AND PHYSIOLOGY

Quickie Starters

How Big Are Your Lungs?

Materials

Dishpan, 2 feet (60 cm) of rubber or plastic tubing, ruler, measuring cup, water, gallon jug, drinking straws

Opening Questions

How much air do your lungs hold?
Do boys have bigger lungs than girls?
Do smokers have more lung capacity than nonsmokers?
Do joggers' lungs hold more air than the lungs of people who don't jog?

Some Possible Activities

Fill the dishpan about one-quarter full of water. Fill the jug to the top with water. Put your hand tightly over the mouth of the jug and invert it in the dishpan, making sure not to let any air get into the jug. Put a clean straw into one end of the tubing and slip the other end into the mouth of the jug. With one continuous breath, keep blowing until you are *completely* out of air.

Slide your hand over the jug's mouth and turn it right side up. To measure how much air you exhaled, do this:

1. Pour in measuring cups of water into the jug until you have refilled the jug.
2. The amount of water you put into the jug to refill it is the amount of air you exhaled.

How Does Your Body Cool Itself?

Materials	2 old wool socks for each child, electric fan
Opening Questions	*Why do you feel cool on a hot summer day when you come out of the pool, ocean, or lake?* *What parts of your body are at work to cool you down when you come out of the water?* *Why does a fan cool us on a hot day?*
Some Possible Activities	Have children remove their shoes and socks. Have children put a dry wool sock on one foot and a wet wool sock on the other foot. Ask: *Which one feels cooler?* To improve cooling effect, use a fan to blow air over the children's feet.

Wet sock Dry sock

Guided Discovery Activities

How Do Humans Breathe? (K–8)

What Do I Want Children to Discover?	When a person exercises, breathing increases. Breathing increases because more **carbon dioxide** is produced. Carbon dioxide causes the diaphragm to work more rapidly. When the diaphragm moves up in the rib cage, it forces air out of the lungs. When the diaphragm moves down, air is pulled into the lungs. Gases and water vapor are exhaled from the lungs.
What Will I Need?	Mirror Rubber bands Stopwatch Small balloons Tape measure Model or chart of the chest cavity

Scissors   Plastic cups
Plastic bag   Plastic drinking straws
Water
½ cup or 100 cc of limewater or calcium hydroxide (obtain in drugstore)

What Will We Discuss?

How many times a minute do you breathe?
How would you go about finding out?

What Must I Know?

This activity should be done in groups of two or three children. For exercise, the children may run in place.

PROCESSES

PART I

What Will Children Do?

1. Do the following with another student: Using a stopwatch, record the number of times he or she normally breathes by counting breaths on a mirror. Let the student also record the number of times you breathe.

	At Rest	After Exercise
One minute	_____	_____
Two minutes	_____	_____
Three minutes	_____	_____

Comparing

What is the average number of times per minute a person breathes at rest?

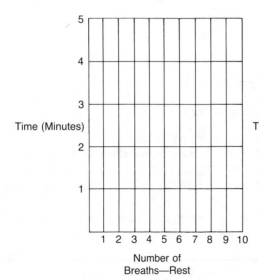

Time (Minutes)

Number of
Breaths—Rest

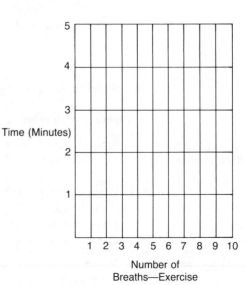

Time (Minutes)

Number of
Breaths—Exercise

Comparing	*What is the average number of times per minute a person breathes after exercise?*
	Graph your rest and exercise record on a diagram like this.
Hypothesizing	*What makes a person breathe faster?*
Inferring	*Why did you count the number of times a person breathes for several minutes rather than for just one?*
Hypothesizing	*What gas do you need from the air?*
Hypothesizing	*What do you exhale?*
Designing an investigation	*How can you prove that you exhale water?*
Designing an investigation	*How can you prove that you exhale carbon dioxide?*
Hypothesizing	*What gas do you breathe from the air that your body does not use?*

What Must I Know? Explain that air contains about 80 percent nitrogen, 17 percent oxygen, 0.03 percent carbon dioxide, and small percentages of other gases. But the body does not use the nitrogen.

Designing an investigation	*How does the size of your chest vary when you breathe?*
	How would you find out?
	2. With a tape measure, check and record these measurements.

	Top of Chest	Lower Diaphragm
Inhale	_____	_____
Exhale	_____	_____

Interpreting data 3. Construct a graph to illustrate these variations.

PART II

1. Obtain a plastic drinking straw, small plastic bag, 2 rubber bands, clear plastic cup, small balloon, and scissors.
2. Cut the straw in half.
3. Punch a hole in the bottom of the cup the same width as the straw. (You can use the heated tip of an ice pick.)
4. Stretch and blow up the balloon a few times.
5. Attach the balloon to the straw with a tightly wound rubber band. Be sure the balloon doesn't come off when you blow into the straw.
6. Push the free end of the straw through the cup's hole and pull until the balloon is at the middle of the cup.
7. Place the open end of the cup into the small plastic bag and fold the bag around the cup, securing it tightly with a rubber band or masking tape if necessary. The plastic bag should be loose, not stretched taut, across the cup's opening.

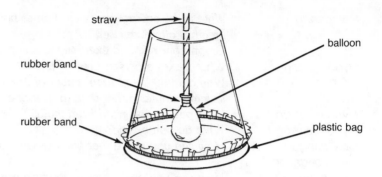

Hypothesizing *What do you think will happen to the balloon if you pull down on the plastic bag at the bottom of the jar?*

 8. Pull down on the plastic bag. Record your observation.

Hypothesizing *What do you think will happen if you push up on the plastic bag?*

 9. Push up on the plastic bag. Record your observation.

Inferring *Why do you see these changes?*

Inferring *Where in your body do you have something that works like this?*

What Must I Know? Introduce the word **diaphragm.** Use a model or a chart of the chest cavity for reference.

Observing *How do the diaphragm, lungs, and chest lie in relation to one another in the chest cavity?*

 10. Diagram and label the parts of the body used in breathing.

PART III

 1. Obtain a mirror.

Hypothesizing *When you breathe, what leaves your mouth?*

 2. Take a mirror and exhale on it. Hold the mirror near your nose.

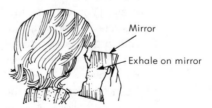

Observing *What do you see on the mirror?*

Inferring *Why does moisture collect on the mirror?*

Assuming *Where does the moisture come form?*

Hypothesizing *What kinds of gases do you think you exhale?*

What Must I Know?   Explain that exhaled air contains about 80 percent nitrogen, 17 percent oxygen, 0.03 percent carbon dioxide, and small percentages of other gases.

Inferring   *What happens to the nitrogen you inhale?*
Inferring   *What gas in air do you need?*
Inferring   *What gas do you exhale more of than you inhale?*

PART IV
1. Obtain a straw and 100 cc of limewater (or some calcium hydroxide). Mix the limewater with water. Let it settle.
2. Blow through a straw into the limewater.

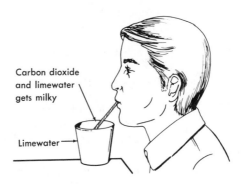

Carbon dioxide
and limewater
gets milky

Limewater →

Observing   *What happens as you blow (exhale) into the limewater?*
Inferring   *Why does it change color?*

What Must I Know?   When carbon dioxide is added to limewater, it changes to a milky color because the carbon dioxide combines with calcium hydroxide to form a white precipitate.

How Will Children Use   1. *How does exercise cause the heart to beat faster?*
or Apply What They   2. *Why does an increase in carbon dioxide in the blood cause the*
Discover?   *heart to beat faster?*
                         3. Explain the hypothesis: "A person needing oxygen naturally breathes faster."

How Does Our Skin Protect Us? (3–8)

What Do I Want   The **skin** protects us from microorganisms that cause disease.
Children to Discover? A cut or wound in the skin can let microorganisms enter the body.
                         Microorganisms sometimes cause infection and disease.
                         A cut or wound in the skin should be properly treated immediately to prevent microorganisms from causing infection.

Antiseptics kill microorganisms; thus they can be used for the treatment of cuts or wounds.
Heat can kill microorganisms.

What Will I Need?

4 unblemished apples   Book of matches
Rotten apple   5 small pieces of cardboard for labels
3 sewing needles   Candle
Small sample of soil   Alcohol

What Will We Discuss?

How is the covering of an apple or an orange like your skin?
What are the advantages of the covering on apples, oranges, and other types of fruit?
How does the covering of your body, the skin, protect you?
What does it mean when a person says he or she wants to sterilize something?
In what ways might you sterilize something?

What Must I Know?

This activity should be done in groups of two to five students.

PROCESSES

What Will Children Do?

Carrying out experiment

1. Obtain five pieces of cardboard for labels, a candle, a match, three needles, and one rotten and four unblemished apples.
2. Put labels *a, b, c,* and *d* with four unblemished apples.

3. Sterilize three needles by heating them in the flame of a candle.
4. Puncture apple *a* with a sterile needle in three places. Apply alcohol over two of the punctures.
5. Push the second sterilized needle into the soil and then into apple *b* in three places.
6. Puncture apple *c* with the third sterile needle but do not apply any alcohol to the three punctures.
7. Do nothing to apple *d* or the rotten apple.
8. Place all four labeled apples in a warm place for several days. *Why was apple d not punctured?*

(a) Three punctures with sterile needle; alcohol applied on two punctures

(b) Puncture with needle stuck in soil

(c) Puncture with needle but no alcohol

(d) Control (no holes)

Rotten

What Must I Know?   If necessary, point out that this is the control in the experiment. Be sure the children understand the term *control.*

Hypothesizing   *What do you think will happen if the apples stand for a few days?*

Comparing   *In what ways do you think they will look alike?*

Comparing   *How will they be different? Why?*

Observing   9. Observe the apples daily. Every other day make a diagram or illustration of the changes taking place. Discuss these with your lab group.

Observing   *What has happened to some of the apples?*

Comparing   *How are the apples alike?*

Comparing   *How are they different?*

Inferring   *What do you think might have caused some of these changes?*

Comparing   *Which spots on the apples seem to be the most prominent? Why?*

Comparing   *Which other apple does apple c resemble most?*

Observing   *What has happened to apple d?*

Inferring   *What was apple d in your experiment?*

     10. Cut all five apples in half.
     Caution: Do not eat the apples because the alcohol is poisonous.

Comparing   *Which apples seem to look most like a rotten apple?*

Inferring   *Why do you think so?*

Inferring   *Why did you apply alcohol over only two punctures on apple a?*

Observing   *What effect did the alcohol have? What about the third puncture?*

What Must I Know?   Alcohol is an **antiseptic.** The alcohol probably destroyed any microorganisms present in the wound.

Inferring   *What happened to all the microorganisms on the needles after they had been heated?*

Comparing   *The skin of an apple is similar to what part of your body?*

Inferring   *Why did the rotten spots seem to grow a little larger each day?*

What Must I Know?   Microorganisms have a fantastic growth rate. As long as there is a substantial amount of food present and space enough for growth, they will continue to reproduce.

Inferring   *What do you think would happen if your skin were punctured?*

Hypothesizing   *What might a person do to a wound or puncture if he or she did not want to get an infection?*

What Must I Know?   The wound should be cleaned, an antiseptic applied, and the wound covered with a sterile bandage.

How Will Children Use or Apply What They Discover?

1. *How might you set up the above experiment using oranges instead of apples? What do you think would happen?*
2. Conduct the same experiment, but this time place the apples in a cool place.
   What effect does temperature have on decay?
3. *In what other ways does your skin protect you?*

How Is Starch Changed in the Food You Eat? (4–8)

What Do I Want Children to Discover?

Large food particles must be broken down into smaller molecules before they can be absorbed.

The breaking down of food by chemical means is called **digestion.**

Food must be dissolved before it can be used by the body.

Starch is a food.

Starch must be changed to dissolved sugar for it to pass through the lining of the small intestine.

What Will I Need?

Cornstarch
Sugar
Iodine (a small bottle with an eye dropper); *Caution:* Iodine is poisonous; keep it away from children. Also, iodine may stain skin, clothing, and other materials.
Spoon
3 glasses
Crackers (two per student)

Funnel
3 paper towels
Scale
100 cc. graduate
Rubber band
4 cubes of sugar
2 jars with covers
Water
Waxed paper
TES-Tape™ (glucose test tape available from drugstore)

What Will We Discuss?

Look at the cracker.
How is the cracker going to help my body when I eat it?
What is going to happen to the cracker?
When will the cracker be ready to be used by the cells?
How is the body going to prepare this cracker for use?
If the body does not use every bit of the cracker, what is going to happen to that which is not used?
Where is the body going to digest this cracker?
What substances does the body contain to break down the cracker into usable substances?

PROCESSES

What Will Children Do?

1. Obtain a teaspoon of cornstarch, two glasses of water, and a teaspoon of sugar. Put the cornstarch into one glass of water and the sugar into the other. Stir each glass with a spoon.

Water and sugar   Water and cornstarch

Observing	*How does the starchy water appear?*
Observing	*How does the sugar water appear?*
Inferring	*Which has dissolved?*
Hypothesizing	*What do you think would happen if you let the glasses stand for a day?*
Inferring	*How would this experiment help to explain why starch has to be changed so your body can use it?*

2. Stir the starch and water again until the starch is mixed with the water. Take a teaspoon of the starch and water mixture and put a drop of iodine into it to dilute to straw color.

Observing	*What color does the mixture turn?*

3. Repeat the above step, substituting sugar water for the starch and water mixture.

Comparing	*How does the result differ?*
	Put a drop of iodine on a cracker.
Observing	*What is the result?*

What Must I Know?   Iodine is used to test for starch. Starch in the presence of iodine turns blue-black.

Summarizing	*How would you summarize this test in terms of the results you have observed?*

4. Obtain a funnel, line it with a piece of paper towel, and set it in an empty glass. Stir the starch in the glass of water again. *Slowly* pour some of the starch water into the funnel.
   After the water has run through, look at the inside of the paper.

Observing	*Is there any starch left inside the funnel?*
Hypothesizing	*How could you test the water to find out if any starch went through with the water?*

5. Perform this test for starch.

Observing	*What color did the mixture turn?*
Inferring	*Is there starch present?*
Hypothesizing	*What do you think will happen if sugar water is poured through filter paper?*
Hypothesizing	*How could you tell if there is sugar in the water before and after you pour it into the funnel?*

Inferring   Which do you think could go through the wall of your intestine better—starch or sugar? Why?

Hypothesizing   6. How can we verify that saliva begins the process of digestion by
Observing   changing starch to sugar?
                     Test one cracker by putting a few drops of iodine on it.
                     What do you observe?
                     Test a cracker for sugar by placing a few drops of water on it and testing it with TES-Tape™.

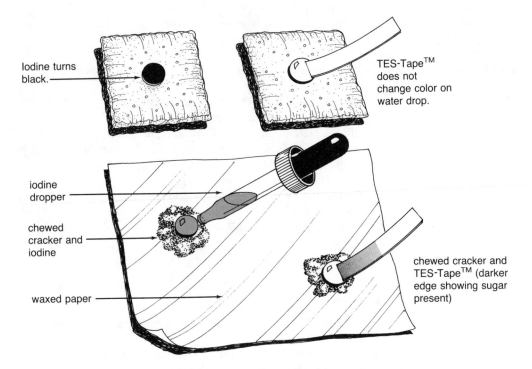

Iodine turns black.

TES-Tape™ does not change color on water drop.

iodine dropper

chewed cracker and iodine

waxed paper

chewed cracker and TES-Tape™ (darker edge showing sugar present)

   7. Use another cracker, place it in your mouth and chew slowly for one to two minutes. Put a small amount of chewed cracker on a piece of wax paper in two small amounts.
      Test one chewed cracker sample for starch using the iodine test.

Observing   *What do you observe?*
                  Test the other chewed cracker sample for sugar using the TES-Tape™.

Observing   *What do you observe?*
                  What has taken place in your mouth?
                  Caution: Dispose of waxed paper and chewed cracker samples immediately. Do not touch other chewed cracker samples.
   8. Obtain two jars with covers. Pour equal amounts of water into each of the two jars. Place two cubes of sugar into each jar and

Observing

screw the covers on tightly. Place one jar aside and let it stand still. Shake the other jar vigorously.
Compare the results occurring in the two jars.

No shaking

Shaking

Inferring
Applying

Why did the sugar dissolve faster in one jar?
What does this activity tell us about chewing your food before swallowing it?

What Must I Know?/
Where Do I Find It?

The more the children chew their food, the more enzymes will mix with the food to break it down chemically. Chewing also helps to break the food down into smaller particles so more of it comes in contract with the enzymes.

How Will Children Use
or Apply What They
Discover?

1. *How does saliva affect other foods such as poultry, fruits, and vegetables?*
2. *Why should diabetics not eat too many starchy foods?*
3. Test other foods for starch content.

What Are the Functions of Bones? (4–6)

What Do I Want
Children to Discover?

Bones are the framework of the body.
Bones are composed of **calcium** and **phosphate salts.**
Bones of an adult are different from the bones of a child.
Bones are classified as round, flat, long, and short.
The function of a bone is limited by its size and shape.
Bones may have defects.
Bones are made of organic and inorganic substances.
Calcium is necessary for the development of bones.
X rays pass through tissue and can be used to tell where a bone is broken.

What Will I Need?

Human skeleton (small model), skeletal chart, or good picture of a skeleton
5 chicken bones (legs or thighs are best)
Small tree twig
Small saw
2 X-ray pictures, one of a good bone and one of a broken bone
Vinegar

Medium-sized beaker or saucepan
½ pint of milk

What Will We Discuss?

How are the structure of a skyscraper and the structure of your body similar?

What is the framework of your body called?

What makes up the skeleton?

If you wanted to determine how bones function, what could you do to find out?

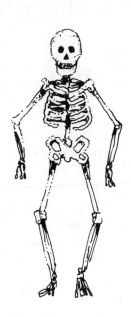

What Will Children Do?

PROCESSES

PART I

1. Obtain a model of a skeleton.

Observing *What are some functions of the skeleton or skeletal system?*

Inferring *How do bones protect the softer parts of your body?*

Name some places in your body where bones cover or protect important organs.

Point to some of these places on your body.

Observing *Where are some places that bones are joined together to allow you to move?*

Point to some of these places on your body.

Observing *Which bones help you to stand up?*

Point to some of these places on your body.

Observing Feel the top of your head. Your head is really made up of several bones.

Inferring *How are they joined to each other?*
Feel the jawbone. Open and close your mouth.

Observing *Does the bottom jawbone or the upper part of the jaw move?*
Feel your spine.

Inferring *From feeling it, what can you say about the spine?*
Observing *How many bones are in the spine?*
Designing an *How could you find out?*
investigation

What is a fracture?
Classifying *What are the different types of fractures?*

What Must I Know? There are two types of fractures, simple and compound. A **simple fracture** occurs when the bone but not the skin is broken. A **compound fracture** is a bone fracture that produces a wound by puncturing soft tissues.

PART II
1. Obtain two chicken bones.
Hypothesizing *How could you fracture a chicken bone?*
2. Fracture one of the chicken bones.
Describing *How would you describe the appearance of the fracture you made?*

What Must I Know? You might have the children compare the fractured bones. Some of them will probably be simple and others compound. Give them the names for the appropriate fractures. (To observe properly a compound fracture, you will need a chicken leg or thigh with the skin and flesh still intact.)

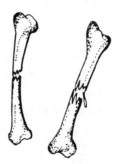

3. Obtain a set of X rays and look at them.
Describing *What do you see?*
Inferring *How do X rays help a doctor treat a broken bone?*
Hypothesizing *What does a doctor do to correct or treat a broken bone?*

4. Obtain a twig and the fractured bone.

Hypothesizing   *How would you use the twig to support the bone and keep it from moving?*

Hypothesizing   *What do you think a doctor does to keep the bone from moving?*
Inferring   Older people fracture their bones more easily than do children.
Designing an   *What can you do to find out why?*
    investigation

PART III

1. Obtain a bone, vinegar, and a beaker. Fill the beaker with vinegar.

Hypothesizing   *What do you think will happen to the bone if placed in the vinegar?*

2. Take the bone out of the vinegar after a minimum of two days.

Observing   *What effect did the vinegar have on the bone?*
Inferring   *How has the strength of the bone changed?*
Hypothesizing   *What could you do to find out?*
    Compare an untreated bone to the treated bone.
Comparing   *How do they differ?*
Inferring   *Which of these two types of bones do you think are similar to those of older people?*

What Must I Know?   Older peoples' bones are more calcified than those of young people. As a result, they are more brittle.

Hypothesizing   *What do you think bones are made of?*
Designing an   *How could you find out?*
    investigation

What Must I Know?   Bones contain organic material and calcium and phosphate salts.

PART IV

1. Obtain one-half pint of milk. Open the carton. Examine the milk.
Observing   *What do you notice about it?*

What Must I Know?   The white material in the milk contains calcium minerals necessary for bones to grow.

2. Obtain a bone and a saw.
Cut the bone in half.
Observing   *What do you notice about the inside of the bone and the dust material produced from sawing?*
What is the center of a bone called?

What Must I Know?   The center of the bone is called the **marrow.** It is important for making blood and for keeping the bone in good health.

Name some foods you need to eat to keep your bones growing and in good health.

How Will Children Use or Apply What They Discovered?

1. *What effect would the lack of milk over an extended period have on a person?*
2. *What are the steps a doctor goes through in setting a bone?*
3. *Why do some people need to have plates or rods attached or fitted to broken bones?*
4. *Why do a person's leg bones curve (or become bowlegged) if he or she has a disease called rickets? What can prevent rickets?*

How Do Our Muscles Work? (4–8)

What Do I Want Children to Discover?

Muscle cells make it possible to move parts of the body.
There are two types of muscles: voluntary and involuntary.

Voluntary muscles are arranged in pairs and work on opposite sides of a bone.
There are three types of levers operated by voluntary muscles, causing the movement of various parts of the body.

What Will I Need?

Uncooked chicken leg and wing, or frog leg, preferably with the feet attached to the legs
Forceps (to pull the skin off the leg)

What Will Children Do?

PROCESSES

1. *Where have you seen a muscle?*
   Hold up an uncooked chicken leg and wing (a frog leg may be used).
   How is the chicken able to move its legs or wings?
   What kind of tissue do you mainly see around the bones of the wing and leg?

Inferring
Observing

What Must I Know?

Most of the tissue seen and most of the meat you eat is muscle. The chicken has several hundred different muscles to move various parts of its body. Muscle tissue covers the body in sheets and bands that lie between the skin and skeleton.

What are the names of some of the voluntary muscles in the upper arm?

What Must I Know?

You may have to explain that muscles that move bones are called **voluntary muscles.** The body also has **involuntary muscles** such as those that are in the wall of the intestines. The involuntary muscles move without a person's having to think about them. Some common voluntary muscles are **biceps** (located in the front of the upper arm), **triceps** (the large muscle at the back of the upper arm), and the **deltoid** (large, triangular muscle of the shoulder that raises the arm away from the side).

2. Obtain some forceps and pull the skin off the chicken leg. Point out several of the different bundles of muscles.

Applying

Can anyone show me one of his muscles?

What Must I Know?

The most common reaction to this is for someone to double up his fist and bring it up close to his shoulder. Have the class take a good grasp of their triceps (underside of the upper arm; see following diagram) and hold it while they raise their lower arms.

Observing

What happens to the triceps when you raise your arm?
Have the class lower their arms.

Observing

What happens to the arm the second time?

Hypothesizing

Why does the upper part of the arm get thicker when the arm is raised?

What Must I Know?

To raise your arm, the muscle has to contract. As it contracts, it becomes shorter and thicker, forming a "bump." Have all the class flex their arms to show their biceps. Teach them the names of these upper arm muscles. The biceps are composed of two muscles connected to the bone by a tendon. The triceps consist of three muscles connected to the bone by one tendon. The triceps lie on the opposite side of the arm from the biceps. The chief characteristic of all muscles is that they can contract. This is because of the special function of the cells that form muscles. When one muscle contracts, the opposing muscle relaxes.

Hypothesizing

3. *If a muscle can only contract how is it possible to return your arm to its original position?*

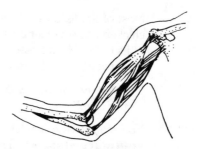

What Must I Know?

Muscles work in pairs. Biceps contract to raise the arms. To lower the arms, the triceps contract and the biceps relax. All bones are moved this way. *Example:* When you show someone how strong you are, you "make a muscle" by contracting your biceps, and your forearm is pulled up toward your shoulder. If you want to lower your arm, you relax your biceps and contract your triceps. As you bend your arm back and forth at the elbow, each of these muscles relaxes and contracts over and over. Draw the diagram of arm muscles on the board to show how skeletal muscles work.

Observing

4. Show the lower part of the chicken bone to the class.
   Where can you see part of a tendon on the chicken leg?

What Must I Know?

If the foot of the bird has been cut off, only part of the shiny white tendon will be seen.

Inferring

5. How is a muscle fastened to the bone?

What Must I Know?

Some muscles are connected directly to the bone, whereas others are connected to a tough, nonstretchable cord, or tendon, which is connected to the bone. (Write *tendon* on the board.)

Where can you feel a strong tendon in your own body?

What Must I Know?

If you reach down and grasp the back of your foot just above the heel, you can feel the strong tendon called the **Achilles tendon** that connects the muscle of your leg to your heel bone. (Write *Achilles* on the board.) Raise yourself on the ball of your foot. You can feel the calf muscles tighten and bulge as they contract and pull upward on your heel.

Hypothesizing

6. *What is the correct way to lift an object so you do not strain your muscles?*
   Have a child demonstrate by picking up a cardboard box as shown in the following diagram.

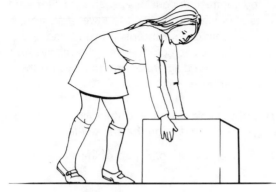
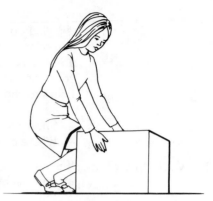

Incorrect (using arms only) Correct (using legs)

Hypothesizing	*Why do you think one method of lifting objects is better than the other?*
What Must I Know?	With the correct method, you use more of your skeleton and many more muscles than in the other, so there is less likelihood of straining any one muscle. Have all the members of the class practice the correct way to lift heavy objects.
Inferring	7. *What kinds of machines make it possible for the body to lift more weight?*
What Must I Know?	A lever is often used. A **lever** is a device consisting of a bar turning about a fixed point, the **fulcrum,** using power or force applied at a second point to lift or sustain a weight at a third point. Our body contains many levers. The joints act as the fulcrum, our muscles act as the force, and the weight is that part we lift.
How Will Children Use or Apply What They Discover?	1. *What are some examples of levers?* 2. *Where are some levers in the human body?* 3. *Why are some weight lifters' biceps so large? Can you enlarge your biceps? How?*

What Does the Heart Do? (4–8)

What Do I Want Children to Discover?	The heart pumps the blood through the body. The heart beats many times per minute. When you exercise, the heart beats faster. The heart has four chambers. Blood moves in an orderly fashion through the body.
What Will I Need?	Balloon Y-shaped glass tubes or a Live goldfish small funnel

Dish with wet cotton
Microscope or microprojector
Funnel
Rubber tubes

Model of heart obtained
from the Heart
Association, or purchase
a calf or sheep heart
(may be stored in alcohol)

What Will We Discuss?

How large is your heart?

What Must I Know?

Have the children make a fist. This is approximately the size of the heart. The heart of an adult is about 5 inches long, 3½ inches wide, and 2½ inches thick.

What does a heart look like?

What Must I Know?

This activity should be done in groups of four children.

What Will Children Do?

PROCESSES

PART I
1. Obtain a model of the heart, Y-shaped tube, a funnel, and 2 rubber tubes.

Observing

How many compartments do you see in the model of the heart?

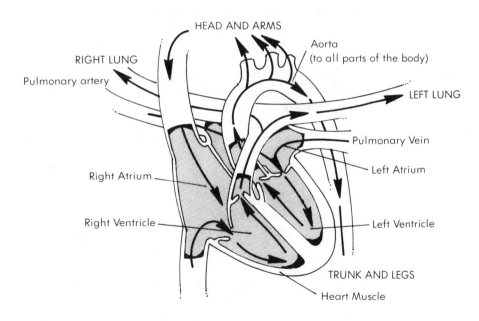

Observing

2. Observe how these compartments are arranged and their similarities and differences.

Observing

Where is the heart located in your body?

3. Place your hand at the center of the rib cage, near the lower edge.

Observing
What do you feel?

Designing an
investigation

4. Make a stethoscope by attaching rubber tubes to the three ends of a Y-shaped glass tube. Attach a funnel to the tail of the "Y" tube.

What Must I Know?
A small funnel with one rubber tube can be substituted if a "Y" tube is not available.

5. Place the funnel on the chest of a friend.
6. Place the other two ends in your ears.
Caution: Use extreme care when placing the tubes in your ears so you do not harm the eardrums.

Observing
What do you hear?

Hypothesizing
Why do you think the heart sounds something like a drum?

Inferring
What makes the drum noise?

Inferring
Why does the heart beat faster?

What Must I Know?
At this point, display a large chart or model. Identify the various parts of the heart and their functions. Trace the route of blood through the heart.

PART II

1. Obtain a balloon. Have your partner fill the balloon half full of water.

Designing an
investigation
How can the balloon be used to demonstrate how the heart pumps blood?

Inferring
What does the water in the balloon represent?

Hypothesizing
What do you think would happen if you released the end of the balloon and pushed on the side of the balloon a little?

2. Gently push some of the liquid out of the balloon.

Inferring
How do you think the heart moves blood out of its chambers?

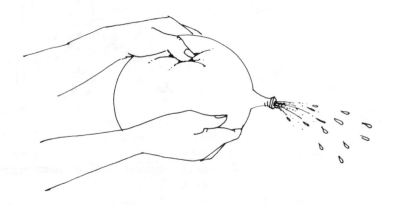

What Must I Know? The heart is similar to the balloon in that it has liquid in it, but the heart actually has two pumps, one on the left side and one on the right side. The sound the students hear is due to the pumping of the heart.

3. Feel your pulse as shown in the diagram.

Observing
Inferring

What do you feel?
What causes the beats you feel?

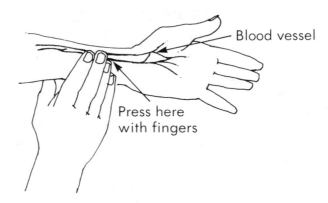

Blood vessel

Press here
with fingers

What Must I Know? The pulse is caused by the surge of blood that passes through the blood vessels each time the heart pumps.

4. Listen to your partner's heart and record the number of its beats per minute. Then have your partner jump up and down 60 times. Record the number of heartbeats after the exercise.

Observing
What happens to the rate of the heartbeat after the exercise?

What Must I Know? When you exercise, your muscles use more oxygen and food energy. Your heart is stimulated because of this activity, and it pumps faster, sending more blood to all parts of the body.

Describing
Designing an
*   investigation*

How does the blood move through the body?
What could you do with a goldfish to see how the blood moves through its body?

How Will Children Use or Apply What They Discover?

1. *Why is it necessary for the blood to continue moving through the body?*
2. *What does the blood do with waste materials picked up from the cells in the muscles?*
3. *What causes the heart to beat faster after exercise?*
4. *What effect would the temperature of the water have on the flow of blood in a goldfish?*

What Makes a Good Diet? (4–8)

What Do I Want Children to Discover?	It is important to consider your diet.
What Will I Need?	Textbook, or some other source listing the "basic four" and other information about nutrition
What Will We Discuss?	*How good is your diet?*

PROCESSES

What Will Children Do?	1. Write down what you think would be a good diet for (1) breakfast, (2) lunch, and (3) dinner.

How Will Children Use or Apply What They Discover?

Inferring	*How many different types of minerals would you get?* Now check your text section on the "basic four."
Observing	*What foods did you leave out?*
Inferring	*How many different types of vitamins would you be likely to eat?*
Inferring	*What foods do you generally eat that might be called "junk foods"?*
Hypothesizing	*Since you should not eat "junk" food, what would be good to eat instead?*
What Must I Know?	Children should have a good, balanced diet. If they eat from the "basic four" categories of foods, this should help to insure that they get the right diet. However, they should be cautioned not to eat too many fatty foods such as meat, cheese, and ice cream, and not to eat too much sugar.

How Do You Play "Check the Label" Game? (4–8)

What Do I Want Children to Discover?	Many foods have lots of sugar.
What Will I Need?	Empty packages, cans, and bottles with labels.
What Will We Discuss?	The contents of food in packages and cans must be labeled. The contents are labeled in order by amount. The first thing on the label is the greatest amount. Often you can be fooled by how much sugar a food has.
What Must I Know?	You have to know that there are many names for the different types of sugars. For example, all of the following are names for different sugar foods:

Sugar	Sucrose
Syrup	Lactose
Corn Syrup	Fructose
Dextrose	Corn sweetener
Maltose	Molasses
Glucose	

What Will Children Do?

PART I

1. Look at the labels on these foods.

   Write the name of each of the foods below. Under each one write the kinds of sugar it contains. Use the preceding list to help you.

   Food Name _____   Food Name _____
   Sugars   Sugars
   Food Name _____   Food Name _____
   Sugars   Sugars
   Food Name _____
   Sugars

How Will Children Use or Apply What They Discover?

PROCESSES

Inferring

What did you find out about these foods? Which food had the most sugar?
Which food had the most vitamins? Which food had the most preservatives? How would you find out?

Evaluating

What will you do in the future so as not to eat too much sugar?

What Must I Know?

A lot of packaged foods also have preservatives in them.

What to Do

PART II

1. Look at the following list. Write on a piece of paper your guess of how much sugar each food contains:

	No. of Parts out of 10		No. of Parts out of 10
Canned peaches	_____	Chocolate ice cream	_____
Canned corn	_____	Catsup	_____
Peanut butter	_____	Italian salad dressing	_____
Yogurt	_____	Russian salad dressing	_____
Cereal sweetened with honey	_____	Dessert type whipped toppings	_____
Chocolate bar	_____	Cracker wafer	_____
Cake	_____	Nondairy coffee creamer	_____
Flavored gelatin	_____		

Which food do you think has the most sugar? _____

Which is next? _____

Which is next? _____

Now look at the table and compare your answers.

Food	Approximate Parts out of 10
Canned peaches	2
Canned corn	1
Peanut butter	1
Yogurt	1
Cereal sweetened with honey	2.5
Chocolate bar	5
Cake	3.5
Flavored gelatin	8
Chocolate ice cream	2
Catsup	3
Russian salad dressing	3
Italian salad dressing	1
Dessert type whipped toppings	2
Cracker wafer	1
Nondairy creamer for coffee	6.5

What Did You Learn?

Which food had the most sugar? _____

Which other foods had a lot of sugar? _____

Using What You Learned

What foods should you avoid eating too much of? _____

What foods do you think have little sugar? _____

How would you find out? _____

Sugar is an important food. Normally, you can get all the sugar you need from fruits and vegetables. Too much sugar from additional sources, however, is not good for your health. It may cause your teeth to decay. Sugar also doesn't have vitamins and minerals. If you eat too much of it, you are less likely to eat other foods that have vitamins and minerals. All parts of your body need these. If you do not get enough of them, all parts of your body suffer. You may then be more likely to get sick. Some people say sugar is "empty" or "trash" food. *Why do you think they say this?*

References—Human Anatomy and Physiology

L. L. Langley, J. R. Telford, and J. B. Cristensen, *Dynamic Anatomy and Physiology* (New York: McGraw-Hill Co., 1980). Ruth D. Brauun and Bertel Brauun, *The Human Body* (New York: Random House, 1982).

ANIMAL ANATOMY AND PHYSIOLOGY

Quickie Starters

What Are the Stages that Insects Go Through?

Materials	Jars with covers (clear plastic, if possible), mealworms (from pet shop), bran or other cereal flakes, hand lenses, spoons, pictures of people and insects at different growing stages
Opening Questions	*What are the stages insects, such as moths, butterflies, and mealworms, go through in their life cycles?* *What are the stages people go through as they grow?* *How are the stages alike and different?*
Some Possible Activities	Using pictures of people and insects at different stages of growth, discuss how they grow. Introduce the mealworms and challenge children to explore how they will grow and change in several stages. Using spoons, you or the children can transfer several mealworms and some bran or cereal flakes into a jar with a lid for each child or group of two or three children. Punch several small holes in lid for air. Observe twice a week and record changes in appearance (color, length, stage, etc.) or behavior and record on a chart or log. At the end of observations, make a chart comparing the stages of insects' lives with humans.[1]

	Stages		
People	Child	Teenager	Adult
Insects	Larva	Pupa	Adult

In addition, make this diagram with your children to visualize the stages of mealworm (and other insect) metamorphosis:

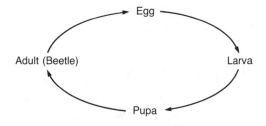

---

[1]For additional information on insect stages and recordkeeping, see appendix O in this text. You are also urged to read John Hall, "Creepie Crawlers," *Understanding the Healthy Body. CESI Sourcebook III,* ed. David R. Stronck (Columbus, OH: SMEAC Information Reference Center, 1983), 83–84.

What Do Fish Need to Live?

Materials	Gallon (4-liter) glass or plastic container, seasoned water (tap water left to stand overnight to remove chlorine), gravel or sand, aquatic plants, 2 or 3 goldfish or guppies, dip net, live or dried fish food
Opening Questions	*What things do fish need to live?* *How can we learn to take care of our fish?* *What must we do to keep the fish healthy?*
Some Possible Activities	Use the index of this text to find out how to set up and maintain a freshwater aquarium, using the materials listed here. Set up the aquarium with children and establish routines for feeding, cleaning, and changing water when it becomes smelly or too cloudy. Point out that guppies and goldfish can be raised at room temperatures. Discuss why these elements are needed for the fish to live: water, plants, food, light. Carefully remove pregnant fish (usually identified by swollen abdomen with dark spot) with dip net and place in separate aquarium. For older children, discuss relationships between variables, parts of aquarium, and effects upon life of fish, such as: amount of light and effect on algae in water, amount of fish one gallon of water will support as observed by fish gulping at top of water, overfeeding and pollution of water, etc.

Guided Discovery Activities

How Many Different Types of Animals Do You Know? (K–6)

What Do I Want Children to Discover?	Each animal lives in a place (**environment**) that best suits it. The way the animal is built depends on where and how it lives. Animals that live on dry land breathe through **lungs.** Animals that usually live in water breathe through **gills.** Land animals usually move by legs and may run, hop, or crawl. Many land animals have claws and sharp teeth. Animals live in water, on land, in the air, and both on land and in water. Animals that fly have wings and light bones.
What Will I Need?	Fish to be dissected (this may be obtained from the local fish market) Aquarium with large goldfish Frog or chicken leg to be dissected Aquarium with a live frog Cutaway model of a human chest cavity showing the lungs As many models of stuffed animals as can be obtained Dry bones from a chicken, cow, and any other animal that may be available Claws, beaks, and teeth from as many animals as possible

Animal's lung in alcohol
Live animals that take a minimal amount of care (such as salaman-
   ders, goldfish, crayfish, and white mice)
Set of scales for weighing bones
Dissecting kit
Pictures (Set I): common animals
Pictures (Set II): rare or unusual animals
Paper towels
Pencil and paper

What Will We Discuss?

How can animals be classified?
How do animals breathe?
What does a gill look like, and how does it function?
What kinds of animals use gills for breathing?
What does a lung look like, and how does it function?
What kinds of animals use lungs for breathing?
How does an animal's body structure affect its locomotion?
How does its body structure affect its diet?

What Will Children Do?

PROCESSES

PART I

Observing

1. Observe the fish in the aquarium. Note their breathing, locomotion, and feeding.
2. Obtain a dead fish, dissecting kit, and paper towels. Carefully dissect a fish. Your teacher will demonstrate the proper method for
   you to follow.

Observing
Inferring

3. Describe what you see in the area of the gills.
   What function do you think the various sections serve?

Gill filaments

What Must I Know?

You may want to demonstrate the proper method for dissecting a
fish. Have the children work in groups of four. Cut the fish along the
ventral side from just below the anus to the throat. Cut up from this
incision to the dorsal side (top) of the fish at both ends of the incision. Using the scissors in the dissection kit, cut the ribs and expose
the air bladder. Also remove the operculum or gill cover on one side.
This will expose the gill filaments. (See diagram.)

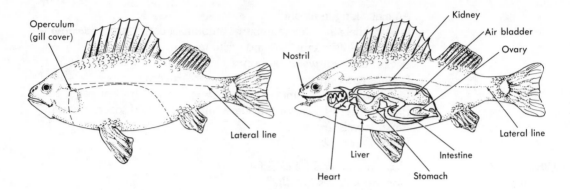

Inferring	*In what ways does a fish use its fins and tail?*
Inferring	*How does their structure affect their use?*
Inferring	*In what manner does a fish ingest its food?*
	Describe the bones of the fish.
Inferring	*How do you think they affect its ability to swim?*

PART II

1. Obtain a frog or chicken leg, two bones from a bird and a cow, and a scale.

   Carefully dissect and record your findings about the frog or chicken leg and how the leg affects the animal's locomotion.

Measuring 2. Measure and weigh two bones of equal length, one of a chicken and one of a cow.

Observing and inferring 3. Obtain and examine at least two sets of claws, beaks, and teeth and describe what you think the diet of each animal might be.

4. Obtain a cutaway model of a human chest cavity showing the lungs.

Observing Describe the lungs.

Hypothesizing *What is their function?*

Name some animals that breathe with the use of lungs.

Comparing *How do human lungs differ from those of other animals?*

Hypothesizing *Why do land animals have lungs rather than gills?*

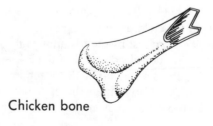

Chicken bone

Beef bone

PART III

1. Obtain a collection of pictures of animals and a pencil and piece of paper.

Classifying

2. Sort the pictures of animals into categories on the basis of the data you obtained from your previous investigations.
3. List the animals down the left-hand side of a sheet of paper by the categories you have determined. Leave two spaces between each entry. Rule your paper into three lengthwise columns. Title the columns as follows:
   a. *How does the animal breathe?*
   b. *How does the animal move?*
   c. *What physical characteristics influence its diet?*
4. Complete the columns for each entry as indicated.

How Will Children Use or Apply What They Discover?

1. *How would you use balloons to show how a lung operates?*
2. *Using the data gathered in your experiments, how would you construct, illustrate, or give a written description of an imaginary animal that can live in water or on land, fly, crawl, and walk?*

What Are the Differences Between a Frog and a Lizard? (3–6)

What Do I Want Children to Discover?

A frog is an amphibian.

Amphibians are animals that spend part of their lives in water and part on land.

As tadpoles, amphibians live in water. They have a slippery skin, and late in their development they have toes without claws.

A lizard is a reptile

Reptiles have skin covered with scales; there is no tadpole stage; toes, if present, have claws.

Reptiles produce eggs with shells because they lay their eggs on land and depend on the sun for hatching them.

What Must I Know?

This activity should be done in groups of five or more students. Commercial-sized mayonnaise jars may be used for terrariums.

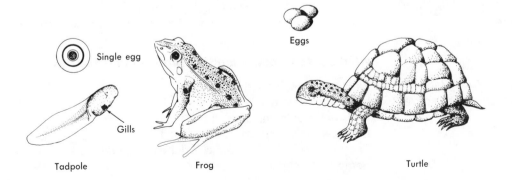

Single egg

Gills

Tadpole

Frog

Eggs

Turtle

What Will I Need?	2 terrariums—1 equipped with water and aquatic plants for the frog; 1 equipped with sand and a rock for the lizard Containers of water for the frogs Frog for each group Lizard for each group Variety of insects for feeding both frog and lizard Eggs or young of both the frog and the lizard
What Must I Know?	If it is not possible to obtain the developmental stages of the frog and lizard, get some pictures of the different stages.
What Will We Discuss?	*To which group of animals do lizards belong?* *To which group of animals do frogs belong?* *What are the general characteristics of each of these groups?* *How are these animals like or unlike each other?* *How does a given environment affect each animal?*

What Will Children Do?	PROCESSES

Observing
Observing
Observing
	1. Observe the frog and the lizard in the two terrariums.
	    How do they breathe?
	    How do they move?
	    Describe their physical characteristics.
	    Do they have any young?

Observing *Observing* *Comparing*	*How do they react to their environment?* *What are the characteristics of the environment?* 2. Compare your observations with those in the classroom reference books. 3. Note any additional differences as indicated in your reading.
Classifying	4. Using the data gathered in steps 1 and 2, list the characteristics of an amphibian in one column and the characteristics of a reptile in another column.
Inferring	5. List the names of some other amphibians and reptiles.
How Will Children Use or Apply What They Discover?	1. Obtain other amphibians and reptiles. Use the same procedure as in the previous activity to compare them. 2. *How would you prepare an environment to raise salamanders?*

What Do You Know about the Birds around You? (K–6)

What Do I Want Children to Discover?	Birds vary in color and size. Birds sing different songs. Birds make different kinds of nests. Birds eat many different kinds of food. The male may have a more colorful plumage than the female. Some birds migrate.

Some birds change color with the season.
Birds care for their young.
Some birds prey on birds.

What Will I Need?

No special materials are necessary; however, the following may be helpful:

Bird book (showing local birds)
Pictures of birds, if birds cannot be observed in nature

What Will We Discuss?

Carefully record on the board the responses of the pupils to the following questions:

What are the names of some birds?
What do these birds look like?
How do chickens and ducks differ?
What are the main differences between a turkey and a robin?
Where do some birds go in the winter?
Where do baby birds come from?
Where do birds lay their eggs?
What kinds of food do birds eat?

What Must I Know?

If the natural environment lends itself to observation of birds, have the children observe birds on the way to and from school or take a field trip in the local area, park, or zoo. If this is not possible, you may provide pictures of different birds, nests, and eggs for the pupils to observe.

PROCESSES

What Will Children Do?

The pupils should report to the class the things they have observed about birds. After the children have made their observations, record their findings by asking and writing on the board their answers to the following questions:

Comparing
Comparing

In what ways are birds alike?
In what ways are birds different from each other?

How Will Children Use or Apply What They Discover?

1. *What advantage is there of laying eggs in nests?*
2. *What could you do to find out more about birds?*
3. On the bulletin board are the lists of the important things you have learned about birds. In the next few days, try to find out as many new things as you can to add to the lists.
4. *What are the different ways birds build their nests?*
5. *How could you find out if there are more birds in the city or in the country?*

What Must I Know?

The following types of questions can be asked about any of the local birds. These questions will have to be modified depending on the kinds of birds that are found in your region.

Redheaded Woodpecker. (1) *Where does the woodpecker build its nest?* (2) *How does it build its nest?* (3) *What kind of food does the woodpecker eat?*

Hummingbird. (1) *How does the male hummingbird differ in color from the female?* (2) *Where do hummingbirds get their food?* (3) *Are hummingbirds as big as the cardinal or sparrow?* (4) *Why do you have difficulty finding their nests?*

Starling. (1) *Why do many other birds prefer not to live near starlings?* (2) *What color is the starling?* (3) *How does the starling vary in color compared to the hummingbird and woodpecker?*

How Do Ants Live? (K–6)

What Do I Want
Children to Discover?

Ants are social **insects.**
All insects have three parts to their bodies.
All insects have six legs.
Ants are beneficial because they help keep the forests and fields clean.
There are different kinds of ants in a colony.
These different ants do different kinds of work in the colony.

What Will I Need?

Large-mouth glass jar (commercial mayonnaise or pickle jar)
Soil to fill the jar two-thirds full
Sponge

Large pan
Sheet of black construction paper
Crumbs and bits of food: bread, cake, sugar, seeds
Colony of ants

What Will We Discuss?

What do the different kinds of ants look like?
In what ways are the ants different?
How does the body of a worker ant compare to that of a queen ant?
How many pairs of legs do ants have?
What are the antennae on the head used for?
What does the egg of an ant look like?
Where do ants make their homes?
How do ants move?
How could you keep ants from leaving a jar?

Ant eggs

Mature ant

What Must I Know?

This activity should be done as a large group activity.

PROCESSES

What Will Children Do?

1. Obtain a large-mouth glass jar, soil to fill the jar two-thirds full, sponge, large pan, sheet of black construction paper, crumbs and bits of food (bread, cake, sugar, and seeds), a colony of ants, and water.

Designing an investigation

How could you arrange these materials to make a home for ants?
What effect will a sheet of black paper placed around the jar have on the ants?

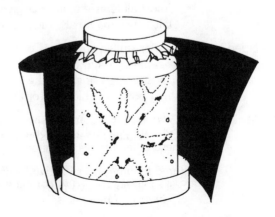

Observing	2. Observe and record what the ants do.
Observing	*How do the ants connect their homes in the jar?*
Hypothesizing	*What would happen to the ants if they did not carry soil to the surface?*
Hypothesizing	*What do you think would happen if there were no queen in the ant colony?*
Comparing	*What changes have been made by the ants since they were first placed in the jar?*

How Will Children Use or Apply What They Discover?

1. *In what ways are ants useful to people?*
2. *What are some other insects that live and work together?*
3. *What are some living things that are sometimes mistaken for insects?*
4. *What would happen if the ant colony were placed in a light, warm place?*
5. *How are ants different from spiders?*
6. *What would be a good description of social insects?*

How Do Birds Differ from Mammals? (4–8)

What Do I Want Children to Discover?

Birds are the only animals that have feathers.
Both mammals and birds are warm-blooded.
Birds have two legs and two wings.
The female mammal has glands for nourishing her young with milk.
Mammals are more or less covered with hair.
Birds do not vary as much in structure as mammals.
The bones of birds are somewhat hollow and light in weight.
Mammal bones are not hollow and are proportionately heavier.
Birds tend to eat approximately the amount of their weight in food each day.
Mammals do not eat as much per body weight as do birds.
Birds use considerable energy in flying and therefore need a great amount of food.
Female birds lay eggs.
Almost all female mammals give birth to live babies.
Only a few mammals, such as the platypus, lay eggs.

What Will I Need?

Live or stuffed specimens of birds and mammals or pictures of them.
Beef and chicken bones (one of each for every two students). If possible, these should be cut in half.
Wing bones of chickens (or any other bird).

What Will We Discuss?

Give as many characteristics as you can that birds have in common.
Give as many characteristics as you can that mammals have in common.
In what ways do birds differ from mammals?
What could you do to compare more closely the differences between birds and mammals?

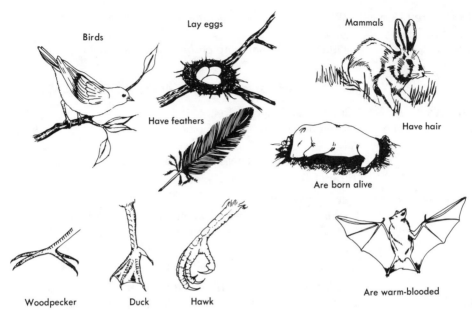

What Must I Know?

The teacher should record on the board the students' ideas on these questions. Or allow the students to divide into groups and discuss the questions. Each group could report its ideas to the class.

What Will Children Do?

Do this activity in groups of two or more students. Encourage children to bring specimens, alive or stuffed, to school. Perhaps a pet day or animal show might be arranged to make the most of this activity. Allow the children to help furnish any of the other supplies, such as beef and chicken bones. Encourage children to bring pictures of animals to class; place these on a bulletin board.

PROCESSES

1. Obtain a cut chicken bone, a cut beef bone, and a wing bone of a chicken.

Classifying
    How did you know which bone was from a chicken and which was from a steer?

Observing and comparing
    Examine the centers of the two bones and record how the structure of the beef bone differs from that of the chicken bone.

Comparing
2. Look at the chicken wing bone.
    How does its structure compare with the arm bones of a person?

Summarizing
3. Make a list of all the characteristic ways birds and mammals differ.

Comparing
4. Compare your list with those made by other members in your class and make any corrections or additions to your list that you think should be made.

How Will Children Use or Apply What They Discover?	1. *What are the main structural differences between birds and mammals?* 2. *How does the structure of the feather help a bird to fly?*

How Does the Lack of Oxygen Affect Animals? (3–8)

What Do I Want Children to Discover?	Animals need **oxygen** to live. Oxygen dissolves in water. Some animals need dissolved oxygen in water. A gas will dissolve better in a cool liquid than in a hot liquid. Fish breathe through gills.
What Will I Need?	2 pint bottles with caps 2 goldfish or any small freshwater fish in a small bottle Burner and a stand or electric hot plate on which to boil water Matches Pan large enough to boil a pint of water
What Will We Discuss?	*What happens to the air dissolved in water when you boil it?* *What do you think would happen to fish if they were placed in water that had been boiled and then cooled?* *What would you do to find out?*
What Must I Know?	This activity may be done in groups of two or more pupils.

PROCESSES

What Will Children Do? *Designing an investigation*	1. Obtain a jar with a fish, two pint-sized jars with caps, a burner or *How would you boil water?* 2. Heat the water to boiling and let it boil for several minutes. 3. While the water is being heated, label one jar "Boiled Water" and the other "Tap Water." 4. After the water has boiled, turn off the burner. 5. *Carefully* pour the boiled water into the jar labeled "Boiled Water," cap it, and allow it to cool to room temperature.
Hypothesizing	*What will happen if you place a fish in tap water?* Place a fish in a jar filled with tap water and cap it.
Observing *Hypothesizing*	6. Observe its movements. *What will happen if you place a fish in the cooled boiled water and cap the jar?*
Observing	7. Place a fish in the jar of boiled water and cap the jar. Observe its movements. (*Caution:* If the fish turns on its side, take it out of the jar quickly, gently shake it in the air by the tail for a second, and place it into a jar of regular unheated water.)

Comparing   *How did the movements of the two fish vary?*
Inferring   *Why did the fish in the cooled boiled water seem to vary in its*
                     movements compared to the other fish?

Tap Water
A

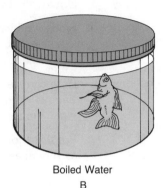

Boiled Water
B

What Must I Know?   When water is boiled, the air molecules dissolved in it move more
                          rapidly and escape into the air. The water lacks air as a result. Fish
                          get the oxygen they need from air dissolved in water. When the air
                          passes over the gills, the oxygen is absorbed by the blood passing
                          through the gills. Fish are not able to survive in the boiled water be-
                          cause it contains little oxygen for the gills to absorb.

Inferring   *Why did you first heat the water and then cool it?*

                          8. If you have not already done so, take the fish out of the jar of
                             boiled water, gently shake it for a second or two by the tail, and
                             place it in a jar of plain water.

Inferring   *Why is it necessary to shake the fish in the air for a few seconds?*

What Must I Know?   The shaking of the fish causes the air to pass over the gills so the fish
                          gets oxygen from the air; the shaking also stimulates the circulation of
                          the blood in the fish.

Inferring   *What do animals in the sea need to live?*
Inferring   *How do they get the oxygen they need?*

What Must I Know?/   Explain to the class that air is composed of a mixture of gases and
Where Do I Find It?   that it is the oxygen in the air that animals need to breathe.

How Will Children Use *What experiment would you do to determine whether other animals*
or Apply What They   *require air (oxygen) to live?*
Discover?

References—Animal Anatomy and Physiology
Dina Humphreys, *Animals Every Child Should Know* (New York: Putnam, 1983).
Ross E. Hutchins, *Insects and Their Young* (New York: Dodd, 1975).

PLANT ANATOMY AND PHYSIOLOGY

Quickie Starter

How Can Some Plants Grow without Seeds?

Materials	Small tumblers (preferably plastic), small sweet potatoes, white potatoes, carrot tops (with some root), toothpicks, cuttings from coleus, philodendron, ivy, and other houseplants
Opening Questions	*How can we get new plants without planting seeds?* *What is needed to get new plants?* *How can we take good care of our new plants?*
Some Possible Activities	Put three toothpicks each in a sweet potato, white potato, and carrot as shown and place in small tumblers of water.

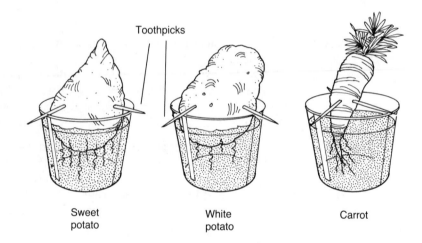

Toothpicks

Sweet potato   White potato   Carrot

Take cuttings of houseplants and place them in small tumblers of water. Put all the tumblers in a well-lit place and make sure the water levels are kept so they touch the plants. Have students observe and measure the changes in the plants, such as root development, height, number of leaves. etc.

What Kinds of Things Can We Do with Plants?

1. Hug and Feel a Tree	Have the children hug a tree trunk, feel its surface, and describe how it feels. Smell the bark. Have the children draw and give a name for their favorite tree or cut pictures of trees out of magazines.

2. Press Plants

Invite the children to collect parts of plants, for example, leaves and flowers. *Caution:* Stress collecting *fallen* plant parts only. Do not pick from living things. Have children press them between newspapers. Place some books or something heavy on the newspapers. After several days, remove the weights and newspaper. Discuss how drying helps to preserve the plants.

3. Make Splatter Pictures of Leaves

Have the children collect different types of leaves and bring them to class. Tell them to place the leaves on colored paper. Dip brushes in poster paint and splatter paint over the leaves to make a picture outline. Have the children compare the different types of leaves and what they had to do to make good splatter pictures. For example, ask how the thickness of the paint affected the quality of the picture.

Guided Discovery Activities

What Are Seeds and How Can We Get Them to Grow? (K–3)

**What Do I Want
Children to Discover?**

Soaked bean seeds are different from dried beans.
A seed has parts: **embryo** (tiny plant), **cotyledon** (stored food),
   seed coat (skin); each part is needed for **germination** and
   growth of the plant.

PART I WHAT ARE THE PARTS OF A SEED?

What Will I Need?

1 lima bean seed soaked overnight
1 unsoaked lima bean
Piece of waxed paper
Hand lens

**What Will We
Discuss?**

What is a seed and what parts does it have?
How can we find out?

PROCESSES

**What Will Children
Do?**

Give each student the materials listed above. Ask them to respond to
the following questions, using their seeds as their sources of observation. List their responses on the board.

Observing
Hypothesizing

How are soaked seeds different from dried seeds?
What do you think you will see when you open your seeds?

Comparing

1. Open your soaked seed. Demonstrate how to do this.
   How does what you see compare with your hypotheses (guesses)?

Labeling

2. Draw and label a picture of an open seed.

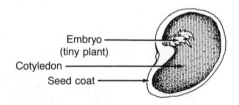

Embryo
(tiny plant)
Cotyledon
Seed coat

Inferring
Inferring
Inferring
*Designing an
   investigation*

Which part of the seed do you think will grow into a plant?
What do you think will happen to the other parts of the seed?
Which parts do you think are needed for the seed to grow?
*How could you set up an experiment to test your ideas in the last
question?*

What Must I Know?

This activity is an important introduction to what a seed is, its parts,
and the functions of those parts in producing a new plant. Activities
that follow will investigate variables that affect seed germination.

PART II WHICH PARTS OF A SEED ARE NEEDED FOR IT TO GROW INTO A PLANT?[2]

What Will I Need?

1 plastic bag
1 paper towel
5 soaked lima beans
Paper clip
Stapler

What Will We Discuss?

Hypothesizing
Designing an investigation

What parts of a seed are needed for it to grow into a plant?
How can we test to see which parts are needed and which are not?
Which parts of a soaked bean can you remove to see if they are needed for growth?

PROCESSES

What Will Children Do?

1. Set up a "germination bag" using a plastic bag, a paper towel, and a stapler. (See diagram)

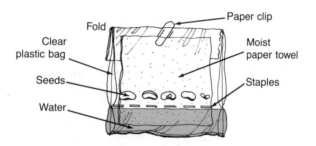

Fold · Paper clip · Clear plastic bag · Moist paper towel · Seeds · Staples · Water

2. Alter five soaked lima beans as follows and put them into the germination bag: a complete bean, bean with the seed coat removed, bean with one cotyledon removed, one cotyledon only, and the embryo only.
3. Put water in the germination bag as shown, close with a paper clip, and attach to bulletin board, wall or chalkboard.
4. Observe your germination bag for several days.

Hypothesizing
Inferring
Observing
Observing
Observing
Inferring

Which of the five seeds, if any, started to grow?
Why do you think that is so?
Were all seeds in your germination bag treated the same?
Which seed grew best?
Which parts did not grow at all?
Why do you think they did not grow?

---

[2]For expanded directions, see "From Seed to Plant," *Elementary Science Supplement to the Syllabus, Level I* (Albany, N.Y.: The State University of New York, The State Education Department, 1986), 39–54.

Observing   *Which parts are needed in order for a seed to grow?*
Observing   *From your germination bag, which part(s) can be removed, so the seeds will still grow?*

Inferring   *Why do you think this is so?*
Inferring   *Do all whole seeds grow? Why or why not?*

How Will Children Use or Apply What They Discover?

1. *Why do seeds die after they have sprouted if they are not planted in soil?*
2. *How long will sprouts live if not planted?*
3. *Why do some kinds of sprouts live longer than others?*
4. *What happens to seeds if they remain wet for a long time?*
5. *Why do seeds not germinate if embryos are removed?*
6. *Why will seeds die if cotyledons are removed?*

PART III HOW DOES TEMPERATURE AFFECT THE SPROUTING OR GERMINATION OF SEEDS?

What Will I Need?

8 lima bean seeds
8 radish seeds
2 plastic bags
2 paper towels

PROCESSES

What Will Children Do?

1. Place four lima bean and four radish seeds in two separate plastic germination bags, with paper towel and water.

2. Put one germination bag in a cool place (i.e., the refrigerator in the teachers' room or cafeteria) and one near a heater or radiator.

Hypothesizing   *How do you think the difference in temperature will affect the germination of the seeds?*

Collecting data and recording data

3. Observe your germination bags each day for one week. Record your observations.
4. At the end of the week, compare the seeds in each germination bag.

Comparing   *What differences do you notice?*
Inferring   *Why do you think these differences occurred?*

What Are Some of the Parts of a Plant and What Do They Do to Help the Plant Grow? (K–8)

PART I WHAT ARE THE PARTS OF A PLANT?

What Do I Want Children to Discover?	Plants have leaves, roots, stems, and flowers. Not all plants have the four parts. **Leaves** are able to make food. The **stems** carry minerals and water from the roots to the leaves and flowers. **Flowers** make seeds that can produce more of the same type of plant. Some **roots** store food.
What Will I Need?	Complete plant such as daisy, geranium, or petunia for entire class
What Must I Know?	Pull up a complete plant for all the children to see. *How do you think roots are useful to this plant?* Expect and accept various ideas. Allow the children opportunities to propose and examine their ideas.

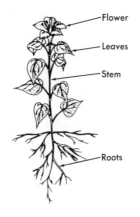

PART II HOW DO ROOTS GROW?

What Do I Want Children to Discover?	Roots move around objects in the soil. Seeds need water to grow. Roots grow downward.
What Will I Need?	Sprouted bean plant Plastic wrap Bean seeds 2 pieces of glass or thick plastic to Small milk carton cut in half place seeds between lengthwise 2 tongue depressors or applicator 4 paper towels sticks
What Will We Discuss?	*What do you think would happen to roots if they were placed so they were growing up instead of down?*

What Must I Know?

In the primary grades, this activity will have to be done as a demonstration because of the difficulty children have in manipulating the equipment. This activity should be done in groups of four students.

PROCESSES

What Will Children Do?

1. Obtain four bean seeds, plastic wrap, a paper towel, a milk carton cut in half, and a cup of water.

   Place the paper towel in the bottom of a milk carton, and press it down. Soak the towel with water from your paper cup. Place four bean seeds on the paper towel. Cover the top of the milk carton with plastic wrap.

Hypothesizing

What are the reasons for preparing the seeds this way?

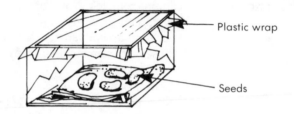

2. When the seeds sprout, place them on several layers of paper towels, between two pieces of glass so the roots point up. Put applicator sticks or tongue depressors between the pieces of glass.

Hypothesizing

What is the reason for putting the tongue depressors between the pieces of glass?

3. Stand the glass so the roots point up and the stems down.

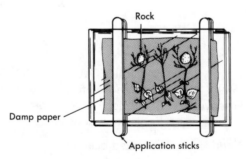

Hypothesizing

What do you think will happen to the growth of stem and roots?

4. Observe the plant growth for several days and record your observations.

Inferring

Was your hypothesis true or false, or does it need to be modified?

Designing an investigation

If you were going to do this activity again, how would you change it to make it better or more interesting?

How Will Children Use or Apply What They Discover?

1. *How would the roots react if objects like cotton, a piece of wood, or a rock were placed in their way?*
2. *What would happen to the roots if the glass were rotated 90° in the same direction every day?*

PART III HOW DOES WATER GET INTO A PLANT?

What Do I Want Children to Discover?

Roots absorb water through small **root hairs.**
Root hairs are damaged when a plant is transplanted or pulled.

What Will I Need?

Radish seeds	Plastic wrap
Pan or dish	Water
Paper towels	Hand lens

What Will We Discuss?

What could you do to determine what a root does (its function) for a plant?

PROCESSES

What Will Children Do?

1. Obtain a paper towel, several radish seeds, and some plastic wrap. Soak the towel so it drips with water. Place the towel in a dish or pan.
   Place several radish seeds on the towel and cover the pan with plastic wrap.

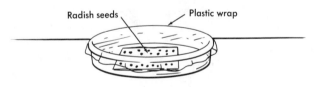

Radish seeds   Plastic wrap

2. Observe for several days and record your observations. Use a hand lens.

Observing
What do you notice about the roots?
What are the small fuzzlike projections from each root called?

Inferring
Why do you think the root has root hairs?

Hypothesizing
What happens to the roots of a plant when it is transplanted?

Hypothesizing
Why is some transplanting unsuccessful?

Designing an investigation
What would you do to determine the function of the root and root hairs?

Hypothesizing
What do you think will happen if you remove the root hairs from the root?

Hypothesizing
What do you think will happen if you expose the root hairs to air and sun?

How Will Children Use or Apply What They Discover?

1. *Why are roots different shapes?*
2. *Why are some roots comparatively shallow and others deep?*
3. *How do people use the roots of plants?*

4. *What are the functions of the root, other than to absorb food materials?*

PART IV HOW ARE ROOTS USEFUL?

What Will I Need?

2 small, healthy coleus, geranium, or petunia plants
2 empty milk cartons

What Will Children Do?

Carrying out experiment

PROCESSES

1. Obtain two petunia plants and remove all the roots from one petunia. Obtain some soil and fill the bottom half of two milk cartons. Place the petunia without roots with its stem down, on top of the soil.

Observing
Inferring

What do you notice about the plant when you let go?
How do you think roots might have helped this plant?

2. Turn the stem right side up and push it to a depth of almost two inches into the soil. Water the plant daily. Allow it to set for four or five days. Set up the other petunia with roots as control as shown.

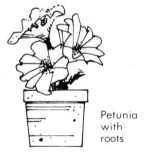

Petunia
with
roots

Petunia
without
roots

Hypothesizing
Observing
Summarizing

What do you think will happen to the plant?

3. After 4 or 5 days, record what happens.

How do you think roots might have helped the plant?

What Must I know?

Some plants develop roots in this situation. If they do, remove the plant and develop the lesson around the function of the newly developed roots.

PART V WHAT ARE THE PURPOSES OF A STEM?

What Do I Want Children to Discover?

Water must move from the roots to the leaves if a plant is to make food and live.

One of the main purposes of the stem of a plant is to carry water from the roots to the leaves.

There are small tubes inside the stem that carry water to the leaves. Water moves up the stem.

What Will I Need?   Geranium, coleus or celery stem   Blotter paper
Red food coloring or ink   Water
Drinking glass

What Will We Discuss?   *How does the water get from the roots to the leaves?*
How do you think a florist obtains a blue carnation?
If you wanted to change a white carnation into a blue carnation, what would you do?
How could you find out if your idea was correct?

PROCESSES

What Will Children Do?

1. Obtain a geranium, celery, or coleus stem with leaves on it, food coloring or red ink, water, and a drinking glass. Put some water in the drinking glass and color it with the food coloring or ink. *Important:* Use a white flower for this activity.

Hypothesizing   *Why do you think you have added coloring to the water?*

2. Cut a small slice from the bottom of the stalk of your stem and set it into the glass of colored water. Allow it to set in a sunny area for two hours.

3. At the end of this period, cut open the stem.

Observing   *What has happened to some of the colored water?*
Observing   *What parts of the stem appear to contain the colored water? Describe these parts.*

Inferring   *What can you conclude about how a stem functions from this activity?*

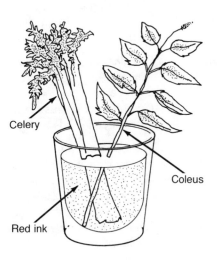

Celery

Coleus

Red ink

How Will Children Use or Apply What They Discover?

1. *What effects might different temperatures have on how rapidly a solution moves up a stem?*
2. *What do you think will happen if you put half of a split stem in one color of water and the other half in another color of water?*

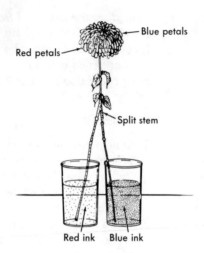

3. *What happens to the upward movement of water in a stem when it is dark?*
   How could you find out?

PART VI WHY DO SOME PARTS OF PLANTS GROW UPWARD?

What Do I Want Children to Discover?

Light and gravity play a role in determining how plants grow.
Roots respond to gravity.
Stems are affected by light.

What Will I Need?

Flat glass or plastic wrap about 4 inches square	Tape
	Light source
2 glasses	Paper towels
Geranium or coleus plant	Cup of soil
3 or 4 bean seeds	Ruler

What Will We Discuss?

What do you think will happen to a plant if its roots are placed in a glass of water?

What do you think will happen if the plant is inverted and the stem is placed in the water?

What effect does light have on the way a plant grows?

What would happen to the way a plant grows if it were placed near a window?

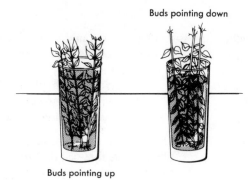

What effect does gravity have on the parts of sprouting seeds?
What could you do to find out?

What Must I Know?   The children should suggest arranging the sprouting seeds and apparatus as shown.

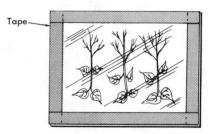

What do you think would happen to the growth of seeds if they were left on the top of some moist soil for a few days?

PROCESSES

What Will Children Do?

Designing an experiment

1. Obtain a geranium or coleus plant, two glasses, a flat piece of glass or plastic wrap, four bean seeds, tape, a paper towel, a cup of soil, and a ruler.
2. Carefully outline the procedure you will follow for investigating the "What Will We Discuss?" questions. After your teacher has checked your outline, proceed with the investigations.

What Must I Know?

The children could make several cuttings of geraniums or coleus or other plants that will root easily in water. Several of these cuttings should be placed right side up and others should be inverted. The inverted ones will not grow roots. To check for the effect of light on plants, the children could take a potted plant and place it on its side near a window. The plant will turn toward the light source.

Observing

3. On a sheet of paper, carefully record any important changes in plant growth during your day-to-day observations.
4. Graph your findings.

Inferring
Inferring
Hypothesizing

Hypothesizing
Applying

Hint: How could you use your ruler in your observations?
What can you conclude from your data?
What would you expect other plants and seeds to do under similar conditions?
What results would you expect if you used different light sources?
Of what value is this experiment to you?

How Will Children Use or Apply What They Discover?

1. What other living things are affected by light and gravity?
2. What are some other factors that affect the growth of plants?
3. Design an experiment to test some of these factors.
4. If you were to do this activity again, how would you change it to make it better?
5. What do you think would happen if you were to scatter mixed parakeet seed on a wet plastic sponge kept in a pan with a little water?
6. What do you think would happen if you obtained two milk cartons filled with soil and planted a handful of seed in one and only four seeds in the other?
Which plants would grow better? Why?

What Is Variation? (K–8)

What Do I Want Children to Discover?

There is tremendous variation in nature.

What Will I Need?

Fallen leaves collected from home or school to show variation
Twigs, stones, and shells to show variation
Ruler

What Will We Discuss?

How do leaves vary?
How could you find out?

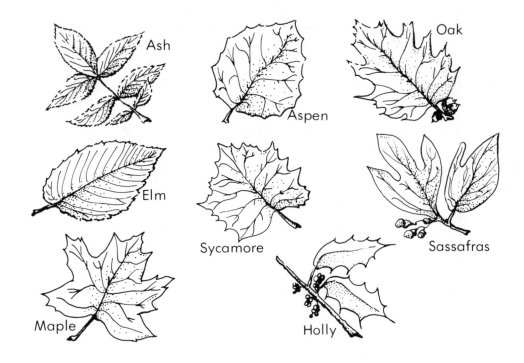

PROCESSES

What Will Children Do?

Inferring
Comparing
Classifying

Inferring

1. Collect different kinds of leaves and obtain a ruler.
2. Place them on your desk and compare them.
   What can you say about the shapes of the leaves?
   How do they differ in size?
3. Place the leaves in groups according to color.
   How many groups did you get?
   Why do you think leaves vary?

What Must I Know?

Leaves may vary because of inheritance, or because of the environment in which they live. For example, the leaves of a particular species may be large if the environment in which the plant grew richly supplied the needs of the plant.

Summarizing

Summarize how leaves vary.

How Will Children Use or Apply What They Discover?

1. *What other things in nature vary?*
2. *How do humans vary?*
3. *How do dogs vary?*

What Is a Cell? (4–8)

What Do I Want Children to Discover?	The smallest unit of life capable of existing independently is the **cell.** The cell consists of many parts. Each part functions in a special way. There are many types of cells, i.e., animal muscle, yeast, red blood, leaf, nerve, etc. All living things are made of cells.
What Will I Need?	Onion Iodine, ink, or methylene blue stain Eye dropper Glass cover slip Water Knife Small paper cup Toothpick Glass slide Microscope
What Will We Discuss?	*How does a rock differ from a plant?* *What do you think living things are made of?* *How would you find out?*

PROCESSES

What Will Children Do?	1. Obtain an onion and a knife. Cut the onion in half.
Observing	*What do you notice about its structure?*
	2. Obtain an eye dropper, a cup of water, a glass slide, iodine, and a glass cover slip. Peel off an inside ring of the onion. From this ring, pull off the outer layer of tissue. This layer should be as thin as tissue paper. Place this tissue in a drop of water on a glass slide.
Hypothesizing	*What do you think will happen if you place a drop of iodine on the tissue?*

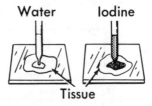

Water   Iodine

Tissue

	3. Place a drop of iodine on the tissue.
Observing	*What effect does iodine have on the onion tissue?*
Inferring	*How will this help you to see the tissue?*
Observing	4. Observe the tissue through the microscope. Record your observations. The small things you see are called cells.
Observing	*How are these cells arranged?*

What Must I Know? The children should see what is illustrated in the diagram.

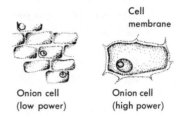

Onion cell
(low power)

Cell
membrane

Onion cell
(high power)

Hypothesizing   *What do you think you will see if you look through the high power?*
                     5. Try the high power.
Observing   *What do you see?*
Designing an   *How could you find out what the parts of cells are called?*
investigation
Designing an   *How could you find out about the functions of these parts?*
investigation
Inferring   *How do you think human tissue is similar to plant tissue?*
Designing an   *How would you find out?*
investigation   6. Obtain a toothpick, a knife, a glass slide, and a cover slip. Gently scrape the inside of your cheek or lip with the toothpick. With a knife, scrape some of the white material on the toothpick into a drop of water on a glass slide. Then add a drop of iodine.
                     7. Spread the material out in the water and place a glass cover slip over it. Examine the material with your microscope under high power.
Observing   *What do you see?*
Comparing   *How are the cells similar to those you saw in the onion tissue?*
Inferring   *From what you have observed, what could you say about living matter?*

How Will Children Use   1. *What are some similarities and some differences of all living tissue?*
or Apply What They
Discover?   2. *How long can living tissues exist without water?*
                            How would you go about finding out?
                            3. *How could you find out what effect prolonged darkness will have on living tissue?*

How Do Leaves "Breathe"? (3–8)

What Do I Want   Leaves have air in them.
Children to Discover?   Gas will expand when heated.
                            Because gases are lighter than water, they will go up through the water and escape.

Leaves have little openings (called **stomata**) through which air enters or leaves the leaf.

What Will I Need?

Elm, coleus, or geranium leaves
Beaker, dish, or saucepan
Lamp or sunlight
Cold and warm water
Hand lens

What Will We Discuss?

What happens when your head is under water and you let some air out of your mouth? What do you see?
What do you think might happen to a leaf if it were placed under water?

PROCESSES

What Will Children Do?

1. Obtain a leaf, a lamp, and a beaker or pan filled with cold water.
2. Place the leaf in the water with the underside up.
3. Place a lamp so its light shines on the leaf, or place the leaf in water in sunlight.
4. Observe the surface of the leaf for five minutes.

Observing
Comparing

What appears on the underside?
How does the appearance of the top and bottom of the leaf vary? Use the hand lens.

Inferring

Why do you think this has happened?

What Must I Know?

Leaves generally have more pores on the lower than on the upper surface.

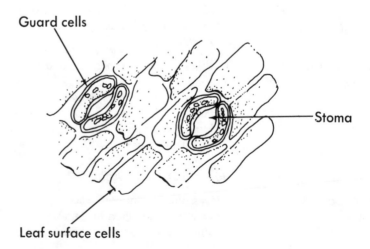

Guard cells

Stoma

Leaf surface cells

Hypothesizing	*What do you think would happen to the leaf if you used warmer water in the above activity?*
Inferring	*What does this indicate about the surface of the leaf?*
Inferring	*If these bubbles are escaping from inside the leaf, how are they able to move to the surface?*

How Will Children Use or Apply What They Discover?	1. *What could you do to improve this investigation?* 2. *What could you do in addition to the previous activity to prove that the surface of a leaf contains holes?*
What Must I Know?/ Where Do I Find It?	Leaves have small pores called **stomata** through which air enters and gases escape.

References—Plant Anatomy and Physiology
Susan Kuchalla, *All About Seeds* (New York: Troll Associates, 1982). Elizabeth Marcus, *Amazing World of Plants* (New York: Troll Associates, 1984).

MICROORGANISMS

Guided Discovery Activities

How Do Bacteria Change Some Foods? (K–8)

What Do I Want Children to Discover?	Milk may be soured by the action of bacteria. Apple juice can be turned to vinegar by the action of bacteria. Bacteria multiply slowly in a cold environment.
What Will I Need?	¼ cup of milk ¼ cup of apple juice 2 pint-sized jars Red and blue litmus paper
What Must I Know?	This activity can be done in groups.
What Will We Discuss?	*What happens to apple juice or milk if it is kept at room temperature for several days?* *What could you do to find out?*

PROCESSES

What Will Children Do?	1. Obtain one-fourth cup of milk and a pint-sized jar. 2. Pour the milk into the jar. 3. Place the jar where directed by your teacher. 4. After two days, look at the milk.
Observing	*What changes do you notice?*

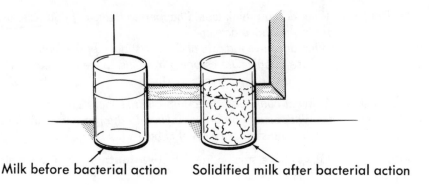

Milk before bacterial action   Solidified milk after bacterial action

Observing	*What do you notice about the smell?*
Observing	*How has the milk changed in appearance?*
Hypothesizing	*What do you think the milk will taste like?*
	5. Taste the milk.
Inferring	*Why do you think the milk soured?*
Designing an investigation	*How could you find out?*
Applying data	*How could you test the sour milk to see if it is acid or base?*

What Must I Know?   Use red and blue litmus paper. This can be obtained from a scientific supply company, high school science teacher, or the local pharmacy. Red litmus paper turns blue in the presence of a base. Blue litmus paper turns pink in the presence of an acid.

Designing an investigation	*How could you find out if the fresh milk was an acid or a base?*
	6. Test fresh milk and your milk sample to see if they are acid or base.
Inferring	*What causes the milk to change?*
Hypothesizing	*How do you think you could have prevented the milk from souring so fast?*

What Must I Know?   Explain to the children that there are bacteria in the air that cause the change in the milk.

Inferring	*Why do you think you cannot see bacteria?*
Inferring	*How do you know bacteria are present in the air?*

How Will Children Use or Apply What They Discover?

1. *If you were a farmer and had to keep milk for two days before the milk truck could come for it, what would you do?*
2. *What would you do to milk to make it sour faster?*
3. *How do people use sour milk in their daily lives?*
4. *What does it mean to get a "yogurt starter culture"?*
5. *How can we make yogurt in class?*

How Do Fungi Grow? (4–8)

What Do I Want Children to Discover?

Fungi are sometimes parasites.
Fungi reproduce by spores.
Mildew is one type of fungus.
Mold is another type of fungus.
Fungi need warmth, moisture, and usually darkness to grow well.

What Will I Need?

Orange	String
Bread (at least 4 pieces)	Microscope or microprojector
2 dishes or plates	Plastic bags
Small pieces of various kinds of cloth (such as wool, rayon, and cotton)	Hand lens

What Will We Discuss?

What would happen to a piece of moist orange peeling if it were put in a dark place and left there for several days? Why?
How could you find out?

What Will Children Do?

PROCESSES

PART I
1. Obtain an orange and a plastic bag.
   What can you do with the orange peeling to make sure it remains moist?
   Where should you store the orange peeling for several days? Why?

Designing an investigation
Hypothesizing

What Must I Know?

If the children do not suggest anything, have them peel the orange, wet the peeling, place the peeling in a plastic bag, and put it in a dark place.

Observing
Inferring

2. After several days, looking at the peeling.
   What do you think the green material on the peeling is?

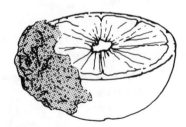

What Must I Know?

This will probably be one of the green penicillin molds that grows well on orange peelings.

PART II

Hypothesizing
Hypothesizing

What effect does light have on mold?
What effect does the lack of moisture have on mold?

1. Obtain four pieces of bread, two plastic bags, and two plates or dishes.

Designing an investigation

What can you do with the bread to see if light and lack of moisture have any effect on mold?

What Must I Know?

The children might do any of the following: Wet one piece of bread and place it in a sealed plastic bag in the dark. Wet another piece and place it in a sealed bag where it will receive a lot of light. Wet another and place it on a dish where it will dry out. Place a fourth piece on a plate; do not wet it.

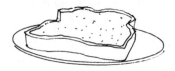 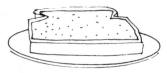

Collecting data

2. Keep a record of what happens to the bread over a four-day period.

Inferring

Did all of your bread tests change in the same way? Why? Use hand lens.

Observing
Inferring
Designing an investigation

What is on some of the bread?
Do you think it is growing? Why?
How could you find out if the mold is growing?

What Must I Know?

The children should leave the bread in the bag for two more days to see if the mold growth increases in size. If it does become larger, it is logical to conclude that it is growing. The idea of measuring the size of the colonies accurately might also be introduced.

Inferring
Summarizing

Why did the bread placed in the sunlight not become very moldy?
What conclusions could you make about mold and its need for light?

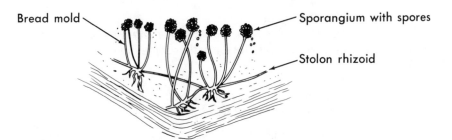

Bread mold — Sporangium with spores — Stolon rhizoid

Inferring
Summarizing

Why did the mold not grow well on the dry plate?
What conclusions can you make about mold and its need for water?

PART III

Hypothesizing

What would happen to damp clothing left in a dark place? Why?

1. Obtain a small piece of cloth, a string, and a plastic bag from your teacher.

Designing an investigation

With these things how could you prove that moisture and lack of light affect cloth?

What Must I Know?

Each student should have a small plastic bag and a small piece of cloth such as wool, cotton, or rayon. All but two of the students should dampen the cloth. Place the dampened cloth in a plastic bag and tie the bag closed. Two students should put a piece of dry cloth in bags and prepare the bags in the same manner. Two or three students should place their bags containing dampened cloth in sunlight. One student should place a bag containing cloth that has not been dampened in sunlight. The rest of the class should place their bags in the dark.

Hypothesizing
Hypothesizing

What do you think will happen to the cloth in each bag? Why?
Which pieces of cloth will change the most? Why?

2. Observe the cloth in the bags each day for several days.

Observing
Inferring
Observing
Inferring

What do you observe?
Why do some of the pieces of cloth appear the way they do?
In which bags did the spots appear first? Why?
Why do some of the pieces of cloth have black spots on them?

Mildew

Inferring
Designing an
  investigation

Use hand lens.
What evidence is there that something is growing on the cloth?
How could you prove whether something is growing on the cloth?

What Must I Know?

Allow the bags to remain in the room and have the students compare the size and number of spots.

What is this type of fungus called?

What Must I Know?

This type of fungus is called a **mildew.**

Inferring

Why is it a good idea to hang your clothes up to dry when they are wet rather than waiting several hours before you hang them?

Hypothesizing
Designing an
  investigation

In what way does mildew affect cloth besides discoloring it?
How could you find out?

Take some of the cloth out of the bag and test its strength by tearing it.
How easily does it rip compared to cloth that has not been infected with mildew?

Summarizing

What does mildew do to clothing?

What Must I Know?

Mildew is a fungus that weakens cloth by producing substances that change the chemicals in the fiber of the cloth.

How Will Children Use or Apply What They Discover?

1. *How does the amount of moisture present affect the growth of a fungus?*
2. *At which temperature does mildew grow the fastest?*
3. *Why will bread stay better and longer in a freezer than a refrigerator?*
4. *What is a dehumidifier? Why are they used in basements?*

How Can Food Be Preserved? (3–8)

What Do I Want Children to Discover?

Spoiling of food is caused by **bacteria** and **molds.**
Food can be preserved by canning, salting, drying, refrigerating, and by chemical means.
Bacteria do not live well in an acid solution.
Bacteria do not reproduce rapidly in a cold environment.
Bacteria will not multiply without moisture.
Sterilization and immediate sealing will prevent spoilage.

What Will I Need?

Package of frozen peas
6 small jars, ½ pint or smaller (milk carton can be substituted for all but one of these jars)
Hot plate

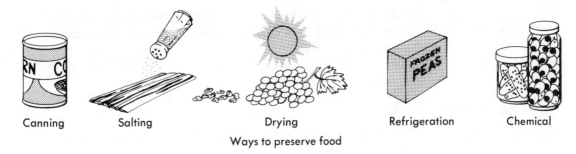

Canning   Salting   Drying   Refrigeration   Chemical

Ways to preserve food

Small saucepan
Enough vinegar to cover the peas in the bottle
Tablespoon of salt
Paper towel

What Will We Discuss?

What causes food to spoil?
How can you prevent food from spoiling?
How could you find out the best way to preserve food?

What Will Children Do?

PROCESSES

What Must I Know?

This activity should be done in groups.

PART I
1. Obtain 6 small jars, enough frozen peas to fill all the jars one-fourth full.
2. After numbering the 6 jars, 1 through 6, fill them one-fourth full with defrosted frozen peas.

Vinegar and peas | Sealed after 15 minutes boiling | Unsealed in sun | Refrigerated | Water and salt | Control (at room temperature)

What Must I Know?

In the following activity, the children are encouraged to devise tests. After the class has written down their tests, discuss their proposals and have them carry them out. Refer to the preceding diagram for suggestions.

Hypothesizing	*What are some possible ways to keep the peas from spoiling?*
Hypothesizing	*What are the best ways to preserve the peas using the materials you have?*
Designing an investigation	*How could you test vinegar, a weak acid, to see if it will prevent the peas from spoiling?*
Designing an investigation	*How could you test to see what effect sunlight has on the peas?*

What Must I Know? The children would have the best results if they spread the peas out on paper to dry.

Hypothesizing	*What effect would boiling the peas for 10 minutes have?* *Caution:* Do not boil a sealed jar with peas. *Why?*
Designing an investigation	*What could you do with peas to test the effect of a low temperature on them?*
Designing an investigation	*What could you do with peas to determine what effect salt and water would have on them?*
Hypothesizing	*What would happen to peas if nothing were added to them?*
Designing an investigation	*How could you find out?*

PART II

Hypothesizing	*How long do you think it will take for bacteria and mold to spoil the peas?*
Collecting data	*How should you record your data so others can see the results easily?*
Observing	1. Observe and record what happened to the peas in the jar with the acid (vinegar).
Hypothesizing	*Why was the acid added to the peas?*
Inferring	*How do bacteria and fungi grow in acid?*
Hypothesizing	*Why did you boil the jar and lid before sealing it?*
Hypothesizing	*Why did you seal the jar after boiling it?*
Observing	*What happened to the peas you placed in the sunlight?*
Inferring	*Why do they look this way?*
Inferring	*Why haven't the mold or bacteria grown well?*
Observing	*What effect did a cold temperature have on the peas?*
Inferring	*Why haven't the mold or bacteria grown well in the refrigerator?*
Observing	*What has happened to the peas in the jar with salt water?*
Inferring	*How can salt water help preserve the peas?*
Observing	*What has happened to the jar to which you added only the peas?*
Inferring	*What conditions contributed to the growth of bacteria and mold in this jar?*

How Will Children Use or Apply What They Discover?

1. *What could you do to preserve peaches?*
2. *How are foods preserved?*

Make a list of common foods and methods of preservation, for example:

Food	Preservation
Milk	Pasteurizing - refrigeration
Meat	
Bread	
Grain	
Tuna	
Eggs	
Peanut butter	

Reference Books—Microorganisms Donald M. Silver, *Library of Knowledge: The Animal World from Single-Cell Creatures to Giants of the Land and Sea* (New York: Random House, 1987). Mary L. Beaney, "Microbiology for First Graders" (Science and Children, vol. 25, no. 1, Sept. 1987), pp. 23–25.

ECOLOGY

Quickie Starters

How Clean Is the Air You Breathe?[3]

Materials

For each group of two to four students: four 10-cm square pieces of waxed paper, four 12-cm square pieces of wood, petroleum jelly (i.e., Vaseline), 16 thumb tacks

Opening Questions

How can we find out if air in some areas has more particles in it than air in other areas?
Where do you think we might find these areas?
What might account for air in some areas having more particles in it than air in other areas?
What effect could dirty air have on your health?

Some Possible Activities

Attach squares of waxed paper to wood blocks with thumb tacks and coat the waxed paper with a *thin* coating of petroleum jelly like this:

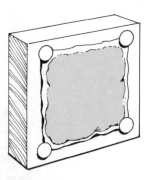

[3]For additional suggestions, see Joe Abruscato and Jack Hassard, "Air Pollution. Making and Using Air Dirt Collectors," *The Whole Cosmos. Catalog of Science Activities* (Santa Monica, CA: Goodyear Publishing Co., 1977), 13.

Put the wood blocks—"Particle Collectors"—outside in places where you think the air is "dirty," such as where there is a lot of bus and car travel, near airports, next to factories, etc. Also, put some in wooded areas, such as parks, and some indoors at home or at school. Make sure no one disturbs your collectors. Write the place and date you placed each collector.

After four or five days, bring the collectors back to class, making sure you don't touch the sticky side of each collector. Look at the waxed paper with a hand lens.

Which collectors (places) had the most particles? Why?
Which collectors (places) had the least particles? Why?

Which Materials Break Down (Decompose) Easily?

Materials

For each group of two to four students, supply a plastic storage bag with snap and seal top 10½ × 11 inches (268mm × 279mm), garden soil, solid wastes; water

Opening
Questions

What happens to our garbage after it is picked up by the garbage people?
Do some things break down (decompose) better than others?
What are they made of?
Do some things resist breaking down (decomposing)? What are they made of?

Some Possible
Activities

Put about 5 inches (12 cm) of garden soil in the bottom of the plastic bag. (Do not use packaged, sterilized soil, since you want bacteria and insects if possible.) Add ½ inch (1 cm) thin pieces of solid wastes from garbage or from the environment, such as leafy vegetables, fruits, aluminum foil, rubber bands, wooden toothpicks, different kinds of cloth and paper, styrofoam and other plastic items. Moisten the soil, seal the bag securely, and leave it at room temperature or near a radiator or heat source. Shake vigorously daily.

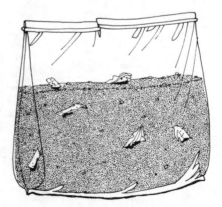

Observe and record what you see weekly for four to six weeks and answer the opening questions.

Guided Discovery Activities

What Do Plants Need to Grow? (K–6)

What Do I Want Children to Discover?

Plants need food to grow.
Plants need water to grow.
Plants need light to grow.
Too much water may kill some plants.

What Will I Need?

Seeds (pea, bean, or lima)
8 small milk cartons
Topsoil

What Will We Discuss?

What do plants need to grow?
If you were going to raise some plants from seeds, what could you do?
If you wanted to find out how light affects plants, what could you do?
If you wanted to find out how water affects plants, what could you do?

What Must I Know?

In the primary grades, it is suggested that the class be divided into groups.
Each group should be assigned to test the effect of only one of the variables listed below, such as water or light.

What Will Children Do?

Carrying out experiment

PROCESSES

1. Obtain eight small milk cartons, topsoil, and bean seeds.
2. Punch four small holes in the bottom of six of the cartons to allow for drainage. Leave two cartons intact.
3. Fill all eight cartons with topsoil.
4. Plant three seeds in each carton one inch deep.

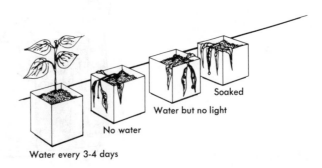

Water every 3-4 days

No water

Water but no light

Soaked

Cover the seeds with soil and pack the soil down with your hand.

5. Water all cartons so soil is damp but not soaking and continue to water them every three or four days until plants are a few inches high.

6. After the seeds sprout, keep the two cartons left intact filled with water so the soil is always soaked.

7. After the plants sprout, stop watering two of your six cartons.

8. Water regularly the two other cartons, but place them in a dark place where they get no light.

9. Keep the other two cartons in a well-lighted place, and water regularly. This is your control.

10. Observe and record your observations daily.

Hypothesizing	*What do you think will happen to the plants being soaked?*
Hypothesizing	*What do you think will happen to the plants not being watered?*
Hypothesizing	*What do you think will happen to the plants that are in the dark?*
Hypothesizing	*What do you think will happen to the plants kept in a lighted room and watered regularly?*
	Why were there two cartons of each condition?
	Two weeks later, answer the following:
Comparing	*Which plants appear to be the most healthy?*
Observing	*What happened to the plants that were kept soaked?*
Collecting and organizing data	*What happened to the plants you did not water?*
Observing	*What happened to the plants kept in a dark place and not exposed to light?*
Observing	*What happened to the plants kept in a lighted room and watered regularly?*
Inferring	What do plants need to grow well?

How Will Children Use or Apply What They Discover?

1. *Why are cut flowers placed in water?*
2. *What would happen if they were not placed in water?*

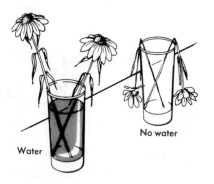

Water   No water

3. *Do all plants need soil, air and water? Explain.*
4. *Of what importance are plants to people?*
5. *Under what conditions do plants grow best in your house?*
6. *What other factors influence healthy plant life?*

What Types of Life Can You Find in a Pond? (K–6)

**What Do I Want
Children to Discover?**

The color in animals or plants usually helps to conceal, disguise, or advertise their presence.

Every living organism has some body parts that are adapted for the life it leads.

Each species adapts to live where it does.

A pond is a small body of water containing many forms of life.

Some forms of life are very small and can be seen only under a microscope.

If a pond is not disturbed, its life forms will remain in balance.

What Will I Need?

Pond that pupils may observe
2 quart jars with lids
Thermometers
Microscope or microprojector and slides
Dip net (may use nylon stocking and hanger)
Magnifying glass
Pencil and notebook

What Must I Know?

This activity should be done in groups of three or four children. When the class collects materials, it would be desirable to have one or two other teachers or parents as chaperones. Since this lesson is designed as a field trip, you may want to collect other specimens for later study. Instruct the children to be on the lookout for cocoons, old birds, nests, leaves, and so on. Respect environment. Do not strip trees or bushes.

**What Will Children
Do?**

PROCESSES

1. Obtain the following materials: 2 quart jars with lids, magnifying lens, thermometer, dip net, pencil, and notebook.

Observing   2. As you approach the pond, notice the different kinds of plant life
                        in the area.
Inferring   *How were you able to tell you were approaching a pond?*
Observing   3. Look carefully for living things.
Classifying   Count the different kinds of organisms you see.
Inferring   *Why was it hard to see some of these things?*
Summarizing   *How many different kinds of insects did you see?*
Observing   *What kinds of things did you find under the water?*
Measuring   4. Determine the temperature of the water at different depths.
Observing   *How does the temperature change with the depth of the water?*

Hypothesizing   *How is the temperature of the water important to the life in a
                        pond?*
Hypothesizing   *What might be living in the water that is so small you cannot see
                        it?*

What Must I Know?   There probably are microscopic organisms in the water.

                     5. Fill a jar with pond water and take it back to school.
Inferring   6. Find an insect (or other animal) that you think could live only
                        near a pond.
Observing   *What is there about this animal that helps it to live where it does?*
Designing an   *How could you find out if this animal could live only near a*
* investigation*   *pond?*
                     7. Take this specimen back to school to find out whether it can live
                        in a classroom. Some animals eat both plants and animals, and
                        other animals eat only animals.
Hypothesizing   *What do you think would happen if someone killed all the plants
                        around a pond?*
                     8. Collect any other specimens to study at home or in school.

What Must I Know?

If the children have had no experience with a microscope, it might be necessary to demonstrate the proper technique before doing the following part of the lesson. A microprojector works well for projecting a microorganism's image on a screen for all to see.

Applying

9. When back in school, have your teacher help you set up a microscope and look at the water you obtained from the pond.
   What looks like it might be alive in the water under the microscope?
   What makes you think it is alive?

How Will Children Use or Apply What They Discover?

1. *How many different kinds of insects can you name that live near a pond?*
2. You may have been lucky enough to have seen some single-celled organisms called **protozoa** under the microscope. You may want to read about them.
   How many different kinds can you find in the pond you studied?
3. *How do different temperatures affect protozoa?*
4. *Could the plants that live under water in a pond live above water?*
5. *How do animals that do not live near ponds adapt to their environments?*

How Does the Environment Affect Life? (3–8)

What Do I Want Children to Discover?

Certain environmental factors determine community types.
Some types of communities are on land and some are in water.
Land communities can be subdivided into forests, bogs, swamps, deserts, and others.
A **community** is a collection of living organisms having mutual relationships among themselves and with their environment.
All living things have certain requirements that must be met by their surroundings.
Habitat is a place where an animal or plant naturally lives or grows.
Different environments are needed to sustain different types of life.

What Will I Need?

3 large, commercial-sized mayonnaise jars; 2 of them with lids in good condition
Cup of coarse-grained gravel
4 cups of beach sand
5 small aquatic plants (approximately 3 to 4 inches in height)
Freshwater fantailed guppy
2 water snails
5-inch square of fine-mesh screening material

Soda bottle cap
2 small cactus plants (approximately 3 or 4 inches in height)
Chameleon, lizard, skink, horned toad, or colored lizard
2 small dried twigs (no longer than three-fourths of the length of the mayonnaise jars)
Small water turtle or frog
Several small ferns, mosses, lichens, liverworts

What Will We Discuss?	*What does environment mean to you?* *What are some things that live around you?* *Name some environments that you know about.*
What Must I Know?	All environments contain geological features, weather, climate, and living things (plants and animals), and all interrelate and affect each other.

PROCESSES

What Will Children Do?	This activity is to be done in groups of four or five children. Each group might be responsible for only one of the habitats.

PART I AQUARIUM

1. Obtain the previous listed materials.
2. Clean the mayonnaise jar thoroughly with soap and water and rinse it well.
3. Wash two cups of sand to be placed in the jar. Spread this over the bottom of the jar.
4. Fill the jar with water and let it stand for several days before adding plants and fish.
5. Place the aquatic plants as suggested by the pet shop owner.
6. Place the guppy and snails in the jar.
7. Now cover the jar with the screening material.

Aquarium

Inferring	*Why do you think it is necessary to clean the jar before using it?*
Inferring	*Why should the sand and gravel be washed before putting them in the jar?*
Inferring	*What would dirty water do to the gills of the fish?*
Inferring	*Why must the gills of the fish be kept clean?*
Inferring	*How do fish breathe?*
Inferring	*Why do you think the water was allowed to stand for several days before the fish were placed in the aquarium?*
Inferring	*What does our health department add to water that might be injurious to fish?*
Inferring	*Why were the snails added to the water?*

What Must I Know? The snails will eat the small green **algae** (the slimy plants that collect on the side of the tank).

Hypothesizing *Why were plants added to the aquarium?*
Inferring *What would the fish eat in nature?*
  Would your guppy live if it did not feed on anything? Why?
Inferring *What do plants make that the fish can use?*
Inferring *What does the fish make that the plants can use?*

What Must I Know? Plants make oxygen and food, and the fish produce carbon dioxide and waste products. The aquarium is not balanced so food must be added from time to time for the fish.

PART II DESERT TERRARIUM
1. Obtain one of the large, commercial-sized mayonnaise jars.
2. Clean the mayonnaise jar with soap and water and rinse it well. Wash and rinse the lid also.
3. Dry off the jar and screw the lid on.
4. With the jar on the floor, pound holes into the lid by hitting a nail through the lid with a hammer.
5. Place the jar on its side.
6. Spread the remaining two cups of sand onto the bottom of the jar.
7. Place the small bottle cap filled with water, the cactus, and one twig into the jar.
8. Place a lizard, skink, chameleon, or horned toad into the jar.
9. Cover the jar with the punctured lid.
10. Water the terrarium once every two to three weeks only if dry. Place the jar so it receives direct sun every day.
11. Feed the animals live mealworms. These can be obtained from a local pet shop.

Desert terrarium

12. Keep the bottle cap filled with water.

PART III BOG TERRARIUM
1. Clean one of the mayonnaise jars with soap and water and rinse it well. Wash and rinse the lid.
2. Dry off the jar and screw the lid on.

3. With the jar on the floor, pound holes into the lid by driving a nail through the lid with a hammer.
4. Place the jar on its side and tape wood strips as shown to keep the jar from rolling.

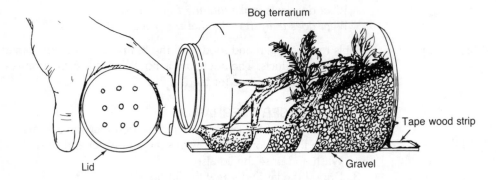

Bog terrarium

Tape wood strip

Lid

Gravel

5. Spread the gravel out on the bottom of the jar so it will be concentrated toward the back of the jar as in the diagram.
6. Place the ferns, mosses, lichens and liverworts over the gravel.
7. Pour some water in (do not put in so much that it covers the back potion of the arrangement).
8. Place a dried twig in the jar.
9. Place a small turtle or frog in the jar.
10. Feed the turtle or frog insects or turtle food every other day.
11. Cover the jar with the punctured lid.
12. Place the terrarium in an area where light is weak.

Comparing and observing
Classifying

How does the life found in the aquarium differ from that found in the desert and/or bog terrariums?
What kinds of conditions do the fish, turtle, frog, or lizard have to have to survive in their particular habitats?

Observing
Observing
Hypothesizing

What kinds of conditions do the bog plants require to grow well?
What kinds of food do the fish, the lizards, or the turtle eat?
What do you think would happen to the turtle if you left it in the desert habitat, or to the lizard if you put it in the bog habitat?

How Will Children Use or Apply What They Discover?

1. *What experiment would you do to find out what happens to plants when grown under different environmental conditions?*
2. *What other kinds of surroundings or environments could you make through the use of mayonnaise jars?*
3. *What does the "environment" have to do with the kinds of organisms found in it?*
4. *Can you name some organisms that are able to live in many different surroundings?*
5. *What would happen to a fern plant if it were transplanted to a desert region?*

6. *What would happen to a penguin if it were taken to live in a desert?*
7. *What would happen to a primitive human being if he or she were suddenly brought to a large city?*
8. *What statements can you make about the effect of environment on a living thing?*

How Do Animals Affect Their Environments? (3–8)

What Do I Want
Children to Discover?

Living things are dependent upon one another for food.

In general, the smaller the animal, the greater the number present in a community.

Larger animals may consume many small animals to satisfy their need for food.

The stronger, better-adapted animals survive.

When the supply of food does not equal the demand in an environment, a change of some kind must occur in the numbers and/or types of organisms present in it.

Water plants are important to an aquatic community.

What Will I Need?

Aquarium	2 or more daphnia
Water from a swamp or lake	Rocks
Green algae	2–6 small fish
2–6 snails	

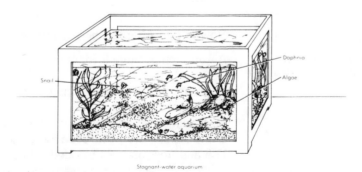

Stagnant-water aquarium

PROCESSES

What Will Children
Do?

1. Obtain an aquarium containing some water from a swamp or lake, green algae, snails, daphnia, rocks, and some small fish. Assemble the material as indicated in the diagram. You now have a **microcosm,** a small world environment. You are not to add anything to the microcosm.

Hypothesizing   *What function do you think the plants serve in it?*

Hypothesizing   *What changes would you expect to take place tomorrow? in a week? in a month?*

Observing	2. Observe and record what the animals eat.
Inferring	*What does the plant do for the animals in the aquarium?*
Inferring	*Where does the plant get its food?*
Hypothesizing	*What might cause the fish to die?*

What Must I Know?

The fish may die if there is not sufficient oxygen dissolved in the water or a sufficient food supply. If one of the fish dies, allow it to remain the aquarium.

Observing	3. Observe carefully what happens to the fish after it is dead.
Inferring	*What effect did the dead fish have on the number of small animals in the aquarium?*
Inferring	*What evidence do you have from the microcosm that one animal may be dependent on another for food?*
Inferring	*Why did the number of organisms start to decrease just after you set up the microcosm?*
Inferring	*Why did the number later increase?*
Inferring	*What effect can the death of an animal have on the microcosm?*
Inferring	*Why is it usually true that the bigger the animal, the fewer of them there are in a particular area?*

How Will Children Use or Apply What They Discover?

1. *What would you do to make a microcosm using a land environment instead of a water environment?*
2. *Why is it important for the numbers of wildlife to be kept in balance?*

How Is Life Affected by Variations in Temperature? (4–8)

What Do I Want Children to Discover?

A warm temperature is more beneficial to life than a cold temperature.

There are maximum and minimum temperatures that living things can stand.

Most animals tend to be more active when the temperature is warm.

Some animals are **cold-blooded,** and others are **warm-blooded.**

Fish and frogs are cold-blooded animals. Their body temperature is about the same as the environment around them.

What Will I Need?

4 quart jars	Paper towels
Thermometer	Candle
Ice cubes	Match
Tadpoles or goldfish	Tripod
Jar of ants	Plastic wrap
Bean seeds	

What Will We Discuss?

What do you think would happen if you were to place goldfish in cold water?

What could you do to find out?

What Will Children Do?

Carrying out experiment

Observing

PROCESSES

PART I GOLDFISH OR TADPOLES

1. Obtain two jars of water, several ice cubes, two goldfish or tadpoles, and a thermometer.
2. Place the ice cubes in one of the jars of water.
   Keep the other at room temperature.
3. Place one goldfish or tadpole in each jar and observe the activity.

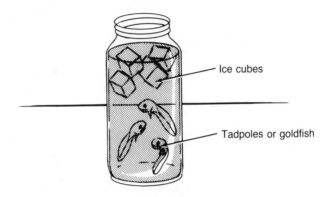

Ice cubes

Tadpoles or goldfish

Collecting data

Observing
Comparing
Hypothesizing
Designing an investigation

4. After 15 minutes, note the temperature of each container and record it.
5. Note the activity of the goldfish or tadpole in each jar.
   Explain what you see and compare it with your first observation.
   What types of animals are more active in warm environments?
   What could you do to find out?

PART II ANTS

Carrying out experiment

Observing
Hypothesizing

Inferring

1. Obtain ants, a candle, tripod, a match, and two jars. Place some ants in each jar. Place one jar in a refrigerator and keep the other at room temperature.
2. After one-half hour, observe the activity of the ants in each jar.
   What do you think would happen if a jar with some ants in it were heated gently with a candle?
3. Place a jar of ants on a tripod over a lighted candle. Heat briefly.
   What effect does a change in temperature have on ants?

What Must I Know?

Do not leave ants over candle more than a few minutes.

PART III PLANT SEEDS

Hypothesizing

Designing an investigation

1. *What do you think would be the effect of different temperatures on plants?*
   What could you do to find out?

2. Obtain two jars. Place water-soaked paper towels in the bottom of the two jars. Add bean seeds to each jar. Cover with plastic wrap.
3. Place one of the jars in a refrigerator and leave the other at room temperature.

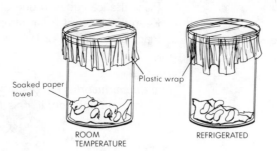

Soaked paper towel

Plastic wrap

ROOM TEMPERATURE

REFRIGERATED

Observing

4. Each day check on what is happening in the experiment and record your observations as indicated below:
   Date you wet them: _____
   Cold temperature environment: _____
   Room temperature: _____
   Date sprouted: _____
   Rate of growth: _____

Comparing

5. At the end of a week, remove the seeds from the jars and measure them to determine which group grew faster.

Observing
Inferring

   Explain what you see.
   What effect does a change in temperature have on the sprouting seeds?

6. Graph your findings.

How Will Children Use or Apply What They Discover?

1. *What would happen in winter if you placed a plant outside?*
2. *Lizards and snakes are cold-blooded animals.*
   How active do you think they would be on a cold day?
3. *Why do you think some people grow plants in a greenhouse?*
4. *How fast do you think plants would grow in a temperature of 200°F?*
5. *What other experiments can you think of to do with plants or animals that might show the effects of temperature?*

How Do Earthworms Change the Soil? (K–6)

What Do I Want Children to Discover?

Earthworms loosen soil so it is more easily aerated.
Earthworms loosen the soil, helping to conserve water.
Earthworms are active in the dark and avoid light.
Earthworms eat the organic materials in the soil.

What Will I Need?

3 jars with lids
Can of sand
Box of cornmeal
Earthworms
Loamy soil
Lamp
Black paper

**What Will We
Discuss?**

Why are earthworms important?
Where do earthworms live?
How do earthworms affect the soil?
How do you think earthworms react to light?
What can you do to find out the answers to some of these questions?

**What Will Children
Do?**

PROCESSES

1. Obtain three jars with lids and fill each two-thirds full with loose, loamy soil.

*Carrying out
experiment*

2. Add some earthworms to *two* of the jars.
3. To all three jars add about one inch of sand and on top of the sand about one-half inch of cornmeal. Cover with lids with holes.
4. Place one of the jars with worms near a window.
   Place a lamp near it that can be turned on at night.
5. Place the other two jars in the dark or wrap with black paper.
6. Add a small amount of water at room temperature to the jars every other day.

Observing

7. Observe the jars each day to note if any changes have taken place. Record in your notebook what happens.

Comparing

8. After four days, compare the jars and determine what is different about the can you kept in the light compared with the two you kept in the dark.

Cornmeal
Sand
Loamy soil

Contains worms
in the light

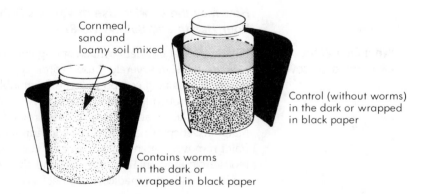

Cornmeal,
sand and
loamy soil mixed

Contains worms
in the dark or
wrapped in black paper

Control (without worms)
in the dark or wrapped
in black paper

Inferring	*What was the purpose of the can without worms?*
Inferring	*Why do you think the soil was moistened with water?*
Inferring	*What conclusions can you make about the sensitivity of worms to light and dark?*
Inferring	*Which of the cans seems to hold water better?*
Inferring	*Why do you think they do?*
Inferring	*What do you think happens to water in the soil containing the worms?*
Inferring	*How do you think worms help conserve water in soil?*
Summarizing	*How do worms condition the soil?*

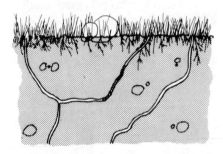

Earthworms help to mix air with the soil.

How Will Children Use or Apply What They Discover?

1. *Why do you not see many worms on the lawns during the day-time?*
2. *Why do you think the cornmeal was placed on top of the soil?*
3. *How do you think worms help to conserve our soil?*
4. *Why was there less moisture in the soil without worms?*
5. *What caused the soil with the cornmeal to change in appearance?*
6. *What would you do to raise worms to sell to people who fish?*
7. *What can you do to determine the kind of soil in which worms will grow best?*

How May the Unwise Use of Various Substances Endanger Your Health and Safety? (K–8)

What Do I Want Children to Discover?

Sink and toilet cleaners contain strong chemical materials that may injure the skin severely if used carelessly.

Some dry cleaning compounds are flammable (burn) and may give off dangerous fumes.

Most germ killers are extremely dangerous if taken internally.

Many insect sprays are poisonous to humans as well as to insects.

Paint removers often burn or give off dangerous fumes.

Household ammonia is poisonous and should be kept in a safe place, not in the medicine cabinet.

The poison label is a skull (skeleton head) with crossbones or Mr. Yuk.

Bleaches should be used in the home with extreme caution.

All poisons should be kept out of reach of children. They can be used by adults, but with caution.

What Will I Need?

Empty containers with poison or warning labels on them:

Bleach bottle	Sink and toilet cleaner cans
Aspirin bottle	Paint remover can
Medicine bottles	Also:
Gasoline can	Full containers of insect spray,
Iodine bottle	bleach, and iodine
Ammonia bottle	Jar of insects
Kerosene can	Piece of cloth

What Will We Discuss?

What is the symbol placed on bottles to indicate they contain poisons?

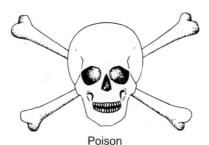

Poison

Mr. YUK

What Must I Know?

Display an enlarged picture of Mr. Yuk and a skull and crossbones, or draw them on the board. Also place many of the containers suggested under "What Will I Need?" on your desk.

Where should the word poison *be placed on the board?*

Why do you think these bottles were placed on the desk?

What Must I Know?

Point to the poison label on the bottles. Explain the reasons for each label. Some poison labels will also have antidotes listed on them. Discuss the purpose of the antidote with the class. Discuss the terms *flammable, antiseptic, bleach, ammonia,* and *medicine.*

PROCESSES

PART I

What Will Children Do?

Caution: The teacher should do this activity *outdoors* and discuss why it is important not to breathe the insect spray. Insect spray should only be handled by adults.

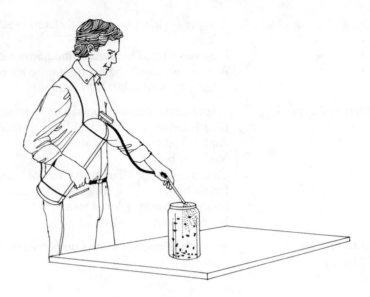

Hypothesizing

1. The teacher holds up the jar of insects and a can of insect spray.
   What do you think will happen to the insects when they are sprayed?

Observing
Inferring

2. The teacher sprays the insects and students observe from a safe distance.
   What do you think the spray would do to you?
   Where should these sprays be kept?

PART II

1. The teacher pours some bleach on a piece of cloth. Allow it to stand for several hours.

Hypothesizing

   What do you think will happen to the material on which the bleach is poured?

Observing
Inferring

2. After two days, have the children note results.
   What does this tell you about bleaches and other chemicals used around the house?

PART III

1. The teacher places iodine on a leaf or skin of a fruit and allows it to stand for several hours.

Hypothesizing
Observing

   What do you think the iodine will do the the leaf?

2. Examine it after several hours.
   What happened?

What Must I Know?

Point out that iodine is a medicine, but it may be harmful to the skin if used for too long on the same spot. Iodine also is very poisonous.

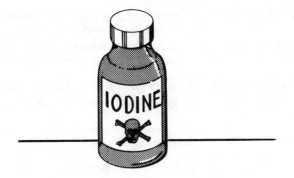

Inferring	*What rule or rules would you make to follow in regard to medicines and the places they should be kept in the house?*
What Must I Know?	Explain that chemicals and medicines kept in the medicine cabinets may be dangerous if not used properly, and children should not use any medicines unless their parents are there to help them.

PART IV

Observing	1. Display the following empty cans: paint remover, gasoline, and kerosene.
What Must I Know?	It may be a good idea to have the children describe the smells these materials give off.
Comparing	*What do all of these have in common?* 2. Write the word *flammable* on the board and ask the children to explain what it means. *What rule can you make in regard to the use and storage of flammable chemicals?*
What Must I Know?/ Where Do I Find It?	Point out they should never be used near fires. Gasoline should particularly never be used to start a fire. It is extremely dangerous to pour gasoline from a container onto a fire because the fire will travel right up the gasoline being poured to the container itself and may cause an explosion resulting in serious burns.
Inferring	*Why should you not play with chemicals you know nothing about?*
Inferring	*From what you observed with the insect spray, why should your parents wash their hands after using an insect spray?*
Inferring	*Why should you not get things from the medicine cabinet in the dark?*
Inferring	*Why is gasoline very dangerous?*

Hypothesizing   *How can you protect babies and small children from the dangers of medicines and chemicals?*

Hypothesizing   *What can you do to protect your family from the dangers of these various substances and make your home a safe place?*

How Will Children Use or Apply What They Discover?

1. *What do you think bleach would do to leather or skin?*
2. *Why is it dangerous to sniff glue, aerosol sprays, and so on?*

References—Ecology Shelly Grossman and Mary L. Grossman, *Ecology* (New York: Wonder, 1981). G. Tyler Miller, Jr., *Living in the Environment* (Belmont, CA: Wadsworth Publishing Company, 1982).

SECTION 3

Quickie Starters and Guided Discovery Activities for Earth and Environmental Sciences

METEOROLOGY (WEATHER)

Quickie Starters

How Are Clouds and Fog Formed?

Materials

Ice cubes; 2 clear, narrow-mouthed bottles; hot and cold water

Opening Questions

What is a cloud and how is it formed?
What is fog and how is it formed?

Some Possible Activities

Fill a bottle with very hot water and let it sit for a few minutes. Now pour out most of the water, leaving about 2 cm (¾ to 1 inch) of water in the bottom of the bottle. For a control, set up an identical bottle with an equal amount of cold water instead of the hot. Place an ice cube in each bottle as shown in the figure.

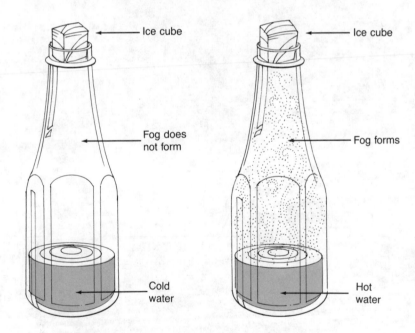

As your students observe the two bottles, ask:
What do you see happening in each bottle?
What do we call what you see in the bottle with hot water?
Why do you think clouds or fog formed in the bottle with hot water and not in the one with cold?
How do clouds and fog form in nature?

What Is the Greenhouse Effect?

Materials	Large-mouthed jar with cover, 2 identical thermometers, 2 large cards, 2 rubber bands
Opening Questions	*How does a greenhouse (where plants are grown) get so warm, even on a cold winter day?* *Why is it so very hot in an automobile in summer when all the windows are shut tight?* *What is meant by "solar heating"?*
Some Possible Activities	Get two thermometers that have identical readings and attach them to large cards with rubber bands. Place one thermometer in a large-mouthed jar and screw on cover. Set up a "heat trap" as shown below to illustrate the principle of the greenhouse, cold frame, or solar house.

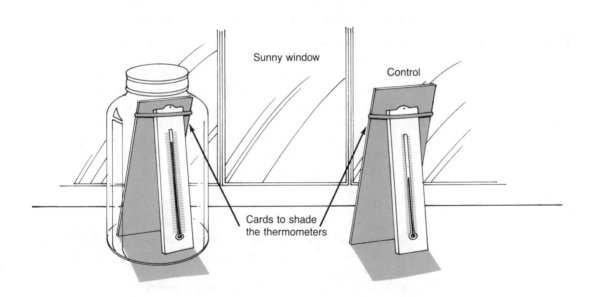

Take readings every half hour.
What differences do you observe on the two thermometers?
Why do you think the one in the closed glass jar is higher?
How is this knowledge used by architects and builders to make solar heated houses?

Guided Discovery Activities

How Can You Measure Temperature Changes?/What Is a Thermometer? (K–8)[1]

What Do I Want Children to Discover?

Thermal energy (heat) gives increased energy to molecules, causing them to exert more pressure or expand.

Warm temperatures make things expand more than cold temperatures.

An instrument that measures changes in thermal energy (heat) is called a **thermometer** (*thermo*—heat and *meter*—to measure).

What Will I Need?

Clear narrow plastic drinking straw   Modeling clay
Small vial or medicine bottle   Red food coloring
Scissors   3 × 5 inch index card
Cold water or rubbing alcohol   Tape

What Will We Discuss?

Where in this classroom would be the warmest places?
Where in this classroom would be the coolest places?
How could we find out the answers to these two questions?
What instrument(s) might we use in our investigation?

What Must I Know?

This activity can be done individually or in groups of two to four children. Thermometers measure the temperature of matter, or how hot or cold it is. Mercury or colored alcohol is usually the liquid used in thermometers. When heated, the liquid expands and moves up the tube. We say the temperature goes up. Conversely, when cooled, the liquid contracts and moves down the tube. We say the temperature goes down. Thermometers are used to measure temperatures in many scientific and everyday personal aspects of life, such as taking body temperatures, measuring air or water, used in cooking, etc.

What Will Children Do? *Measuring*

PROCESSES

1. Put 2.5 cm (1 inch) of cold water into the small vial or medicine bottle and add red food coloring. (*Note:* Rubbing alcohol responds more quickly to temperature changes and can be used instead of water.)
2. With scissors cut the end of the drinking straw at a slight angle. (*Note:* Your results will be best if you get the narrowest straw you can. Also changes in air pressure and evaporation may affect your thermometer so put a few drops of oil into the top of the drinking

---

[1]For excellent directions on constructing several different types of simple thermometers, see Marvin N. Tolman and James O. Morton. *Earth Science Activities for Grades 2–8. Science Curriculum Activities Library, Book III* (West Nyack. NY: Parker Publishing Company, 1986), 79–82.

straw or seal it with modeling clay, after setting up the thermometers.)
3. Put the straw into the vial and completely seal the top of the vial with modeling clay, making sure it is air tight.
4. Tape a 3 × 5 inch index card to the drinking straw and mark the level of the colored water in the straw like this:

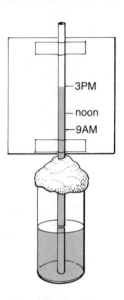

Hypothesizing   5. *What do you think will happen to the colored water in the drinking straws if you put your thermometer in a warmer spot?*

Observing   Put your thermometer in a warmer spot or in a pan of warm water and observe what happens. Mark your card on your drinking straw to the new height of the colored water.

Recording data   Draw a picture of what happened to the colored water in the drinking straw.

Inferring   *Why do you think the colored water moved up the drinking straw?*

Hypothesizing   6. *What do you think will happen now if you put your thermometers in a cooler spot?*

Put your thermometers in a cooler spot or in a pan of cold water.

Recording data   Draw a picture of what happened to the colored water in the drinking straw.

Inferring   *Why do you think the colored water moved down the drinking straw?*

What Must I Know?   Check each student's drawings to see if they observed that as temperatures go up, so does the colored water in straw, and down when temperatures go down. Discuss the concept of interrelations between expansion and contraction of molecules and temperature or amount of molecular motion.

How Will Children Use or Apply What They Discover?

Comparing

Extrapolating

Hypothesizing

Measuring/ Comparing

Measuring

Predicting

Describing

1. Have your students observe and record where the level of their colored water is each day for a week at the opening, lunch, and closing time of school and answer these questions:
   a. *Of your three thermometer readings each day, which one was the highest and which one the lowest?*
   b. *During a week, which was the warmest morning, lunch, and afternoon?*
   c. *Can you predict where tomorrow's levels of colored water will be for your three thermometer readings?*

2. Take thermometer readings and compare where the level of the colored water will be in the coolest and warmest spots in your classroom.

3. Using a commercial thermometer, measure air temperature. Now have children mark their cards on the drinking straws with the actual numerical reading. Have children take their daily readings on their thermometers for a week with you giving them the actual numerical reading each time.

4. After one week, ask your children to predict what the actual numerical temperature will be for your three daily readings.

5. Make a list of various jobs where people use thermometers. Describe how thermometers are used in each job.

How Can You Measure Air Pressure Changes?/What is a Barometer? (K–8)

What Do I Want Children to Discover?

Air exerts pressure.
Air pressure changes.
Air pressure may indicate the type of weather.
Low air pressure usually indicates rainy or cloudy weather.
High air pressure usually indicates fair weather.

What Will I Need?

Coffee can with plastic snap top
Large balloon
Straw
Glue
Straight pin
Card

What Will We Discuss?

Have each child blow up a balloon and ask:
What is in the balloon?
How do you know there is pressure exerted in the balloon?
How can you discover whether or not air has the same pressure at all times and at all places?

What is a barometer?
What is it used for?
How might location affect the readings of the barometer?

What Must I Know?

The room temperature will affect the barometer the children will make in this activity. It does not, therefore, only measure air pressure differences. It might be desirable to have some students keep their barometers outside class and compare their readings with those in class.

PROCESSES

What Will Children Do?

1. Obtain a coffee can with a plastic snap top, straw, glue, straight pin, and a card.
2. Cover the coffee can with the plastic snap top, making certain the can is sealed completely. *Caution:* Often the plastic snap top will *not* sufficiently seal the can. A piece of a large balloon and a tight rubber band is much better.
3. Place a small amount of glue in the center of the drum and attach a straw as shown in the diagram. Place another drop of glue on the end of the straw and attach the pin.
4. Mark a card with some lines that are the same distance apart. Tack it on the wall as shown in the diagram.

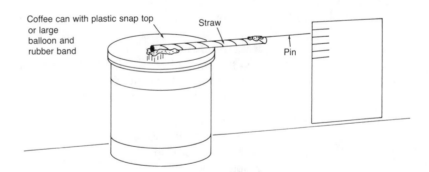

Coffee can with plastic snap top or large balloon and rubber band — Straw — Pin

Hypothesizing

What will happen to the plastic snap top or balloon if the air pressure on it increases?

Hypothesizing

What will happen to the plastic snap top or balloon if the air pressure decreases?

What Must I Know?

When air pressure increases, it pushes down on the plastic snap top or balloon, causing the straw to give a high reading. When the air pressure is low, the opposite will happen. A falling barometer may indicate that a storm is approaching.

5. Record the readings of the barometer three times a day for a week.

Comparing   *How do the readings of the barometer differ during the day?*

Comparing   *How do the readings differ from day to day?*

Inferring   *What causes the readings to vary?*

6. Record the type of weather existing at the time the barometer readings were made.

Inferring   *What kind of air pressure generally exists during fair weather?*

Inferring   *What kind of air pressure generally exists during stormy weather?*

7. Compare the readings of barometers in different locations.

Inferring   *What reasons can you give for the readings?*

Applying   *By using the readings of the barometer, predict what the weather will be.*

How Will Children Use or Apply What They Discover?

1. *Does air travel from an area of high pressure to an area of low pressure or from an area of low pressure to an area of high pressure? Why?*

2. *What would you do to improve the barometer?*

3. *What other materials could you use to make a barometer?*

How Can You Measure Humidity Changes?/What Is a Hygrometer? (4–8)

What Do I Want Children to Discover?

Air contains moisture.

Pressure and temperature affect the amount of moisture air can hold at any given time.

Relative humidity is the amount of water vapor actually contained in the atmosphere divided by the amount that could be contained in the same atmosphere.

Relative humidity can be measured.

What Will I Need?

2 thermometers
Wide cotton shoelace
Small bottle or dish
Empty milk carton
Thread

What Will We Discuss?

What instrument is used to measure the amount of water or humidity in the atmosphere?

How does it work?

PROCESSES

What Will Children Do?

1. Obtain an empty milk container, two thermometers, a cotton shoelace, and some thread.

2. Cut a four-inch section from the cotton shoelace and slip it over the bulb of one of the thermometers. Tie it with thread above and

below the bulb to hold it in place. Put the other end of shoelace in a small bottle or dish inside the milk carton.

3. Attach both thermometers to the milk carton as in the diagram.

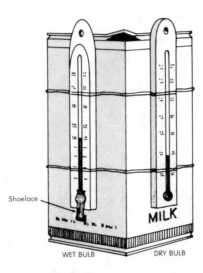

Shoelace

MILK

WET BULB   DRY BULB

You now have a **hygrometer**—an instrument for measuring the relative humidity in the atmosphere.

Caution: The two thermometers should register very clearly the same temperatures when placed side by side before the shoelace is placed over one of them, or the difference must be considered a constant that is part of all computations.

4. When the shoelace is wet, fan it with a piece of cardboard for one minute.

Hypothesizing

What do you think will happen to the thermometer with the shoelace? Why do you think so?

Observing
Hypothesizing

5. Check the temperature readings of the two thermometers.

*How do you account for the difference between the thermometer with the shoelace (called the "**wet-bulb**") and the one without the shoelace (called the "**dry-bulb**")?*

What Must I Know?

When the shoelace is wet, the evaporation of the water will result in a cooling of the "wet-bulb" thermometer while the "dry-bulb" thermometer will continue to read the temperature of the air around it.

6. Compute the relative humidity by recording the temperature of the "dry-bulb" thermometer and the difference between the readings of the two thermometers, and applying these to the relative humidity table on page 216.

Observing

7. Take readings on your hygrometer every day for two weeks and record your findings. Also try readings in different places.

FINDING RELATIVE HUMIDITY IN PERCENT
Difference in Degrees between Wet-Bulb and Dry-Bulb Thermometers

Air Temperature (Reading of Dry-Bulb Thermometer) in Degrees Fahrenheit

	1	2	3	4	5	6	7	8	9	10	11	12	13	14	15	16	17	18	19	20	21	22	23	24	25	26	27	28	29	30
30°	89	78	68	57	47	37	27	17	8																					
32°	90	79	69	60	50	41	31	22	13	4																				
34°	90	81	72	62	53	44	35	27	18	9	1																			
36°	91	82	73	65	56	48	39	31	23	14	6																			
38°	91	83	75	67	59	51	43	35	27	19	12	4																		
40°	92	84	76	68	61	53	46	38	31	23	16	9	2																	
42°	92	85	77	70	62	55	48	41	34	28	21	14	7																	
44°	93	85	78	71	64	57	51	44	37	31	24	18	12	5																
46°	93	86	79	72	65	59	53	46	40	34	28	22	16	10	4															
48°	93	87	80	73	67	60	54	48	42	36	31	25	19	14	8	3														
50°	93	87	81	74	68	62	56	50	44	39	33	28	22	17	12	7	2													
52°	94	88	81	75	69	63	58	52	46	41	36	30	25	20	15	10	6													
54°	94	88	82	76	70	65	59	54	48	43	38	33	28	23	18	14	9	5												
56°	94	88	82	77	71	66	61	55	50	45	40	35	31	26	21	17	12	8	4											
58°	94	89	83	77	72	67	62	57	52	47	42	38	33	28	24	20	15	11	7	3										
60°	94	89	84	78	73	68	63	58	53	49	44	40	35	31	27	22	18	14	10	6	2									
62°	94	89	84	79	74	69	64	60	55	50	46	41	37	33	29	25	21	17	13	9	6	2								
64°	95	90	85	79	75	70	66	61	56	52	48	43	39	35	31	27	23	20	16	12	9	5	2							
66°	95	90	85	80	76	71	66	62	58	53	49	45	41	37	33	29	26	22	18	15	11	8	5	1						
68°	95	90	85	81	76	72	67	63	59	55	51	47	43	39	35	31	28	24	21	17	14	11	8	4	1					
70°	95	90	86	81	77	72	68	64	60	56	52	48	44	40	37	33	30	26	23	20	17	13	10	7	4	1				
72°	95	91	86	82	78	73	69	65	61	57	53	49	46	42	39	35	32	28	25	22	19	16	13	10	7	4	1			
74°	95	91	86	82	78	74	70	66	62	58	54	51	47	44	40	37	34	30	27	24	21	18	15	12	9	7	4	1		
76°	96	91	87	83	78	74	70	67	63	59	55	52	48	45	42	38	35	32	29	26	23	20	17	14	12	9	6	4	1	
78°	96	91	87	83	79	75	71	67	64	60	57	53	50	46	43	40	37	34	31	28	25	22	19	16	14	11	9	6	4	1
80°	96	91	87	83	79	76	72	68	64	61	57	54	51	47	44	41	38	35	32	29	27	24	21	18	16	13	11	8	6	4
82°	96	91	87	83	79	76	72	69	65	62	58	55	52	49	46	43	40	37	34	31	28	25	2	20	18	15	13	10	8	6
84°	96	92	88	84	80	77	73	70	66	63	59	56	53	50	47	44	41	38	35	32	30	27	25	22	20	17	15	12	10	8
86°	96	92	88	84	80	77	73	70	66	63	60	57	54	51	48	45	42	39	37	34	31	29	26	24	21	19	17	14	12	10
88°	96	92	88	85	81	78	74	71	67	64	61	58	55	52	49	46	43	41	38	35	33	30	28	25	23	21	18	16	14	12
90°	96	92	88	85	81	78	74	71	68	64	61	58	56	53	50	47	44	42	39	37	34	32	29	27	24	22	20	18	16	14

Example:

Temperature of dry-bulb thermometer	76°	
Temperature of wet-bulb thermometer	68°	
The difference is	8°	

Find 76° in the dry-bulb column and 8° in the difference column. Where these two columns meet, you read the relative humidity. In this case, it is 67 percent.

Inferring
Applying

What reasons can you give for different readings?
Using your hygrometer, can you predict which days are better for drying clothes outside?

How Will Children Use or Apply What They Discover?

1. *Can you find other instruments that will indicate or measure relative humidity?*
2. *How is the relative humidity used by weather people to predict weather?*
3. *Why were you asked to fan the "wet-bulb" thermometer?*

How Can Solar Energy Be Used? (3–8)

What Do I Want Children to Discover?

Water in a solution absorbs the sun's energy and evaporates, leaving the salt behind.

Water vapor when cooled is **condensed** and changed into water.

What Will I Need?

Salt   Ring stand (See diagram)
2 dishes   Ring clamps

Water   Spoon
Plastic bag   Rubber band

What Will We Discuss?

What ways can you make the sun do work for you?

What Must I Know?

This activity should be done in groups of five.

PROCESSES

PART I

What Will Children Do?

1. Obtain two small dishes and some salt.
2. Pour a spoonful of salt into one dish, add water, and stir with a spoon until all the salt is dissolved.
3. Cover both dishes with a plastic bag, setting up the equipment as shown in the diagram. *Caution:* Fasten a rubber band around the collector dish and plastic bag, otherwise water will run down the plastic and collect *under* the collector dish.

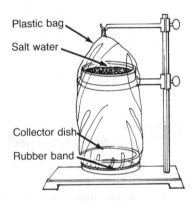

Plastic bag

Salt water

Collector dish

Rubber band

4. Place your equipment in the sunlight.

Hypothesizing   What do you think will happen to the salt water?

Hypothesizing   *Why do you think you were told to cover the salt water with a plastic bag?*

Observing   5. Record your observations every day.

What Must I Know?/ Where Do I Find It?

When there is only salt remaining in the top dish and the water is in the bottom dish, the following steps should be done by the group:

PART II

Taste the water in the bottom dish.

Comparing   How does the water taste?

Inferring   *Where did the water in the bottom dish come from?*

Inferring   *What happened to your salt solution?*

Inferring   *Where did the water go?*

Inferring   *Why did the water disappear?*

Applying   *How does the sun's energy (solar energy) benefit people?*

Applying   *How could this method be helpful to people who live near the ocean but do not have enough drinking water?*

How Will Children Use or Apply What They Discover?

1. *What are some other uses for this method of obtaining drinking water?*
2. *What are some other ways in which the sun's energy (solar energy) can be used to help people?*
3. Explain how this solar water heater works:

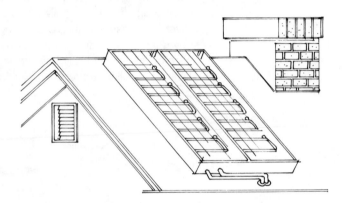

How Much Water Will Snow Make? (K–6)

What Do I Want Children to Discover?

When snow falls lightly on the earth, the crystals leave air spaces between them.

When snow melts, it becomes water.

When a substance changes from a solid state of matter to a liquid state, it absorbs heat.

Heat affects the rate of melting.

Water molecules occupy less volume as a liquid than as a solid.

What Will I Need?

Glass jar

Meter or centimeter stick

Crayon or pencil

Cup full of snow or crushed ice

Hot plate

Pan with water

Clock (with second hand)

What Will We Discuss?

Show the following illustration to start the discussion:

What can you tell about this picture?

Why is the man in the picture measuring the depth of the snow?

What will the snow change to?

When it melts and changes to water, how much water will this snow make?

Why does a soil conservationist want to know how much water snow will make?

What is he measuring that will help tell him how much water he is going to get from the snow?

What could you do to find out how much water the snow would make?

What Must I Know?

This activity should be done in groups of two. If snow is not available, substitute crushed ice, but tell the class that snow varies from ice in the amount of water it contains.

What Will Children Do?

Carrying out experiment

PROCESSES

1. Obtain a jar and fill it with snow or crushed ice.
2. Mark the level of the snow with a crayon.

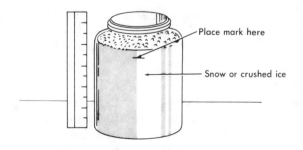

Place mark here

Snow or crushed ice

3. Let the snow or crushed ice melt.
4. Time the rate of melting in minutes and seconds, using the clock on the wall or your wristwatch.

Observing *As the snow melts, what do you see collecting in the bottom of the jar?*

Inferring *What causes the snow to melt and change to water?*
Hypothesizing *How might you make the snow melt faster?*

5. Fill another jar with snow or crushed ice.
6. Mark the level of snow or crushed ice.
7. Obtain a hot plate.
8. Place the jar in a pan of water and set on the hot plate.
9. Time the rate of melting in minutes and seconds as you did with the first jar.
10. When the snow in each jar finishes melting, record the time it took.
11. For each jar mark the level with a crayon.
12. Measure the water level in centimeters and record your findings.

Inferring *What can you conclude about snow when it melts?*
Observing and *Did heating the snow affect the amount of water produced?*
inferring *Why?*

How Will Children Use or Apply What They Discover?
1. *What happens to water when it freezes?*
2. *What do you think would happen if other substances such as dry ice were heated?*

References—Meteorology (Weather) Adam Ford. *Weather Watch* (New York: Lothrop, 1982). Janet Palazzo, *What Makes the Weather* (New York: Troll Associates, 1982).

GEOLOGY (EARTH'S CHANGING SURFACE)

Quickie Starters

How Can You Build Stalactites and Stalagmites?

Materials Paper towel, Epsom salts, water, spoon, 30 cm (1 inch) of thick string, large tin can, 2 small jars or paper cups, 2 heavy washers

Opening Questions *How are some rocks formed in caves?*
What is a stalactite and how is it formed?
What is a stalagmite and how is it formed?
Where else are stalactites and stalagmites formed?

Some Possible Activities Fill the large tin can about three quarters with water. Add spoonfuls of Epsom salts and stir vigorously until no more Epsom salts will dissolve. (*Note:* Epsom salts crystals will fall to the bottom of the can when no more will dissolve.) Fill the two small jars or paper cups with the Epsom salts solution and place them 5 cm (2 inches) apart on the paper towel. Tie a heavy washer on each end of the string. Place one washer in each of the small jars or paper cups with the Epsom salts solution. *Note:* Arrange the string in the cups so that you leave at least 5 cm (2 inches) between the string and the paper towel.

After several days, mineral deposits will form on the paper towel and string in this manner:

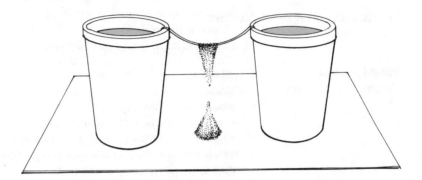

Note: Help children learn the differences between stalactites and stalagmites. Point out that the Epsom salts solution deposits that hang down (C for ceiling) are called **stalactites**, while those that point up (G for ground) are called **stalagmites**.

How Are Rocks Broken Up?

Materials

2 plastic vials or medicine bottles with snap lids, bean seeds, water

Opening Questions

How can seeds break up rocks and soil?

How can we set up an experiment to test if seeds can break up rocks and soil?

Some Possible Activities

Fill both vials or medicine bottles with as many of the same beans as will fit in. Add as much water to only one vial of beans as you can get in. Snap lids on tightly to both vials like this:

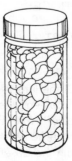

Ask children what they think will happen to the two vials. Observe both vials the next day. In the one with the water, the beans will have expanded and lifted the lid off. In the vial without water (called the control), there will be no observable change. Help children to infer that swelling and growing plants change the land by breaking up rocks and soil just as the swelling beans lifted the vial's lid off.

Guided Discovery Activities

How Are Crystals Formed? (K–6)

What Do I Want Children to Discover?

Crystals are nonliving substances that grow into bodies of various shapes.

Crystals grow by adding on more layers of the same substance, keeping the same shape at all times.

Crystal size is determined by differences in the rate of crystallization.

If crystals are disturbed in the growing process, they will break apart into hundreds of microscopic pieces.

True solids are crystalline in form.

Crystalline form is important in determining some of the properties of substances

What Will I Need?

Tablespoon	Sugar
2 jars	2 pieces of clear silk thread
2 jar lids	Copper sulfate
Salt	2 pencils
Water	Plastic wrap
2 small glasses	Magnifying glass or hand lens

What Will We Discuss?

What are crystals?
How could you grow a crystal?
What happens when a crystal is growing?
Why is a study of crystals important?

What Must I Know?

This activity will involve one or two students.

PROCESSES

PART I

What Will Children Do?

1. Obtain a tablespoon of salt, jar lid, and a small glass. Mix a tablespoon of salt in the glass of water. Stir the water well. Let the solution stand for a few minutes until it becomes clear.

Observing

What happens to the salt?

2. Very gently pour some of the salt solution into the jar lid and let it stand for several days where the lid will not be disturbed.

Hypothesizing

What do you think will happen to the salt solution?

3. After several days have passed, look at the materials in the lid using your magnifying glass.

Communicating   4. Describe what you see.

Comparing   5. *How are the materials in the lid different from your original salt solution?*

Inferring   *Why do you now have a solid when you started out with a liquid?*

Hypothesizing   *What name could you give to the formations in the lid?*

What Must I Know?

The salt dissolved in the water and when the salt water stood for several days, the water evaporated leaving salt crystals. Crystals are nonliving substances that are found in various geometrical shapes.

Salt crystals

PART II

1. Obtain a tablespoon of sugar, a jar lid, and a small glass of water. Be sure the tablespoon is clean. Mix a tablespoon of sugar in the glass of water. Stir the water well. Let the solution stand for a few minutes until it becomes clear.

Observing   *What happens to the sugar?*

Comparing   *How is the sugar solution similar in appearance to the salt solution?*

2. Obtain a lid and very gently pour some of the sugar solution into the lid and let it stand for several days.

Hypothesizing   *What do you think will happen to the sugar solution?*

3. After several days have passed, look at the materials in your lid using your magnifying glass.

Sugar crystals

Communicating

Comparing

Inferring

4. Describe what you see.

   How are the materials in this lid different from the materials in the lid containing the salt crystals? How are they alike?

   What happens to the sugar solution?

What Must I Know?

When the sugar water stood for several days, the water evaporated, leaving sugar crystals.

PART III

Caution: Copper sulfate is poisonous, therefore, Part III should be done by the teacher as a demonstration for students to observe.

1. Wash your hands carefully. Obtain two pieces of clear silk thread, two jars, copper sulfate, two pencils, plastic wrap; and water.
2. Fill the two jars three-fourths full of hot water and add copper sulfate until the water is saturated with it. Make sure you stir the water constantly while adding copper sulfate.
3. Obtain two seed crystals of copper sulfate and tie each one to one end of separate pieces of silk thread. (Seed crystals, which should be ⅛ inch to ¼ inch in length, can be prepared in the same way as sugar crystals.) Tie the free end of each piece of thread to separate pencils. Rest each pencil on a separate jar, allowing the crystals to fall into the copper sulfate solution. Place the jar where it will not be disturbed.

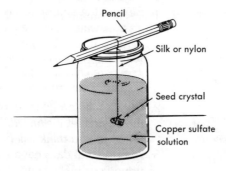

Pencil

Silk or nylon

Seed crystal

Copper sulfate solution

Hypothesizing

Hypothesizing

Why was it necessary for me to wash my hands?

What do you think the copper sulfate solution will do to the crystals?

4. Watch the crystals carefully for several days.

Observing

Record what happens to the crystals.

What Must I Know?

The copper sulfate solution causes the seed crystals to grow. **Crystals** grow by adding on more layers of the same substance, keeping the same shape at all times.

Hypothesizing

How could larger crystals be grown?

What Must I Know?
Hypothesizing

The slower crystals grow, the larger they become.
How could the growing process of the crystals be slowed down?

What Must I Know?

Reducing the rate of evaporation causes the crystals to grow at a slower rate.

Hypothesizing

How could the rate of evaporation of the copper sulfate solution be slowed down?

5. Remove one of the pencils. Obtain some plastic wrap, and cover the top of the jar from which you removed the pencil. Be sure to pierce a hole in the plastic wrap large enough for the suspended crystals to pass through when the pencil is returned to the top of the jar.

Comparing
Observing
Inferring

6. Compare both jars closely over several days.
How do the crystals formed in the two jars differ?
Explain why the crystals are different.

What Must I Know?

The crystal in the closed jar will be larger since the plastic wrap slowed down the rate of evaporation, causing the crystal to grow at a slower rate. The open jar will have a smaller crystal since the faster rate of evaporation causes the crystal to grow at a faster rate.

Hypothesizing

After the third day, what do you think would happen if the crystals were disturbed during their periods of crystallization?

Observing

7. Gently shake the jar without the plastic wrap and explain what happens.

What Must I Know?

If crystals are disturbed in the growing process, they will break apart into hundreds of microscopic pieces.

Inferring
Summarizing
Classifying

Where are crystals found in nature?
How are crystals grown?
Explain how crystalline form is important in determining the properties of substances.

Hypothesizing

Why do some rocks have large crystals and some have small crystals?

What Must I Know?

True solids are crystalline in form. Crystals grow by adding on more layers of the same substance, keeping the same crystalline form at all times. Crystalline form is important in determining some of the properties of substances. Differences in the rate of crystallization determine differences in crystal size.

How Will Children Use or Apply What They Discover?

1. *What other experiments could you devise that would involve growing crystals?*
2. *How are crystals used in industry?*
3. *If there were no crystals on earth, how would people's way of living be affected?*
4. *How would you grow large crystals?*

How Are Rocks Alike and Different? (K–6)

What Do I Want Children to Discover?

Some rocks are heavy and some are light.
Different rocks have different colors.
Some rocks are smooth and some are rough.
Some rocks are hard and some are soft.

What Will I Need?

Knife	Hammer	Conglomerates
Penny	Cloth	Igneous rocks
Glass	Magnifying glass	Metamorphic rocks
Newspaper	Sedimentary rocks	

What Will We Discuss?

Where could you find different kinds of rocks?
When you feel rocks, how do they differ?

What Must I Know?

This activity should be done in groups of two or more children.

PROCESSES

What Will Children Do?

1. Obtain the following materials: knife, penny, glass, newspaper, hammer, cloth, magnifying glass, and several types of rocks the teacher has available for you.
2. Place these materials on your newspaper.

Observing
Comparing
Comparing
Comparing

3. Observe the rocks closely.
   In what ways are the rocks alike?
   In what ways are the rocks different?
   When you feel the rocks, how do they differ?
   Compare two rocks of the same size.

Comparing
Inferring
Inferring

   How does their weight compare?
   Why do you think some rocks are rough and jagged?
   What do you think has happened to the rocks that are smooth and rounded?

Classifying

4. Place your rocks in groups.
   In what other ways could you group the rocks?

Designing an investigation

   How do you think you could tell the hardness or softness of a rock?
   (Scratch with knife, penny, fingernail, and so on.)

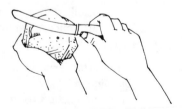

5. Try some of your ideas on the rocks.

Hypothesizing

   If two rocks were the same size, how could you find out which rock was heavier?

Designing an investigation

How could you tell whether a rock looked the same on the inside as it did on the outside? (Place in newspaper and hit with hammer.)

Designing an investigation

How would you find out how rocks become smooth and rounded? (Place rocks in plastic jar of water and shake vigorously.)

Inferring

Why are some of the rocks made of many smaller rocks or pieces?

Observing

Are the pieces of the rock rounded or jagged?

Observing

Are the pieces dull or shiny in the rock?

Hypothesizing

Why do you think they are like that?

How Will Children Use or Apply What They Discover?

1. *In what ways are soft rocks used?*
2. *In what ways are hard rocks used?*
3. *How is concrete made?*

How Do Limestone, Marble, and Granite Differ? (3–8)

What Do I Want Children to Discover?

A **sedimentary rock** can be changed by compression and compaction.

This change may cause lower rocks in a sedimentary bed to become harder.

Limestone and marble are chemically the same.

What Will I Need?

Pieces of granite
Pieces of limestone
Pieces of marble
Vinegar
Knife

What Will We Discuss?

How are limestone and marble alike?
How are limestone and marble different?
Why do you think these rocks could be different colors?

What Will Children Do?

PROCESSES

1. Obtain 3 or 4 pieces each of limestone, marble, and granite, 20 cc. of vinegar, and a knife.
2. Look at the rocks closely.
   How can you tell which is limestone and which is marble?

Designing an investigation

Limestone

Marble

Comparing	*How does the granite compare with the others?*
Hypothesizing	*In what way could you tell that the rocks are related?*
Hypothesizing	*Which of these would scratch the other rocks?*
	3. Scratch the different pieces across each other.
Classifying	*Which are harder?*
Hypothesizing	*What do you think will happen if you place a few drops of vinegar on your rocks?*
Observing	4. Place a few drops on the pieces and record what happens.

What Must I Know?

Explain to the class that **geologists** determine the similarity of substances by scratching them and by using chemical tests such as dropping acid on the rocks to see if they react chemically. They also have many other tests. Explain that limestone through heat and pressure in the earth is compacted into a harder substance called marble. Although its physical properties have changed, its chemical composition has remained the same. Marble may vary in color because of the various types of minerals that may be mixed with it.

Caution: Have children wash hands thoroughly after handling vinegar.

How Will Children Use or Apply What They Discover?

1. *How do people use limestone, marble, and granite?*
2. *Which substances are the most common?*
3. *If you saw a substance you thought was salt, how would you prove it was salt?*
4. *What other ways do you think geologists identify substances? How could you find out?*

How Does Erosion Affect the Soil? (3–6)

What Do I Want Children to Discover?

Soil consists of several layers.
Soil is made from rock.
There are many kinds of soil.
Erosion is the wasting away of soil.
Soil has **organic material** (material that is living or had been living) that enriches it.

What Will I Need?

Hammer
Newspapers
Rock, about the size of a tennis ball, which can be easily chipped
Quart jar, three-fourths filled with soil; lid
2 cans (preferably the size of soup cans): 1 three-fourths filled with soil; and 1 three-fourths filled with soil, dead grass, leaves, and peat moss
2 milk cartons, quart-size
Soil, approximately 8 cups
2 aluminum pie pans

Grass seed, 1 teaspoon
Scissors
Damp cloth large enough to cover a quart milk carton
Tap water, ½ gallon
2 blocks of wood, each 1½ × 3 inches
Measuring cup

What Will We Discuss?

You have all played with dirt (soil) or at least handled it in some way, such as washing it off your feet or hands.
Where does soil come from?
How could you make soil here in the classroom?

What Must I Know?

This activity may be done in groups of two or more pupils.

What Will Children Do?

PROCESSES

PART I

1. Obtain a rock about the size of a tennis ball, two sheets of newspaper, and a hammer.

What Must I Know?

For safety reasons, have the children wrap a rock in newspaper before hitting it so the chips do not fly.

2. Place the covered rock on a hard surface. Hold it in place with one hand and with the other hit it gently five or six times with the hammer. Unwrap the newspaper.

Observing
Observing
What do you observe?
Does the rock appear the same?

Observing
Inferring

Comparing

What do you see that looks like soil?
Soil varies from one place to another. Can you suggest from this activity any reasons why?
How does the soil on the desert or beach differ from the soil in the mountain?

What Must I Know?

Soil varies because it is made from different types of rocks, and its particle sizes may also vary. Some soils are made of coarse grains and others are composed of fine grains.

PART II

1. Obtain a quart jar three-fourths filled with soil and decayed plant material, one-half gallon of water, and a lid for the jar.

Hypothesizing

If you add water to this jar and cover it and shake it, how do you think the soil will settle?

2. Add water (about three cupfuls) to the jar until it is about two inches from the top. Shake the jar for about a minute. Then place the jar on the table and allow the soil to settle. Do not disturb the jar.

Observing — *What do you notice about the way the soil is settling?*

Inferring — *Why do certain particles of the soil settle to the bottom first?*

Observing — *In which layer is the organic material (material that is living or had been living) mainly found?*

Inferring — What can you say about layers of soil?

PART III

1. Obtain two soup cans filled with different kinds of soil (like humus and sandy), about one-half gallon of water, and a measuring cup.

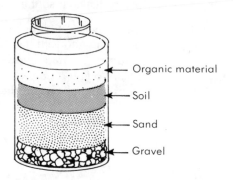

— Organic material

— Soil

— Sand

— Gravel

2. Pour about one cup of water into each can.

Hypothesizing — *What do you think will happen to the water in the soil of both cans?*

Comparing and observing — *Which can seems to be able to hold moisture best?*

Comparing and observing — *What difference do you notice in the soil in the two cans?*

Comparing and observing — *Which has more organic material?*

Interpreting — *Why is organic material good for the soil?*

PART IV

Carrying out experiment

1. Obtain two quart-size milk cartons, eight cups of soil, one-half gal-lon of water, a measuring cup, a package of grass seed, two alu-

minum pie pans, two blocks of wood, a damp cloth, and a pair of scissors.

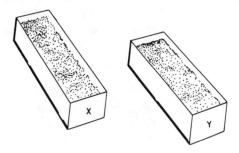

2. Using the scissors, cut out one of the long sides of both milk cartons. (See preceding diagram.)
3. Fill the milk cartons with soil, leaving about one-half inch from the top, and label the cartons X and Y.
4. In carton X, plant the grass seed just under the surface of the soil.
5. Water carton X and place the damp cloth over it to keep the moisture in. Continue to water the seeds until they have sprouted and are one inch high.
6. When carton X is ready, place one block of wood under one end of each carton. Carefully make five holes in each of the bottoms of the lower ends of cartons X and Y, and place these ends into the aluminum pie pans. (See diagram.)

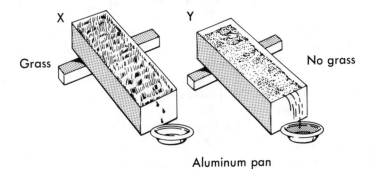

Aluminum pan

7. Place these cartons in an area out of direct sunlight and wind.
8. Measure one cup of water and gently sprinkle this water over carton X. Do the same to carton Y.
   Repeat this each day for three days and write what you see.

Measuring and observing
Collecting and organizing data
Inferring

Why are the cartons set up in such a position?

Hypothesizing   *Which carton do you think will lose the most soil?*
    After three days:
Observing   *Which carton has lost the most soil?*
Interpreting   *Why does one carton lose less soil than the other?*
Interpreting   *How can you prevent erosion (washing or wearing away) in soils?*
Applying   *What, other than grass, can be planted to prevent erosion?*
    9. Draw a diagram to show what you would do to control erosion.

How Will Children Use or Apply What They Discover?

1. Make a "mountain" of pebbles, soil, and sand.
   What do you think will happen if you pour water down on it?
   Pour water over the mountain and observe what happens.
   What erodes first?
   What conclusions can you draw from this activity?
2. Take a walk around the schoolyard.
   What signs of erosion are there?
   What could be done to prevent this erosion?
3. *How do you know there are many kinds of soil?*
4. *What are some of the ways by which erosion can be controlled?*
5. *Where is organic material mainly found in the soil?*
6. *In the experiment you did with the milk cartons, why did you not plant seeds in both cartons?*
7. *Why is erosion control important to farmers?*
8. *What are terraced rice fields? Why are they necessary and important?*

What Is a Fault? (4–8)

What Do I Want Children to Discover?

Some land has been formed by **sedimentation,** causing layering.
When too much force is applied to the earth's layers, they crack.
The point where the earth's crust cracks and moves is called a **fault.**
A **normal fault** is where the earth's crust drops.
A **thrust fault** is where the earth's crust rises over an adjacent part of the earth.
Earthquakes may be caused by the earth's crust sliding along a fault.

What Will I Need?

Quart jar
Quart of water
Sand
Several types of soil—light, dark, and so on
2 plastic cups
Balance
2 cigar box molds filled with layers of colored plaster of paris
Knife to cut the plaster mold
2 × 4-inch piece of wood cut along a sloping line

What Will We Discuss?

If great force is applied to a rock or parts of the earth's structure, what will happen to the rock or the structure?
What is an earthquake?
What causes an earthquake?

What Must I Know?

This activity should be done in groups of two or more students. The molds should be made by mixing two or three pints of plaster of paris with different food coloring. The wet plaster of paris should be layered in the cigar boxes and allowed to dry partially before cutting as indicated below. Do not let the plaster of paris become too dry or it will be too hard to cut.

PROCESSES

PART I

What Will Children Do?

1. Obtain a quart jar, some sand, and several types of soil. Half fill the quart jar with water. Add sand to the jar until it is 1 inch thick in the bottom of the jar.

Observing
Hypothesizing

What happens to the sand?
What will happen if you pour soil onto part of the sand?

2. Add several other types of soil to the jar and observe.

Comparing
Inferring

How do the materials in the jar resemble parts of our earth?
Explain how you think parts of our earth have become layered.

3. Obtain a balance, a plastic cup half filled with water and another cup half filled with sand. Place the cup of sand on one side of the balance and the cup of water on the other side.

Hypothesizing

What ways can you balance the sand and water?

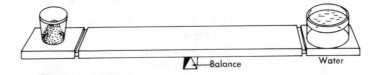

Balance   Water

4. Use one of your methods to balance the sand and water.

Hypothesizing

Now that these are balanced, what will happen if you take some sand from one side of the balance and place it on the other side by the cup of water?

5. Do this and observe.

Inferring

How is what you did with the balance similar to some of the things that happen in the earth's crust?

What Must I Know?

The land surface of the continents is always being worn away. The particles formed from this wear often flow into streams and are carried to the sea. When the material gets to the ocean floor, it causes that part of the floor to become heavier and may cause the crust of the earth and the layers to bend. If they bend far enough, faults may appear. This is an explanation for one type of fault, although it is a rare type.

6. Rebalance sand and water and let stand undisturbed for several days.

Inferring

Why does the sand side go down?

PART II

1. Obtain a cigar box mold from your teacher and remove the plaster block. Using the knife, cut the block in two. Raise one of these blocks above the other as indicated in the diagram.

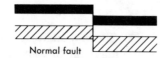

Normal fault

A place where the earth's crust and layers have broken similar to your cut is called a **fault.**

Comparing

How is the appearance of the block similar to the appearance of the earth in some places you have seen?

Summarizing

Explain how you think a rock structure could reach the condition similar to the one you have arranged in your model.

What Must I Know?

The rock structure could have formed a fault owing to stresses within the earth that drew the sections of rock apart. This stress could have caused one section to fall. This kind of fault is called a **normal fault.**

2. Obtain a 2 × 4-inch piece of wood that has been cut in two along a sloping line.

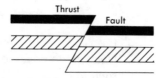

Thrust
Fault

Comparing

How is this fault different from the normal fault?
What would you call this type of fault?

What Must I Know?

Explain that this type of fault is called a **thrust fault.** The fault occurs when compression pushes sections of rock closer together, forcing one section of rock to move or slide up.

Inferring
Summarizing

How could this structure have been formed in nature?
How would you define a thrust fault?

What Must I Know?

Other faults, such as the one that caused the San Francisco earthquake of 1906, may be caused mainly by horizontal movement of the earth. The San Andreas fault in California is of this type.

Hypothesizing

What connection is there between an earthquake and a fault?

What Must I Know?/
Where Do I Find It?

Explain that earthquakes may be caused by the earth's crust sliding along a fault or by the forming of a fault.

How Will Children Use or Apply What They Discover?

1. *What effects do faults have on our earth?*
2. *Could faults be prevented? How?*

How Does a Geyser Work? (2–8)

What Do I Want Children to Discover?

Geysers are hot springs that throw up hot water and gases with explosive force from time to time.

Geysers are formed when ground water, heated by hot rocks or gases, gets so hot that it expands and releases dissolved gases in the water, which exert pressure.

The expansion of water forces the water to the surface through partially obstructed cracks in the earth.

Geysers are found in volcanic regions or areas where there used to be volcanoes.

What Will I Need?

Saucepan
Water
Pyrex funnel
3 bottle caps
Hot plate

What Will We Discuss?

What is a geyser?
How does a geyser work?
Where are geysers found?

What Must I Know?

This activity should involve one or two students. For younger students, it should be a teacher demonstration.

What Will Children Do?

PROCESSES

1. Obtain a saucepan, water, a funnel, three bottle caps, and a hot plate. Fill the saucepan half full with water. Place the funnel in the saucepan, resting it on the three bottle caps. Set the saucepan on the hot plate and heat the water. *Caution:* Stand several feet away as the water heats. Boiling water can burn your skin.

Hypothesizing
Observing

What will happen to the water?
2. As you observe the water, record what you see.

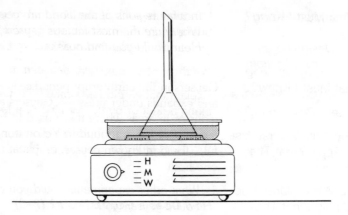

Observing	*What happens to the water when it is heated?*
Inferring	*Why do you think this happens?*
Hypothesizing	*How does the funnel affect this experiment?*

What Must I Know? Water expands when heated. When the water at the bottom of the pan boils, it is forced by pressure out through the top of the funnel.

3. Remove the saucepan from the hot plate.

Hypothesizing   *What will happen to your experiment if the source of heat is removed?*

What Must I Know? When the water is allowed to cool, pressure will be reduced, thus causing the water to remain in the saucepan.

Hypothesizing   *How does water inside the earth become heated?*

What Must I Know? Ground water beneath the earth's surface is heated by hot rocks or gases.

Hypothesizing	*What happens to the water inside the earth when it becomes heated?*
Applying	*Why does hot water inside the earth escape?*
Hypothesizing	*How does the water inside the earth escape?*
	What is this type of geological feature called?

What Must I Know? A geyser is an underground spring that releases hot water with explosive force from time to time. When ground water heats, it expands and releases dissolved gases in the water, which exert pressure. This forces the water to the surface through cracks in the earth, thereby forming a geyser.

Summarizing	*Explain how your experiment demonstrates what happens in nature when a geyser occurs.*
Hypothesizing	*How could you cause your geyser to erupt again?*
Applying	*How do geysers in our earth erupt again and again?*

Hypothesizing	*In what regions of the world are geysers found?*
	Where are the most famous geysers located?
Designing an investigation	*How would you find out?*

What Must I Know?

Geysers in the earth erupt periodically as the ground water is heated and expands under pressure. Geysers are found only in volcanic regions or in areas where there used to be volcanoes. The most spectacular geysers are found in Yellowstone National Park. "Old Faithful," the best known geyser, erupts at fairly regular intervals of about one hour.

How Will Children Use or Apply What They Discover?

1. *What other experiments could you devise that would demonstrate how a geyser works?*
2. *What would you do to make your geyser shoot higher? Why might it not be a good idea to do this?*
3. *Why are geysers not found everywhere?*
4. *In what ways are geysers helpful to people?*
5. *In what ways are geysers a problem?*

What are Fossils and Fossil Beds? (3–8)

What Do I Want Children to Discover?

A **fossil** is remains or evidence of previous life preserved in the earth's surface.

A fossil may have been buried in mud; covered by sand, volcanic ash, or other material; or frozen in ice or soil.

Some types of fossils are actual remains found in ice, amber, asphalt pits, oil shale, coal, and other carbonaceous remains.

Other fossils are petrified wood and casts, including tracks, molds, and coprolites (hardened feces).

Fossil beds occur in areas containing sedimentary deposits. These are areas where soil has washed or blown over the organism.

What Will I Need?

2 ice trays	Model of an animal or a cutout of an animal
Fruit such as cherries and grapes	
Water	Several sheets of paper
Soil	Actual fossils if available
Small cardboard box	Pictures of fossils if available

What Must I Know?

This activity should be done in groups of five.

What Will Children Do?

PROCESSES

PART I

Carrying out experiment

1. Obtain two ice trays, fruit, water, and soil.
2. Place some fruit in an ice tray and put the tray in the freezing compartment of a refrigerator.

3. Place soil and water in another ice tray and add some fruit to it. Put the tray in the freezing compartment of a refrigerator.
4. Place some of the same kind of fruit in the refrigerator on a shelf and in the classroom on a shelf.

Hypothesizing   *What do you think will happen to the fruit in the water in the ice tray?*

Hypothesizing   *What do you think will happen to the fruit in the soil and water in the ice tray?*

Hypothesizing   *What do you think will happen to the fruit on the shelf in the refrigerator?*

Hypothesizing   *What do you think will happen to the fruit on the shelf in the classroom?*

Hypothesizing   *How long do you think the fruit will last (be preserved) in each place?*

Observing   5. Take your ice trays out each day and record what you see in them.

Cherries in ice

Cherries at room temperature

Cherries in refrigerator

Communicating   6. Record information about the fruit in the refrigerator and on the shelf.

Observing   *What has happened to the fruit in each instance?*
Observing   *How long did the fruit last in each instance?*
Hypothesizing   *If an animal were to die in the Artic and were covered by snow and ice, what do you think would happen to that animal?*

Some years ago, part of a mammoth (an animal that looks like an elephant) was found buried in the ice in Siberia.

Inferring   *What does this tell you about the area?*
What do we call the remains of an animal or plant from an earlier geological period?

What Must I Know?   Explain terms when necessary. Point out to the children that this is one way that fossils are formed.

PART II
1. Obtain soil and a small cardboard box.
2. Add water to the soil, making mud that is fairly thick.
   Place it in the bottom of the small cardboard box. Smooth it out; press your hand in the mud so you get a good impression. Cover the mud with a layer of sand several inches deep.

Hypothesizing   *What do you think will happen to the impression of your hand?*

3. After two or three days, carefully remove the sand.

Observing   *What has happened to the impression of your hand?*

Inferring   *What would you call this impression?*

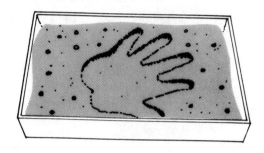

Inferring   *What kinds of impressions similar to this help geologists find out about life in previous geological times?*

Inferring   *In what types of materials do you find imprints such as these?*

Inferring   *Where could you find imprints such as these?*

What Must I Know?   Point out that this is another way in which fossils are formed. If possible, have some fossils and pictures of different kinds of fossils in the classroom. The children can examine and discuss them and discover more information.

PART III

1. Obtain a model of an animal or a cutout of an animal and cover it with several sheets of paper.

   What have you made?

   What would each layer of paper be in nature?

Applying   *What do you think would happen to the animal?*

   What do you think a fossil bed is?

Inferring   *Why do you think a fossil bed usually must have several layers of soil in it?*

How Will Children Use or Apply What They Discover

1. *Where would you expect to find fossils?*
2. *Why are more fossils not found?*
3. *Explain why you could or could not expect to find fossils in the area in which you live.*
4. *What evidence is there that fossils are being formed today?*
5. *What information can you discover from fossils?*

How Can You Make a Fossil? (K–6)

What Do I Want Children to Discover?   A **fossil** is any remain, impression, or trace of an animal or plant of a former geological age.

Fossils can be found in sedimentary rock.

Sedimentary rock is formed from mud and silt.
Organisms whose fossils are uncovered lived and died in a period
    when the layers in which their remains are found were laid down.
Older layers of rocks have fossils that are unlike the animals and
    plants now living.

What Will I Need?

Pictures of fossils and extinct animals
Fossils
Plaster of paris
Assorted leaves
Shells
Petroleum jelly
Cardboard
Water

What Will We Discuss?

What is a fossil?
Where could you find a fossil?

What Must I Know?

If possible, hold up some examples of fossils or show pictures of fossils. Show pictures of extinct animals. Ask the children how we know that these animals existed if they are no longer present on earth.

What Will Children Do?

Designing an investigation

PROCESSES

1. Obtain some plaster of paris, petroleum jelly, a leaf or shell, and a piece of cardboard.
   What could you do with these materials to make an imprint of a leaf or shell?
2. Mix a small amount of water with about 3 tablespoons of plaster of paris until the plaster is smooth and fairly thick.
3. Coat the leaf with petroleum jelly and place the leaf on about ¼ inch of plaster. Press the leaf gently into the plaster. Let the plaster and leaf dry on the window sill.
4. Remove the leaf.

Comparing

    What have you made?

What Must I Know?

Point out that the plaster would be like small particles of dirt (sediment) dropped by a river and that it takes millions of years to make hard rock out of sediment.

Inferring	*How do fossils help scientists to tell the kinds of life on earth before written history?*
Summarizing	*What evidence is there that life has changed in a million years?*
Inferring	*Why?*

How Will Children Use or Apply What They Discover?

1. *What other things could you use to make imprints?*
2. *Where do people get the oil they use in their cars?*

References—Geology (Earth's Changing Surface) Robert J. Foster, *General Geology,* third edition (Columbus, OH: Merrill Publishing Co., 1978). Illa Podendorf, *Rocks and Minerals* (New York: Children's Press. 1982).

ASTRONOMY (EARTH IN SPACE)

Quickie Starters

How Can You Change Your Shadow's Size?

Materials

Flashlight, 2 pieces of white paper, scissors, paste, funnel, pencil or crayon

Opening Questions

How can you make shadows larger or smaller?

What are some of the things (variables) that affect the size of shadows?

Why do shadows change shape and size during a day?

Some Possible Activities

Have children work with a partner. Put a funnel on a large sheet of white paper. One student shines the flashlight on the funnel and the other one traces and cuts the shadow out with scissors, in this sequence:

1. First hold the flashlight *high,* trace and cut out the shadow of the funnel.
2. Next, put a new piece of white paper under the funnel, hold the flashlight *low,* trace, and cut out the shadow of the funnel.

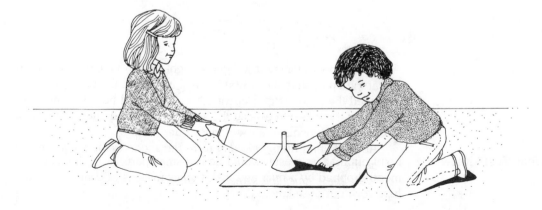

3. Compare the size and shape of the two cut-out shadows of the funnel.

   Why do you think the shadow made when the flashlight was held low was longer?

   During what part(s) of the day are shadows this way outdoors?

How Can Shadows Help You Tell Time?

Materials

For each child or group of two to four students:
Long nail, hammer, 8½ × 11 inch pieces of white paper, square board big enough to hold the paper, pencil

Opening Questions

Do you think that shadows outdoors change during the day? How might we find out?

If shadows change, at what time will they be the shortest? The longest?

Why do you think so?

Some Possible Activities

Put the paper in the middle of the board and drive the nail into the board and paper like this, making sure the nail will not easily come out of board.

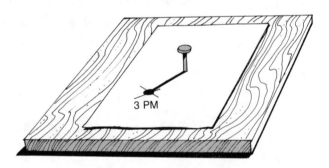

Place the board where it will get sunlight all day. Every hour put an X at the tip of shadow cast by the nail as well as the time you marked the shadow tip. Repeat this every school hour for one week, keeping the board in exactly the same spot. At the end of the week, assist your students to answer these questions:

At what times during the day were the shadows the longest as well as the shortest?

Were these times the same each day?

What Is the Shape of the Earth? (K–3)

What Do I Want Children to Discover?

The earth is round like a globe.
The earth is very large.

What Will I Need?

Globe of the earth
Several rubber balls of various sizes
Pictures taken of the earth's surface from outer space

What Will We Discuss?

What shape do you think the earth is?
How do you think you could find out?

What Must I Know?

This activity is to be done as a demonstration.

What Will Children Do?

PROCESSES

Observing
Comparing

1. Obtain a world globe and several rubber balls of different sizes.
   What do you notice about each of the balls?
   If the earth is round, what is there about the earth that is like the balls?

What Must I Know?

Each ball has a different curve according to the size of the ball. A large ball would have a very slight curve.

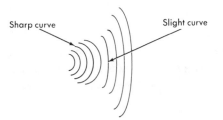

Sharp curve   Slight curve

Observing

Inferring
Hypothesizing
Hypothesizing

2. Look out the window and observe the place where the sky and the earth meet.
   What do you think the horizon is?
   What could you do to see more of the earth's surface?
   If you were to see a ship sail into the distance, what part of it would you see last? Why?

What Must I Know?

They would see the top of the mast last since the earth is curved and the ship would be moving over the earth's curvature.

Classifying

Hypothesizing

Would you see more or less of the earth's surface if you were flying in a plane?
Why can a person in a space capsule take a picture of so much more of the earth than someone on a mountain?

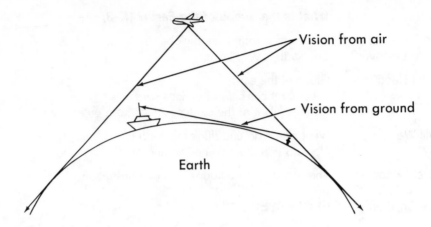

Vision from air

Vision from ground

Earth

Observing

3. Look at some pictures of the earth's surface taken from rockets.
   What shape is the earth's horizon?
4. Go to the second story of a building.
   Observe the different things you did not see on the ground floor.
   What do you see that might prove the earth is round?

Inferring

How Will Children Use or Apply What They Discover?

1. *If you were observing an eclipse of the moon, what could you find out about the shape of the earth?*

Why Is There Day and Night? (K–6)

What Do I Want Children to Discover?

The earth **rotates** or turns around.
It rotates from west to east.
It takes 24 hours for the earth to make one complete turn or rotation.
The rotation of the earth explains why part of the 24-hour period is night and part is day.
The sun is always shining.

What Will I Need?

Strong flashlight or filmstrip projector
Knitting needle
Clay or styrofoam ball

What Will We Discuss?

It is daytime here; where would it be night?
When it is night here, where would it be day?
What could you do to find out about daytime and nighttime on the earth?

PROCESSES

What Will Children Do?

1. Obtain a strong flashlight or filmstrip projector, a knitting needle, and some clay. Make a clay ball as large as a baseball; use it as a model of the earth. A styrofoam ball may be used.
   In what way do you think the ball is like the earth?

2. Push the knitting needle through the clay or styrofoam globe. Darken the room. Let the flashlight or filmstrip projector shine on the ball.

The flashlight represents the sun.

Inferring   *What side of the globe do you think is having night?*

Inferring   *What side of the globe do you think is having day?*

Inferring   *What tells you that the sun is always shining somewhere on the earth?*

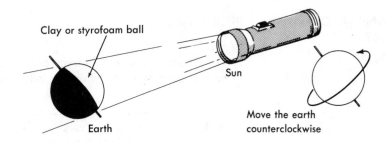

Clay or styrofoam ball

Sun

Earth

Move the earth counterclockwise

3. Stick a pin in the globe to represent the place where you live. Turn the globe slowly to the sunlight side.

Hypothesizing   *Using the globe, how could you make night come to the place where you live?*

What Must I Know?   The globe is turned slowly to show where night would begin to fall and where it would be midnight and sunrise. To show this, the globe must be turned counterclockwise.

Inferring   *What time of day is it when your pin is on the same side as the*

Inferring   *sun?*

When your pin is away from the sun, what time of day would it be?

How Will Children Use or Apply What They Discover?
1. *What would happen if the earth did not turn?*
2. *If the earth did not turn, which side would you rather be on? Why?*

How Do the Planets Move? (4–8)

What Do I Want Children to Discover?
Planets move around the sun.
There are nine planets that move around the sun.
Planets vary in size and distance from the sun.
The planets farthest from the sun have the longest years and the longest paths to follow.

What Will I Need?
Lamp
Ruler
Clay or Styrofoam balls

What Will We Discuss?

On what planet do you live?
How does the earth move?
How do you think the movement of the earth corresponds to the orbit of the other planets?
How can you show the planets and how they move?

What Must I Know?

Some things cannot be seen, felt, or measured. Therefore, a scientific model must be formed. The pupils may select Styrofoam balls to make the planet models. They can hang these from the inside of a cardboard box.

What Will Children Do?

PROCESSES

PART I

1. Obtain some clay or Styrofoam and shape it into balls so they vary in sizes as indicated on the following scales:

Planet	Small Scale Size in Diameter (inches)	Large Scale Size in Diameter (inches)
Mercury	$\frac{1}{16}$	$\frac{1}{4}$
Venus	$\frac{2}{16}$	$\frac{5}{8}$
Earth	$\frac{2}{16}$	$\frac{5}{8}$
Mars	$\frac{3}{32}$	$\frac{3}{8}$
Jupiter	$1\frac{5}{16}$	$6\frac{3}{4}$
Saturn	$1\frac{1}{16}$	$5\frac{1}{2}$
Uranus	$\frac{1}{2}$	$2\frac{1}{4}$
Neptune	$\frac{9}{16}$	$2\frac{1}{4}$
Pluto	$\frac{7}{16}$	$\frac{1}{4}$
Sun	15	60

The scales of $\frac{1}{16}$ or $\frac{1}{4}$ inch are equal to about 4,000 miles. Make a ring of paper to place around Saturn.

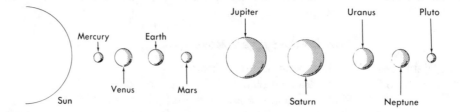

Inferring   *Where does the earth get its light?*
Inferring   *Where do the other planets get their light?*
Applying   *How can you show that planets reflect their light from the sun?*

Hypothesizing	*Where should the sun be placed?*
Hypothesizing	*What planet should be placed next to the sun?*

2. Attach the balls to paper clips and hang them from a tackboard. Write the names of planets on small paper and fasten the names below the planets.

Observing	*How many planets are there?*
Comparing	*How do the planets differ in size?*
Comparing	*Which is the largest planet?*
Comparing	*Which two planets are the smallest?*
Inferring	*Why can't you have an accurate comparison of the planets with the sun?*
	What is the name given to the sun and the planets?
Applying	*Why is it called the solar system?*

What Must I Know?

Pupils may use a reference book, or you may need to explain to some pupils that the word *solar* comes from the Latin word meaning sun. Distance *between* planets is difficult to simulate if the same scale of $\frac{1}{16}$ or $\frac{1}{4}$ inch = 4,000 miles is used. For instance, the earth's average distance from the sun is about 93 million miles. At $\frac{1}{4}$ inch = 4,000 miles, you would have to place the earth about *485 feet* from the sun!

PART II

1. Work with your planet models and refer to resource materials to determine answers to the following questions:

Observing	*Which planet has rings?*
Observing	*Which planet is closest to the sun?*
Observing	*Which planet is farthest from the sun?*
Inferring	*Which planet takes the longest to go around the sun?*
Inferring	*Which planet would have the longest year?*
Inferring	*Why would that planet have the longest year?*
Applying	*Which planet do you think would be the warmest?*
Designing an investigation	*How can you determine if all the planets move in the same direction?*

How Will Children Use or Apply What They Discover?

1. *What else could you do with your planet models to show how they move around the sun?*
2. *How could you construct an apparatus that would show all nine planets revolving around the sun?*

What Must I Know?

The planets that children made could be fastened onto a wire that is attached between spools on dowel rods as shown in the diagram below. Another way is to attach the wire to corners of the ceiling in your classroom.

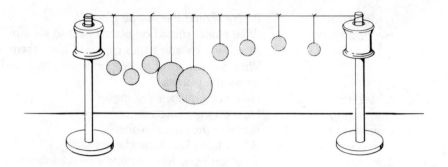

What Size Is the Sun Compared to the Earth? (K–3)

What Do I Want Children to Discover?

The sun is many times larger than the earth.

Objects of similar size appear smaller when they are far away and larger when they are near.

Stars are very big in size, bright, and far away.

What Will I Need?

Basketball
Several radish seeds

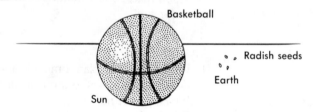

What Will Children Do?

PROCESSES

1. Look at the basketball and the seeds.
   Which would you have represent the earth and which the sun? Why?

Comparing

2. *As you look at the stars on a clear night, how do they differ from each other?*

What Must I Know?

Some are brighter than others; some are different colors.

3. Darken your classroom. If this is not possible, go with your teacher into a darkened gymnasium, auditorium, or hallway, and have one of your classmates hold a flashlight at the opposite end of the room. He or she should walk slowly toward you.

Observing

How does the light change as it gets closer to you?

What Must I Know?

They should notice that the light gets brighter and bigger.

Inferring

Knowing this, why do you think some stars look different?

What Must I Know? Some stars look closer to us than other stars because they are brighter or they are bigger.

How Will Children Use or Apply What They Discover?

1. *If you had two flashlights giving off the same amount of light, what would you do to one to make it look dimmer than the other in a large, dark room?*
2. Get two children of very different heights (a kindergartner and a sixth grader). Have the kindergartner stand 2 feet from the class on the playground and the sixth grader, 100 yards away. Compare their heights.
   Why do they appear as they do?

What Does the Sun Do for Us? (K–3)

What Do I Want Children to Discover? The sun gives off energy in the form of heat and light. The light of the sun can be brought to a point by using a lens.

What Will I Need? Hand magnifying glass (one for every two students)
Sheet of paper

What Will Children Do?

PROCESSES

1. Obtain a magnifying glass and a piece of paper.
2. Hold the magnifying glass over a piece of paper outside in the sunlight. Move the magnifying glass up and down above the piece of paper until the light comes to a point. Hold it there for a few seconds. *Caution:* Do *not* stare at point of light or put hands on focused point.

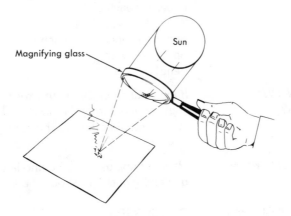

Observing *What happens to the paper?*

What Must I Know? The paper will begin to smoke and burn.

Hypothesizing *Why does the paper react as it does?*

What Must I Know?   The paper burns because the magnifying glass concentrates the sun's heat rays into a small point of intense heat.

Observing

3. Try the same experiment with the light from a light bulb.
   What happens to the paper?

What Must I Know?   Nothing happens to the paper because the light is not intense enough.

Hypothesizing
Inferring

Why does the paper react as it does this time?
What do these activities tell you about the sun?

What Must I Know?   This shows that the sun gives off a great deal of heat and light.

How Will Children Use or Apply What They Discover?

1. *If you wanted to melt some wax and did not have any matches, how would you do it?*
2. *On a cold day, why do you feel warm in sunlight but very cold when in a shadow?*

How Long Is a Year? (3–6)

What Do I Want Children to Discover?

The earth moves around the sun (revolves).
It takes one year for the earth to make one trip around the sun.
An earth year is 365¼ days.
The earth rotates as it revolves around the sun.
The earth moves around the sun in an elliptical path.

What Will I Need?

Globe	Masking tape
Lamp	Chalk
Cardboard for each child	Lamp
Paper for each child	Overhead projector
2 pins for each child	Transparency of the planets in orbit
String—15 inches for each child	Opaque circles to represent the sun and earth
String—24 feet	
Pencils	Planetarium if available

What Will We Discuss?

If the rotating of the earth explains the length of day, how can a globe and a lamp be used to show the length of a year?
What kind of path does the earth make when it revolves around the sun?

What Must I Know?   Have a pupil use a globe and lamp to review how rotation causes day and night. This should be a demonstration activity.

What Will Children Do?

PROCESSES

1. Obtain a piece of paper, cardboard, two pins, string, and a pencil.
2. Try to draw a circle by sticking two pins 7 inches apart in the middle of the paper, which is resting on the cardboard. Form a loop from a piece of string 9 inches long. Slip the loop over the pins.

Pull the loop tight with a pencil and, using the string as a guide, draw a line around the pins.

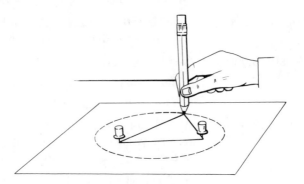

Comparing	*How does the shape you made differ from a perfect circle? What might you call this shape?*
What Must I Know?	If the children do not know, tell them it is called an *ellipse*.

3. Use a longer string loop, masking tape, and chalk to make an ellipse on the floor.
4. Place a lamp in the center of the ellipse.

Inferring	*What does the lamp represent?*
Inferring	*What does the ellipse you drew around the sun represent?*
Hypothesizing	*What could you use to represent the earth?*
What Must I Know?	A child should walk on a line around the sun (the light) and should rotate as he or she follows the line.

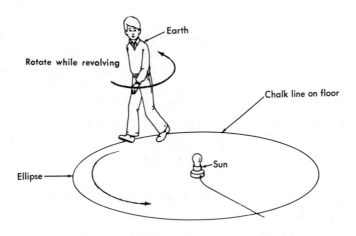

Applying	*In what way should the earth move around the sun?*

What Must I Know?	Children should take turns rotating as they revolve around the sun. You might tell them that rotation is like spinning; but in revolving, one object must go around another object.
Hypothesizing	*What is the process of the earth moving around the sun called?* *When something revolves, what is it doing?*
What Must I Know?	One trip around the sun is called a **revolution.**
Inferring	*How many days make a year?* *How can you find out?*
What Must I Know?	After they have checked the number of days in a year, the children might investigate why some of the statements say there are 365 days and others say 365¼ days.
Summarizing	5. Rotate like the earth. *How long does it take the earth to rotate on its axis to make a day?* 6. Demonstrate how the earth revolves around the sun. *How long does it take for the earth to make one complete orbit around the sun?* *What is the name of the imaginary line on which the earth travels around the sun?* *How long is an earth year?*
What Must I Know?	"Convert" the overhead projector into a planetarium by placing on the stage of the projector an opaque circle to represent the sun and a smaller opaque circle to represent the earth. Have a child show how the earth revolves around the sun by moving the earth correctly.
How Will Children Use or Apply What They Discover?	1. *What else revolves around the sun?* 2. *How could you determine if other planets have the same length of year as the earth?* 3. *Which planet has the longest year? Why?* 4. *Which planet would have the shortest year?* *How could you demonstrate the revolution of the planets?* *What effect would the various lengths of years have on birthdays of people if all planets were inhabited?*
What Must I Know?	If a planetarium is available, use it as a visual aid. The overhead projector also may be used. Focus a transparency of the planets in orbit onto the ceiling and discuss the solar system.

What Causes the Seasons? (4–8)

What Do I Want Children to Discover?	The sun gives off light and heat. The more sun rays that hit a section of the earth, the warmer that section will get.

When it is light on one side of the earth, it is dark on the other side of the earth.

The rotating of the earth causes night and day.

The earth makes one revolution around the sun in one year.

What Will I Need?

Flashlight or filmstrip projector
2 thermometers
Black paper
2 plastic or rubber balls
Globe

What Will We Discuss?

How do the four seasons differ?

Why does the continental United States have different seasons?

How could you use simple apparatus such as used in this activity to demonstrate night and day and to show the cause of the seasons?

What Must I Know?

This investigation should not be crowded into a single period.

What Will Children Do?

PROCESSES

PART I

1. Shine a flashlight as shown in diagram 1.

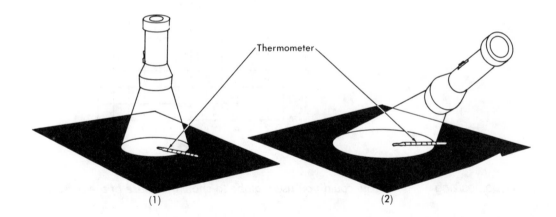

Thermometer

(1)   (2)

Observing

What do you notice about the way the light shines on the paper?

Observing

What kind of area is covered by the light as it shines on the paper?

Trace this area on the paper.

Hypothesizing

If you shine the light as shown in diagram 2, what do you think will happen to the area covered?

Trace this area. Compare the areas traced.

Hypothesizing

In which way, direct or slanted, do you think the temperature would be greater? Why do you think so?

*Designing an
investigation*

How could you determine whether your answer is correct?

2. Take two flashlights or filmstrip projectors and two thermometers and shine them as in diagrams 1 and 2. Place a thermometer on the paper to see if you can detect a difference in the temperature.

Comparing — *How do the temperatures differ?*

Inferring — *What do you think causes the variation?*

Comparing — *How does the temperature vary with the seasons?*

Graph your results as shown below.

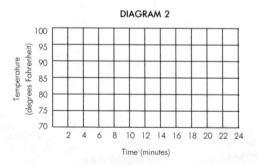

PART II

Hypothesizing

How could you use a globe to show the cause of the seasons?

1. Obtain two plastic or rubber balls. Place each ball on a nail as shown in the diagram. A globe of the earth may be substituted for the second ball. Shine a flashlight beam directly on each globe.

Observing	*What do you notice about the way the light hits the two globes?*
Hypothesizing	*What would you have to do to the globes to show what causes day and night?*
Hypothesizing	*If the earth were not inclined as in the second globe, how could you determine if there would be any seasons?*

2. Point the flashlight at the second globe, and move the globe around the flashlight.

Observing	*What do you notice about the way the light strikes the globe as you move the globe, stopping at several places?*
Inferring	*What do you think the season would be at each point where you stop?*
Hypothesizing	*Why does the United States get more sunlight in summer than in winter?*
Hypothesizing	*Why does the sun not shine on the earth the same way every month of the year?*
Observing	*Which covers a larger portion of the earth, the slanted rays or the direct rays?*
Applying	*How can you determine which rays are cooler on the earth's surface—direct or slanting?*
Summarizing	*How long does it take for the earth to make one trip around the sun?*
Observing	*When it is winter in New York, what season is it in Argentina?*
Inferring	*How does the angle of the earth affect the seasons?*

What Must I Know?   Parts of the earth receive more heat from the sun at one time of the year than at another time because of the tilt of the axis. Place the following diagram on the board after the lesson and have the children point out the various seasons and explain them.

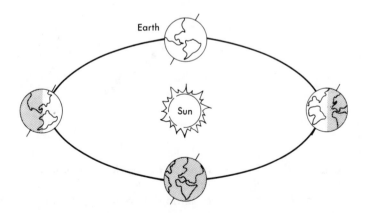

How Will Children Use or Apply What They Discover?

1. *What other investigations can you use to show why the earth has seasons?*
2. *In what way would a knowledge of seasonal variations help you better understand the peoples of the world?*

3. *How do you explain portions of the earth being warmer in summer even though they are farther away from the sun than in winter?*

Why Do Stars Appear Close or Far Apart? (K–4)

What Do I Want Children to Discover?

There are millions of stars, and they are tremendous distances from each other.

The earth's great distance from the stars makes the stars appear closer together.

What Will I Need?

50 bottle caps or 50 marbles

What Will We Discuss?

How do the stars appear to you as you look into the sky?
Explain why they look near to each other or far apart.
Why do they look small?
What can you do to show how things look at a distance?

What Will Children Do?

PROCESSES

1. Obtain and place 50 bottle caps in a cluster so no bottle cap is less than 1 inch from its nearest neighbor. Stand in front of the bottle caps, facing them.

Hypothesizing

What do you think will happen as you move away from these objects?

2. Move away from the caps.

Observing

How do the bottle caps appear as you move 5 steps away from them?

Observing

3. *How do the bottle caps appear as you move 10 steps away from them?*

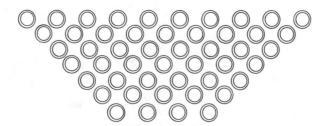

Observing

4. *How do the bottle caps appear as you move 15 steps away from them?*

Summarizing

How do the bottle caps look as you move away from them?

Observing

5. Draw how the bottle caps look when you see them in front of you and then how they look when you take 15 steps away from them.

Designing an investigation

In what way could you go about finding how the stars look in the sky?

What Must I Know?

The more immature pupils will need more guidance. They may be asked to observe the night sky. The next day you and the pupils could discuss the results of their observation and investigation.

Inferring

> *How could you use this investigation with bottle caps and observation of the sky to explain why the stars look so close together?*

Inferring

> *Why do you think stars look close together yet are so far apart?*

Summarizing

> *What do you know now about how far away the stars are?*

How Will Children Use or Apply What They Discover?

1. *If you were to fill a Chinese checkerboard with marbles, would it make the shape of a star, or would it represent many "little" stars? Why?*
2. *If you were to look at cars at different distances, which would appear smaller, the near ones or those far away?*

What Causes Some Stars to Be Different Colors? (4–8)

What Do I Want Children to Discover?

When objects are heated, they may change color.

White-hot objects are hotter than red-hot objects.

White stars are believed to be hotter than yellow stars, and yellow stars are hotter than red stars.

A **star** is a giant mass of tremendously hot, glowing gases.

White stars have temperatures of 40,000° F at their surfaces; yellow stars, 10,000° F; and red stars, 3,000° F.

Color is related to the age of a star.

Young stars are white.

Old stars are red.

What Will I Need?

Pliers

Copper wire

Bunsen or alcohol burner

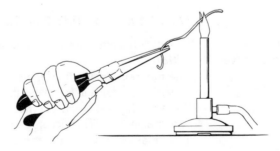

What Will We Discuss?

> *If you saw two pieces of iron, both of which had been in a furnace, and one piece was red and the other was white, which one would you think was the hotter?*
>
> *Why would one be hotter than the other?*

What Must I Know?	Because of the equipment used and the possible danger of a child being burned, this activity should probably be done as a demonstration.
What Will Children Do?	**PROCESSES**
Hypothesizing	1. With a pair of pliers hold a wire above a Bunsen burner. *What do you think will happen to the wire as it is heated?*
What Must I Know?	The wire will change color, becoming red, then yellow, and finally white as the temperature increases.
Inferring	*What do you notice about the way the wire changes color?*
Inferring	*What makes it change color?*
Summarizing	*What are the different colors that the wire gives off in the process of being heated?*
Inferring	*What color do you think is the hottest? The coldest?*
Hypothesizing	*If you saw a red and yellow star through a telescope, which of these do you think would be the hottest? Why?*
What Must I Know?	Red stars are cooler than yellow stars, and white stars are hotter than either red or yellow stars. Explain from this demonstration how it is possible for an astronomer, a scientist who studies the stars, to tell how hot a star is without ever going to it. Explain that the color of the stars cannot be detected with the naked eye. The astronomer must use astronomical instruments in order to do this.
How Will Children Use or Apply What They Discover?	1. *If you were going to heat some charcoal, which of the following types of light do you think it would give off first: red, yellow, or white?*
	2. *What color is radiated from the hottest source in your home?*
	3. *What other things might an astronomer study in the laboratory to help him or her better understand the stars?*

What Causes the Tides? (4–8)

What Do I Want Children to Discover?	Gravitational attractions of the moon and sun on the earth cause **tides.**
	The moon is smaller than the sun, but because it is closer to the earth, its tidal pull is greater than that of the sun.
	Tides are highest when the moon and sun are pulling on the earth in a straight line. This occurs twice a month.
	Low tides occur when the moon and sun are pulling at right angles to each other.
	Gravity decreases with the increase of distance between two objects.
What Will I Need?	Horseshoe magnet
	Ring stand

String
Book
Paper clip
Styrofoam ball, 9 inches in diameter
Styrofoam ball, 2 inches in diameter
Small round-shaped balloon

What Must I Know?   This activity should be done by groups of three or more students.

**What Will Children
Do?**

PROCESSES

1. Obtain a ring stand, a horseshoe magnet, some string, a paper clip, and a book.
2. Set up the equipment as shown in the next diagram.

Inferring   *What holds up the paper clip?*
Observing   *Are you able to see this force?*
Assuming   *How do you know it is there if you cannot see it?*

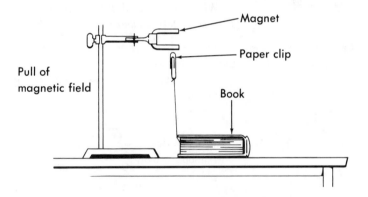

What Must I Know?   This is a **magnetic force**. It is shown here to illustrate what a force is and that a force may be invisible. Tides are not caused by magnetic force but gravitational force. The children should have done some activities involving gravity before they do this lesson.

Hypothesizing   *Knowing this, what effect do you think the moon's gravitational force has on the water of the earth?*
Hypothesizing   *How will it pull the water?*

3. Obtain two Styrofoam balls, 9 inches and 2 inches in diameter, and a small balloon.
4. Ask two partners to help you.
5. Blow up the balloon and tie the end closed. Have the two partners each hold one of the Styrofoam balls. You should hold the balloon in the same position as in the following diagram.

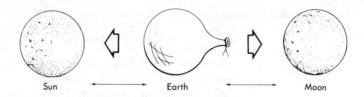

6. Pull the balloon with one hand toward the sun.
   Pull with the other hand toward the moon.

Inferring *What would the pull being exerted on the balloon represent?*

Hypothesizing *What do you think will happen if the sun and moon are placed at right angles to the earth?*

Hypothesizing *How will the gravitational forces vary?*

7. Pull the balloon mostly toward the moon and exert much less force in the sun's direction.

Comparing *From the way the balloon is being pulled, which has greater gravitational pull on the earth—the moon or the sun?*

Hypothesizing *Why do you think the moon has greater pull on the earth when it is so much smaller than the sun?*

What Must I Know? The moon has greater effect because it is much closer to the earth than the sun is.

For summarization, draw the following diagram on the board and discuss it with the class.

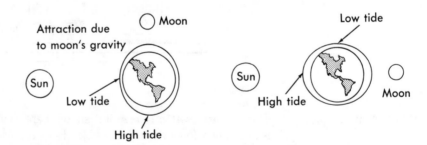

At the conclusion of the activity, discuss with the class the following concepts to be sure the students understand them:

Force is either a push or a pull exerted on an object. **Gravity** is a force you cannot see.

The greater the mass of an object, the heavier it is, and the more gravitational force it has.

The closer an object is to another, the greater the gravitational attraction there will be between them.

Mass is defined as the amount of matter a body contains.

How Will Children Use or Apply What They Discover?

1. Draw the positions of the moon, earth, and sun when there is a very high tide on part of the earth.
   How does the water around that part of the earth look?
2. *When there is low tide at a place on the earth, how does the water look?*
3. *Why does the moon have a greater effect on the tide than the sun does?*
4. *What holds you down in your chair?*
5. *What effect do the gravitational forces of the moon and sun have on the world's continents?*

Why Does the Moon Shine? (K–6)

What Do I Want Children to Discover?

Objects are seen when they give off their own light or when they **reflect** light from another source.

The moon does not give off its own light. Its light is reflected light from the sun.

What Will I Need?

Flashlight	Small foil ball, about 1 inch in diameter, with attached string
Masking tape	
Large ball	Larger styrofoam ball, about 3 inches in diameter, with attached string
	Box with tight fitting lid (shoe box)

What Will We Discuss?

Place a ball on the table, darken the room, and ask:
What is on the table?
What do you need to be able to see the object?
Turn on the lights.
Why do you see the ball now?
Do you see it because it is giving off its own light or because it is reflecting light?
Look at the ceiling lights.
Why is it possible for you to see the lights?
How is this light different from the light you see when you look at the ball?
Darken the room.
What are two reasons why you may not see any lights in the room?

What Will Children Do? *Hypothesizing Inferring*

PROCESSES

How do you think the moon shines?
What is reflected light?

1. Obtain the following materials: box with tight fitting lid, foil made into a ball with attached string, flashlight, and masking tape.
2. Suspend the small ball on a string 1 inch long from inside the lid of the box as shown in the diagram. Insert flashlight in the end of

the box and seal any space around it with masking tape. Make a small eyehole at the end of the box under the flashlight.

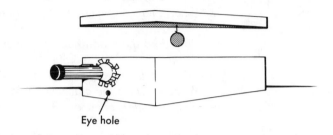

Eye hole

Put on the lid with the ball suspended inside the box. Seal the edges around the lid.

Observing and inferring   *What do you see when you look through the eyehole? Why?*

Observing and inferring   3. Turn on the flashlight.

Inferring   *What do you see when you look through the eyehole? Why?*

Do you see the ball because it reflects light or because it gives off light of its own?

Classifying   *What two kinds of light do you see?*

Inferring   *What is the source of each kind of light?*

4. Look out the window.

Inferring   *Why are you able to see some objects?*

Inferring   *What is the source of the light on the objects?*

Inferring   *Do the objects seen outside the window give off reflected light or light of their own?*

Inferring   *What does the sun give off?*

Inferring   *Why does the moon shine?*

5. Obtain a styrofoam ball, 3 inches in diameter, with attached string. Use your box, flashlight, suspended foil ball, but add the larger styrofoam ball suspended 2 inches down, as shown in the diagram. Seal the edges again. Seal the old eyehole and make a new eyehole as indicated in the drawing.

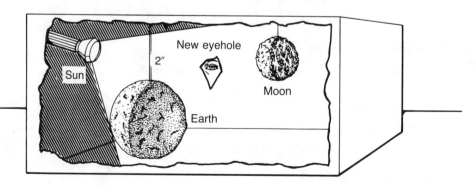

Formulating a
model

Inferring

Inferring

Inferring

Inferring

Summarizing

If the small ball is the moon, what does the flashlight represent?

6. Turn on the flashlight and look through the new eyehole.
   What does the large ball represent?
7. Look at the ball representing the earth and tell which side is day and which side is night.
   On which side would you be if you could see the moon?
   How is it possible for you to see the moon if you are on the dark side of the earth?
   Why does the moon shine?

How Will Children Use or Apply What They Discover?

1. *If you lived on another planet, would you be able to see earth?*
2. *What are the positions of the sun, moon, and earth (a) when it is night for you, (b) when it is day for you?*

Why Does It Appear That There Are Phases of the Moon? (4–6)

What Do I Want Children to Discover?

Sometimes the moon appears fully round.
The moon seems to change shape.
Sometimes the moon seems to get smaller and smaller.
Sometimes the moon seems to get larger and larger.

What Will I Need?

Black construction paper
Soft white chalk
Globe
Small ball
Basketball
Flashlight or filmstrip projector

What Must I Know?

Before the experiment, consult the local newspaper to see when the moon's quarter will be visible during the day.

PROCESSES

What Will Children Do?

Observing

1. Obtain a large piece of black construction paper and some white chalk.
2. Take this home and observe the moon for the next five days. Draw the shape of the moon as you see it each night.
   In what way does the moon's shape seem to change?
3. Obtain a globe, small ball, and a flashlight or filmstrip projector. Using this equipment, make the following arrangement.
4. Place a pin on the night side of the earth as indicated in the diagram. The pin represents you.

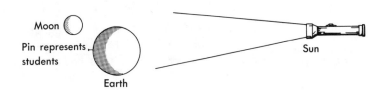

Moon

Pin represents students

Earth

Sun

Inferring Draw how much of a moon you would see if you were where the pin is.

5. Move the moon around the earth.

Inferring *On which side of the earth is the moon when you cannot see it?*

Inferring *Where is the moon when it is full?*

6. Make diagrams to help you explain the last three questions.

7. Look at the following diagram showing some phases of the moon.

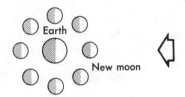

8. Prepare eight drawings showing how the moon would appear to you during the eight phases as indicated in the diagram.

9. Obtain a basketball and flashlight.

10. Choose two partners to help you. Have one partner hold the flashlight and shine it on the basketball being held by your second partner as he or she walks in a circle around you.

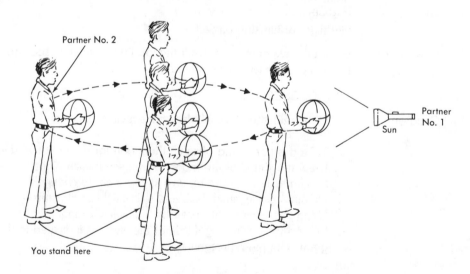

Inferring 11. As you observe the ball, diagram on a piece of paper how the light on the ball is similar to the phases of the moon.

Inferring *In what position is the ball when it is covered by the shadow?*

Inferring	*Where would the moon have to be when it is covered by a*
Inferring	*shadow?*
	When the ball shows no shadow, what phase of the moon would this represent?
Summarizing	12. Draw how the full moon looks from earth.
Summarizing	*What causes the phases of the moon?*
How Will Children Use or Apply What They Discover?	1. *If the moon is not out at night, on what side of the earth must it be located?*
	2. *If the moon could remain still in the sky, how would it look every night?*

What Is an Eclipse? (4–8)

What Do I Want Children to Discover?	The shadow of the moon on the earth causes a **solar eclipse.**
	The shadow of the earth on the moon causes a **lunar eclipse.**
	To see a solar eclipse, one has to be on the sunny side of the earth.
	To see a lunar eclipse, one has to be on the night side of the earth.
What Will I Need?	(For each 3–5 students)
	Flashlight, slide projector, or similar light source
	Styrene (or similar) ball approximately 8 inches in diameter
	Styrofoam (or similar) ball approximately 2 inches in diameter
What Will We Discuss?	*What does the word eclipse mean?*
	If something is eclipsed, what does it mean?
	What would it mean to say the sun is eclipsed?
What Will Children Do?	PROCESSES
	1. Investigate the following questions, letting the flashlight represent the sun; the large ball, the earth; and the small ball, the moon.
Hypothesizing	2. *How must the sun, earth, and moon be arranged for a solar eclipse to occur?*
What Must I Know?	The moon must be between the earth and the sun.
Observing	3. Describe the shadow that falls upon the earth.
Inferring	*When a solar eclipse occurs, would everyone on earth be able to see it? Explain your answer.*
What Must I Know?	No, because the moon's shadow only touches a small part of the earth.
Inferring	*Can a solar eclipse be seen at night? Explain.*
What Must I Know?	No, it can only happen in the daytime when the moon can block out the sun's light.

Hypothesizing	*How must the sun, moon, and earth be arranged for a lunar eclipse to occur?*
What Must I Know?	The earth must be between the sun and moon for a shadow to fall upon the moon.
Hypothesizing	*When is it possible to see a lunar eclipse?*
What Must I Know?	Only at night.
How Will Children Use or Apply What They Discover?	1. The almanac indicates solar and lunar eclipses do not occur regularly each month as it seems they should. Use your equipment to see if you can discover an explanation to determine why this is so.
What Must I Know?/ Where Do I Find It?	The children's activity should show that if the moon passes above or below the plane of the earth's orbit, the earth's shadow could miss the moon entirely, or the moon's shadow could miss the earth. In either case, the eclipse might be visible only from some point in space. The formulated hypothesis should be similar to the following: The plane of the moon's orbit is tilted away from the plane of the earth's orbit: eclipses can only occur when the earth, sun, and moon are in a straight line, and this does not happen each month.

References—Astronomy (Earth in Space) Franklyn M. Branley, *The Planets in Our Solar System* (New York: Harper and Row, 1981). Roy A. Gallant. *Once Around the Galaxy* (New York: Watts, 1983).

SECTION 4

Guided Discovery Science Activities for Special Needs Children

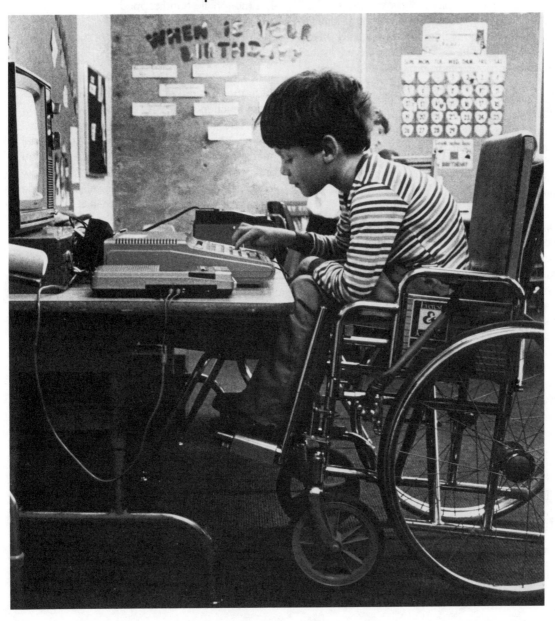

This section contains guided discovery science activities for special needs children. These activities supplement those presented in chapter 11. The reason for additional activities for special needs children is based on the fact that you either have, or soon will have, such children in your classroom. There are over 8 million youngsters in schools today (one in ten) with some form of handicap. Public Law 94–142 allows for mainstreaming handicapped students in the regular classroom whenever practical. Whether the handicap is sensory, mental, emotional, or social, it is important for you to find ways to include special needs students in your class.

Guided discovery science activities can provide a sense of achievement to handicapped children who seldom enjoy such success in school. It is not easy to accomplish this task. However, by becoming aware of the kinds of "specialness" *each* child possesses and possible ways of helping the child best function within these limitations, you will begin to individualize your science program.

Labels often get in the way of looking at individuals. "Special" individuals differ significantly in what they need to succeed in the world. They have, as Norris Haring says, "*special needs,* a phrase that is becoming more and more popular as a description of these members of our society."[1]

Guided discovery science activities are presented for children with these handicaps or disabilities.

1. Sensory handicapped
2. Mentally retarded
3. Visual perception problems
4. Emotionally handicapped
5. Hearing impaired

Although other handicaps and disabilities are prevalent and important, these activities are limited to the above four categories of children most frequently encountered by classroom teachers.

These activities are not meant to be exhaustive but are ways to meet the special needs of your students in science. As you practice using them, you will get to know these students better and find ways to provide successful science/learning activities for them. You can modify the guided discovery science activities in section 5 for this purpose. Learning to be more sensitive to children with special needs will help you respond the same way to all of your students. The unexpected gain to you of focusing upon "special needs" children will be to see all your students as special.

The format used in this section is the Quickie Starter format in the activities in sections 1 through 3. This less formal format was selected because special needs children generally respond better when activities are hands-on, concrete, and more open ended. This format also allows the teacher to have more flexibility in modifying the activities to the special needs of individual children. As you become more confident with science activities for special needs children, you will be able to modify some of the activities in sections 1 through 3.

---

[1] Norris G. Haring, ed., *Behavior of Exceptional Children. An Introduction to Special Education,* 2nd ed. (Columbus, Ohio: Merrill Publishing Co., 1978), 1.

SENSORY HANDICAPPED CHILDREN

How Can Blind or Visually Impaired Children Learn about Magnets? (K–8)

Materials

Assorted magnets, common objects attracted and not attracted by magnets (paper clips, rubber bands, plastic and metal zippers, pencils, paper, wire, and so on), 2 shallow boxes. (*Important Note:* Avoid sharp or pointed objects.)

Opening Questions

What are magnets?
What things do they pick up?

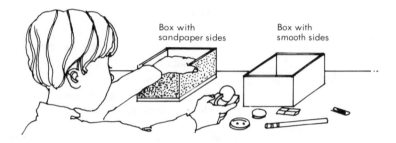

Box with sandpaper sides

Box with smooth sides

Some Possible Activities

Have the children handle magnets and describe the shapes (bar, disc-shaped, horseshoe, U-shaped, cylindrical, and so on).

ASK:

How will you know if a magnet picks up (attracts) an object?

They will readily discern by touching the magnet that something was attracted as it "sticks" to the magnet. Ask them to name the objects on the table and then test to "see" (find out) if they are attracted by the magnet. They can sort objects tested by the magnet into two shallow boxes. One with smooth sides can be called "Objects attracted by magnets." Sandpaper glued to the other box can facilitate *tactile* sorting in this box called "Objects not attracted by magnets." Once they understand the sorting system, they can verify the contents of both boxes by themselves and even test new objects with magnets.

In What Ways Can the Blind or Visually Impaired Identify Objects in the Environment? (K–8)

Materials

Masks to cover eyes, pairs of noise makers (rattles, party horns, "clickers," and so on)

Opening Question

Can you find your partner if you cannot see him or her? How?

Some Possible
Activities

Take a group of sighted and blind or visually impaired children out-side your classroom on a relatively open (free of trees, shrubs, or other obstacles) lawn area. Use other students or adults to keep the children from moving outside the area as they engage in the activity. Play a game in which the children assume the roles of limited-vision animals. Sighted children wear masks on their eyes. One child is a predator, the other prey. Each prey has one of a variety of paired noisemakers (two clickers, party horns, and so on). At a signal, preys try to find their partners who have the same noisemakers. Predators in the meantime try to capture the noisy prey.

After the fun game, have the children all sit quietly and listen to the environmental sounds.

ASK:
Which sounds can you identify?
Which sounds are made by the same source?
In which direction do you hear the various sounds?
Which sound do you like the best? Why?
Which sound do you like the least? Why?
How do you think a particular sound was made?

For more information about this and other life science activities for the visually impaired student, see Larry Malone and Linda DeLucchi, "Life Science for Visually Impaired Students," *Science and Children,* 16, no. 5 (February 1979): 29–31.

What Are Some Ways for Blind or Visually Impaired Students to Find Out about Their Bodies? (K–8)

Materials

Stethoscopes, braille-faced clocks

Opening Question

Does your heart beat faster when you lie down or stand up or run?

Some Possible
Activities

After raising the question with blind or visually impaired children, give simple instructions on how to use the equipment and carry out the activity. Introduce the term *variable* and explain that the variable they will investigate is body position and how it affects their heart rate. Have the children learn to listen to their heartbeats through the stethoscope and count the beats on the braille-faced clock. An adult or older child can help younger children with the numbers.

After they have completed taking and recording their heart rates in lying and standing positions, discuss this and help them to see the effect of body position on heart rate. You can extend the activity by asking further questions.

ASK:
What other variables could be investigated in this activity?
What effect would these things have on heart rate: age, amount

of movement, time of day, drinking soda pop, smoking, and so on?

Encourage the children to explore the variables without your giving them directions on how to do it. You might also introduce animals and see if the children can use them to compare and do further exploration.

How Can Blind Students "See" and Compare Polluted Water? (4–8)

Materials

4 jars of water containing different pollutants, light sensor (available on Federal Quota from the American Printing House for the Blind, P.O. Box 6085, Louisville, KY 40206), light source (sunlight, filmstrip projector, and so on)

Opening Question

How can we (blind students) find out (by using our hearing) which jars contain the most polluted water?

Some Possible Activities

Prepare four jars of water with varying amounts of pollutants (soil, debris, egg shells, and so on). Introduce and demonstrate to the students the **light sensor device.** This device produces an *auditory* signal of varying pitch and volume as a result of its exposure to the intensity of light. Set up the four jars of varying pollutants with a light source behind it in this way.

Light sensor

Light source

Have students examine each jar at close range by pointing the light sensor directly at each jar, as shown above. A beeping sound is emitted, which becomes higher and more frequent with the greater amount of light coming into the sensor. Students will discover that the fewer pollutants in each jar, the greater amount of light coming through the jar, and, therefore, the more shrill and rapid the beep from the sensor. More pollutants result in much less light coming through the jar to the sensor and a slower and lower pitched beep. *Note:* For an excellent expanded description of the use of the light sensor with blind students, see Frank L. Franks and LaRhea Sanford, "Using the Light Sensor to Introduce Laboratory Science," *Science and Children* 13, no. 6 (March 1976): 48–49.

MENTALLY RETARDED CHILDREN

How Can Mentally Retarded Children Learn to Develop a Thermic Sense (Sense of Temperature)? (K–8)

Materials

Several metal bowls, water of varying temperatures

Opening Questions

How do hot things feel?
How do cold things feel?

Some Possible Activities

Prepare several metal bowls with varying temperatures of water from ice cold to very warm. *Caution:* Do not have the hot water hot enough to scald or injure any child. Let the water set in the bowls for a few minutes and then have the children feel the *outside* of the bowls.

> **ASK:**
> *Which bowl feels cold?*
> *Which one feels warm?*
> *Which one feels hot?*

If a child does not know the difference, repeat it.

> **SAY:**
> *This bowl feels cold.*
> *Does it make your hand cold?*
> *This bowl is hot.*
> *Is your hand hot?*
> *Where else have you felt hot and cold things?*

Relate this activity to their immediate lives by comparing it to holding a glass of iced drink, a cup of hot soup, and so on.

Point out the dangers of hot and cold.

> **ASK:**
> *Why should we use this potholder if we are holding something hot from the oven or stove?*

Why should you wear a coat and gloves when it is very cold outside?

Where are very hot things in our homes?

Have pictures of oven, stove, radiators, etc.

ASK:
Which things are very cold in our school?

Take the children to the cafeteria and have them tell or show you (or you show them) the refrigerator or freezer.

How Can Mentally Retarded Children Learn the Concept of Weight? (K–8)

Materials

Small blocks of wood of the same size but different woods such as balsa (model airplane wood), oak, pine, or mahogany

Opening Questions

Which of these blocks do you think would be the heaviest? Lightest?

Some Possible Activities

Ask the children what it means when people say something is heavy. Have them use whatever words will help them to develop the concept as long as the words do not connote misconceptions. They might say, "It's harder to lift." If they have difficulty with this concept, help them to develop it. Do the same with the idea of something lighter in weight. Now give them the blocks.

ASK:
Do you think they all weigh the same?
Which one might be the heaviest? Lightest?

Have the children feel the blocks and place them in order from heaviest to lightest.

Label the heaviest block with an H and use an L for the lightest one. Ask the children what things in the classroom are heavy and light.

Place an H and L on the objects selected (heavy: desks, cabinets, teacher; light: paper, pencils, paper clips; and so on.) Explain why it is dangerous to lift very heavy things.

How Can Mentally Retarded Children Learn to Discriminate Tastes? (K–8)

Materials

Box of cotton swabs and a bottle of solutions of common liquids that are salty, sweet, sour, bitter, acid, and neutral

Opening Questions

How many of you would like to play a game?
Are you a good detective?

Some Possible Activities

Tell the children they are going to play a detective game to try to find out what is in the bottles you have. Caution them never to taste anything they don't know about. Ask why they should not do this and explain the dangers of poisons. Tell them that none of the things in the bottle are poisonous and are things they taste everyday.

Have all children use a different swab and explain why they should do this (germs, colds, other diseases, and so on). Have all children get a sample of something sweet (syrup).

ASK:
What kind of taste is this?

Have them agree that it is *sweet* and if possible have them identify the source (syrup). Toss the cotton swabs away and give them a second one. This time use a sour solution. Repeat the procedure in identification and invent the word *sour* orally and, if appropriate for the group, in writing on the chalkboard. Repeat this procedure for all of the solutions.

Ask the children what kinds of foods they eat that are salty, sweet, sour, bitter, acid, or neutral. Have them cut out pictures from magazines for each category. Discuss their lunch in school and visit the cafeteria to observe the foods and note which category each food is in.

Note: For older or less retarded children, you can show them that different places on the tongue react more strongly to certain tastes. Touch solutions to these four sensation areas of the tongue.

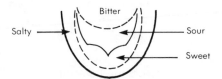

How Can Mentally Retarded Children Learn to Recognize Common Odors? (K–8)

Materials

Common odors in jars: onion, perfume, alcohol, pepper, cinnamon, peppermint, and so on.

Opening Question

Who can tell us what this odor (smell) is?

Some Possible Activities

Have the children smell a familiar odor (peppermint) by bringing the jar at least one foot below their noses and raising it slowly until they can smell it. (This avoids overwhelming the child with the odor and with some odors that might injure the child's sensitive nose.) *Note:* At first, for some mentally retarded children, it is best to help the children learn to recognize various odors by presenting the smell with the appropriate label, having them see the material, and then asking them to discriminate among various odors while blindfolded.

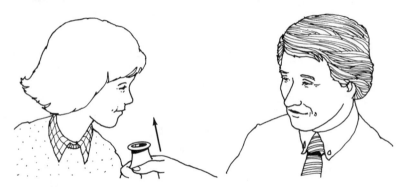

Label the odors either before or after identification, depending upon the children's level. Use words both orally and written for the names of odors as appropriate. Have the children identify odors in their homes, school, and outdoors. Have them cut pictures from magazines for common odors and label them: gasoline, flowers, paint, smoke, etc. Have the children identify odors they like and dislike. Stress that some odors are dangerous, such as gas and smoke.

CHILDREN WITH VISUAL PERCEPTION PROBLEMS[2]

Observing Properties of Leaves (K–3)

Materials

Variety of leaves (maple, oak, elm, birch, etc.)

---

[2] The authors are indebted to the following article and others in the *Science and Children* issue devoted to "Science for the Handicapped": Marlene Thier, "Utilizing Science Experiences for Developing Perception Skills," *Science and Children* 13, no. 6 (March 1976), 39–40.

Opening Question

What do you notice about the shape of this leaf?
Have each child look at a maple leaf.

ASK:
What is this?
Where do you think it came from?
How many points does it have?
What color is it?
How many large lines (veins) are there coming from the stem?

Let the child experience the leaf through sensory activities, that is, feeling with hand, against cheek, smelling it, and crushing it.
What does the smell make you think of?
How else would you describe the leaf?
Ask the children to think of other properties. Invent the word *property* for the children to refer to the leaf's attributes. Introduce another species of leaf.

ASK:
How are the leaves alike? Different?
What properties are the same?
What properties are different?

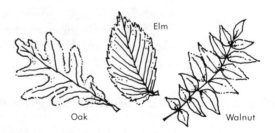

Comparing Properties of Shells or Buttons and Classifying Them (K–3)

Materials

Assortment of shells or buttons

Some Possible
Activities

Give each child a handful of shells or buttons.

ASK:

How are these things alike?
How are they different?
Group them together by the same property.
Which properties might you use?

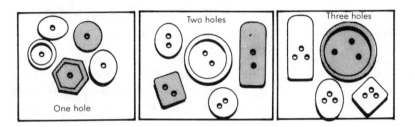

Let the children group them.

ASK:

How can you group the buttons using a different property?

Note: In this activity the child not only makes the visual discriminations, but acts upon them.

Using Plants to Teach Visual Sequencing (K–3)

Materials

Some Possible
Activities

Milk cartons, soil, pea seeds, chart paper

Have each child plant a pea in a milk carton. Make certain the children keep the soil moist, and have a time each day when they observe the plant and record their observations. Mark on your chart any changes that take place each day. As soon as germination takes place and plants break through the soil, set up a chart for the children to record the growth of each of their plants. They can measure plant height using gummed paper to show the various stages of growth over a six-week period, like this.

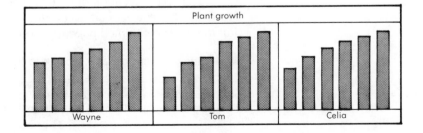

When working with younger children, plant an additional seed each week so they can see plants ranging in growth from one to six weeks, to help them with visual sequencing. They begin to observe a natural phenomenon and learn to record small changes over a period of time and in a sequenced progression—something they need to know.

Learning Relative Position and Motion (K–6)[3]

Materials

Mr. O for each child, white pipe cleaners, gummed white dots, blocks

Some Possible Activities

Children with perceptual problems usually have poor directionality concepts. "Mr. O" from the SCIIS Relative Position and Motion unit can help these children with learning position in space, relative position of the child in the environment, directionality, and figure-ground relationships.

Here is Mr. O. He sees things only from his point of view.

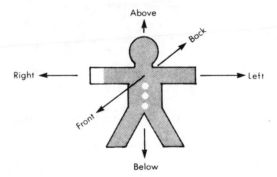

Cut out a Mr. O for each child. For younger children, after introducing Mr. O, play a game to familiarize them with his parts and invent words for directions in relation to him, as shown on the Mr. O sketch above. Younger children can also hang Mr. O around their necks at this point and you can point these things out to them:

Mr. O's right hand is white.
Put a white pipe cleaner around your right hand.
Mr. O has three white buttons on the front of him.
Put three white gummed paper dots on the front of you.

Now ask the children to place a block to the right of Mr. O.

---

[3] For a detailed description of Mr. O, see Robert Karplus et al., *Relative Position and Motion (Level 4),* Teacher's Guide SCIIS (Chicago: Rand McNally & Co., 1978), pp. 29–39.

ASK:

Where is the block in relation to Mr. O?
Where is the block in relation to you?
Is it near or far?

Do the same with the left side, in front of, in back of, above, and below using only one variable at a time. Gradually build to more than one variable.

Once the child begins to understand this use of Mr. O, take Mr. O from around the child's neck and turn Mr. O to face him or her.

ASK:

Where is Mr. O's hand now in relation to yours?

Place the block to the right, left, front, and back of Mr. O, and ask the child to report the position relative first to Mr. O and then to himself or herself.

Note: Children become aware of changes needed in describing directionality from a non-ego-centered frame. They begin to develop direction giving through awareness of relative position in space and figure-ground relationships. Children with visual perception handicaps have great difficulty with this task and need the systematic help shown here.

Outside-the-Classroom Walk to Develop Visual Scrutiny and Analysis (K–6)

Materials

Small envelopes or plastic bags, paper, pencils

Some Possible Activities

Select a site outside your classroom where you and your students can take a walk. Before going, instruct the children to observe, record, or collect the following. Task cards, 3″ × 5″ index cards, can be used to write down what the children will look for.

A sample of five different colors of any *natural* object that has fallen to the ground (caution children not to pick anything from living organisms)

Places (to be listed on their recording sheets) where they saw
  a. 3 different colors on the same plant
  b. 5 different shades of any one color (green, for instance) along the path
  c. 6 different textures on living organisms
  d. as many different colors as they can find

Samples of evidence that animals have inhabited the environment
Samples of dead insects
Samples of evidence that people have been in the area
Samples of different kinds of seeds in the area
Other samples that are applicable to your outdoor site

Have the children place their samples in small envelopes, plastic bags, or other suitable containers. With younger children or children who have severe visual perception handicaps, it is best to use one of the activities at a time, so they focus on one variable in their environment and filter out distractions. The activities also are progressive, moving from observing many different plants (looking at plants and finding colors) to finding the same variable on only one plant (how many different colors on one plant).

Later, in the classroom discussions, help the children describe their samples and share them with their classmates. Further activities in pasting samples on paper, writing descriptive words for each object, and talking about their findings aid children with visual perception handicaps in developing skills they will need for further exploration of their environments and for reading, writing, and spelling.

EMOTIONALLY HANDICAPPED CHILDREN

Learning about Our Environment by Touching (K–6)

Materials
Paper, crayons, chalk, soft pencils, tin foil

Opening Question
How can our fingertips give us different kinds of information than our eyes?

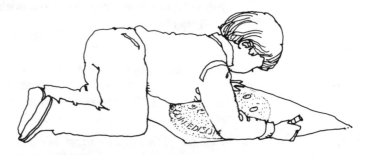

Some Possible Activities
Direct contact and the understanding and mastery of everyday living experiences under a sensitive teacher's guidance can produce an extensive and exciting learning environment for the emotionally handicapped child. One such activity can be a tactile experience. Take your students (with assistance from parents) on a walk around the school. Have the children select surfaces and have them do rubbings of those surfaces using the materials listed above. In urban areas they can do rubbings of sidewalks, manhole covers, grates, signs, and fences. The rubbings can be used to create texture panels and are also effective when they are individually matted and mounted. You might also attempt to get your students to talk about how the objects felt, whether they were rough, smooth, soft, hard, wet, or dry.

You can find many more activities for emotionally handicapped children in this practical book: *An Outdoor Education Guide for Urban Teachers of the Emotionally Handicapped* (Proceedings), presented by the State University of New York State Education Department Division for Handicapped Children and the Division of Health, Physical Education and Recreation, in co-sponsorship with State University College of Arts and Science at Plattsburgh and Clinton, Essex, Warren, and Washington Counties BOCES, Special Study Institute, Funded Through: PL 91–230, June 1974.

Learning about Our Environment by Listening and Moving (K–6)

Materials

A walking trip in the community

Opening Questions

What people-made sights and sounds can you identify?
How can you use your body to reproduce the sights and sounds?

Some Possible Activities

Sitting or working in a confined space (a desk and chair, for instance) makes static learning experiences This is especially true for emotionally handicapped children. They need to stretch and expand their bodies and minds, probably more than other children. These children can also begin to feel the same freedom of clear movement outside as they would in a gymnasium. Take them into the community and ask them to identify these people-made sights and sounds.

Taxi cabs	Ambulances
Cars	Fire engines
Fire alarms	Construction machines
Buses	Trucks
Airplanes	Motorcycles
Helicopters	Air hammers

ASK:

What are the sounds of each vehicle?

*How can you show the intensity and rhythm of each one with
  your body?*

How is the fire engine sound different from the ambulance sound?

Show us the differences with your movements.

*Would you move fast, slow, or jerky if you sounded like an air-
  plane? A dump truck?*

How are car horn sounds different? Make the sounds to show us.

*How do various sounds make you feel? Happy? Sad? Show us by
  your movements.*

Imitate with your body a vechicle starting and stopping.

HEARING IMPAIRED CHILDREN

There are many benefits for hearing impaired children in the regular
classroom, if they are about the same chronological and mental age,
and if there is an attempt to individualize instruction.

All of the guided discovery science activities described for other
handicapped or disabled children are applicable for the hearing-
handicapped, as are the guided discovery activities in sections 1
through 3, when you use these minimal adaptions of your regular
classroom procedure.

1. Seat the children where they can see your lip movements easily.
   Avoid seating them facing bright lights or windows.
2. Speak naturally, in complete grammatical sentences. Do not
   overemphasize lip movements or slow your rate of speech. Do
   not speak too loudly, especially if the child is wearing a hearing
   aid.
3. Avoid visual distractions such as excessive make-up and jewelry
   that would draw attention away from your lips.
4. Do not stand with your back to a window or bright light source.
   This throws your face in a shadow and makes speech reading
   difficult.
5. Try not to move around the room while speaking or to talk while
   writing on the board. If possible, use an overhead projector,
   which allows you to speak and write while keeping eye contact
   with the children.
6. During class discussions encourage hearing-handicapped children
   to face the speaker. Allow them to move around the room if
   necessary to get a better view.
7. In some cases, a manual interpreter will be assigned to the child.
   Allow the interpreter and child to select the most favorable seating arrangements. The manual interpreter should interpret every-

thing said in the classroom as precisely as possible. The interpreter may also be asked to interpret the child's oral or signed responses to the teacher and class. Interpreters are not tutors or classroom aides, but rather professional personnel who are facilitators of classroom communication.

8. When possible, write assignments and directions on the chalkboard or distribute mimeographed directions to the class. If assignments are given orally, a hearing student may be asked to take notes for the hearing-handicapped child.

9. Ask handicapped children to repeat or explain class material to make sure they have understood it. Embarrassed by their handicaps, hearing-impaired children might learn to nod affirmatively when asked if they understood, even though they may not have understood the instructions at all.

10. If a child has a hearing aid, familiarize yourself with its operation and ask the child or the child's special teacher to demonstrate it to the class. The child should assume responsibility for the care of the aid.

11. Maintain close contact with the other professional personnel who have responsibility for the child's education. If possible, regularly exchange visits with the special class teacher or therapist to observe the child in other educational settings.[4]

---

[4] Adapted from Haring, *Behavior of Exceptional Children,* 318–319.

SECTION 5

Piagetian Types of Guided Discovery Activities

Outlined below are a few special Piagetian types of activities to help you see how Piaget's theory may be applied to the different elementary school levels. These activities are outlined under specific operational cognitive abilities such as classification and conservation to show you how to take an operation and devise activities to involve children in these processes. Many of the other activities in this discovery activities section are also Piagetian in design but are not organized around specific operations as these Piagetian activities are. To get more ideas for activities, look at the Piagetian interviews in chapter 2. These interviews may also be given as activities. You should realize, however, that perhaps one-half or more of your students may not attain the tasks correctly. If this happens, the children who did not achieve them need further involvement with similar experiences. The children who do not achieve the tasks should *not* be told they failed. Piaget stated that the children themselves will know when they get the tasks cor-

rect. He believed, for example, that appropriate reinforcements for physical knowledge can come only from the objects themselves.

These activities are not included specifically to teach some operation but to demonstrate how children might be involved in physical experiences relative to their approximate development.

Each child will get out of the activity what he or she is cognitively ready to assimilate. The suggested questions are provided to illustrate how you *might* interact with children to determine what they are focusing on and how they reason. Practice in giving these activities should sensitize you to listening better to children and learning how to intervene with questions to cause them to think about what they are doing. Learning this style of teaching should help you to develop better the children's thinking and science knowledge.

Chapter 2 also describes activities involving class inclusion, conservation, ordering, and reversibility.

Class Inclusion: Do Children Know That Subclasses Are Included in a Major Class? (Ages 6–7)

1. Show several pictures of plants and animals.

   ASK:
   How many plants are there?
   How many animals are there?
   Are there more animals than plants?
   Are there more living things than animals?

2. Invite students to collect pictures of animals that move fast and slow, for example, a fly or rabbit and a turtle or a snail. Try to get more examples of fast animals than slow ones. Place the pictures of the fast and slow ones on the tackboard.

Which moves faster?

   ASK:
   What are all the pictures of?
   How many slow animals are there?
   Are there more fast animals than slow animals?

DISCUSSION:

Class inclusion is a very important operational ability. It is a good indicator that a student is developing representational thought, which is essential in using symbols such as letters of the alphabet. A child that has difficulty with class inclusion probably has problems with reading.

Spatial Relations (Ages 6–7)

1. Give students pieces of straw and ask them to construct the diamond shape as best they can. Their construction should be accurate, with the points at the top and bottom.

2. Ask children to duplicate the following:

DISCUSSION:
If they do not duplicate objects to the correct shape or size, they do not have good geometrical spatial conceptualization.

Also have students read words with letter combinations (words) such as "park," "bath," "dad," "quiet," "man," and "woman." If they do not perform well on these tasks and the letter discrimination, involve them with activities found in the Elementary Science Unit: Attribute Games and Problems, Webster Division, McGraw-Hill, 1974, or Material Objects Unit SCIS II, Rand McNally, 1976. Both of these units involve activities to help students discriminate better and develop class inclusion.

Ordering: Placing Objects in Order (Ages 6–8)

Give the children ten cards showing different animals. Each drawing should be larger than the previous one. Tell them: "Place the animals in order. Start with the smallest. Number the animals in order." Have the children check their answers with the other children. Note if they seem to order mainly by trial and error or have some organized procedure for doing this. If the students do this well, you may want to give them four more pictures that fit in between these ten animal sizes. Have them place these four where they think they belong.

DISCUSSION:
If they do this well, they probably are able to order relatively well.

Associativity: Realize That It Does Not Matter How You Arrange Things; the Number or Area Will Remain the Same (Ages 6–8)

1. Place ten counters, blocks, or buttons in a straight line and have students count them. Then move the counters to form a circle.

ASK:
Are there more, fewer, or the same number of counters now as when they were in a straight line?
How would you prove you are right?

Note that this activity is also related to conservation of substance and number, but here you are trying to find out if students know that reorganizing the counters doesn't change their number.

2. Invite students to count counters in two directions, for example, from left to right and then right to left, to see if they get the same number. Have them count two groups of objects, for example, three and two, and then count all of them to see what number they get. Then have them count first the group of two and then three to see what they get.

DISCUSSION:

If they have associativity, they will realize that three and two equals five objects and that two and three equals five objects.

One-to-One Correspondence (Ages 6–8)

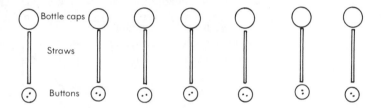

Obtain five bottle caps, buttons, straws, or any other type of marker that you want to use. Have the students line up the buttons in a row and then do the same with the bottle caps directly across from the buttons.

ASK:

Are there more, fewer, or the same number of buttons as bottle caps?

Then move the buttons so they are spread out, but do not move the bottle caps.

ASK:

Are there now more, fewer, or the same number of buttons as bottle caps?
Why?

If the children think there are more buttons than bottle caps,

ASK:

Please count them. Now what do you think?

If they still do not realize that each button corresponds with each bottle cap, have them connect each pair by placing a straw between them.

ASK:

Are there more, fewer or the same number of buttons as bottle caps now?

DISCUSSION:

If students still do not conceptualize one-to-one correspondence, have them place the materials in a box to be collected. Repeat this activity several times using different markers until the children do correspond.

Coordinating Systems—Horizontal and Vertical (Ages 6–12)

This is an exercise in reproducing and estimating the length of a line. Give the children a meter stick, compass, string, small triangle that has one angle similar to the one shown, rulers, and paper strips.

ASK:

What is the length of the line?

Draw a picture just like this one.

Remove the picture from the students' vision. Tell them that they may refer to it if necessary.

DISCUSSION:

Children of	6–7	Usually use no measurement.
	7–8	Measure the length of the lines.
	9–10	Superimpose ◺ to measure angle.
	10–12	Begin to use measurement to accurately reproduce the angle.

Children unable to coordinate the horizontal and vertical as presented here may have problems in geometry and in understanding certain science concepts, particularly in geology and astronomy.

Conservation by Length (Ages 7–8)

Take two strips of paper of the same length.

ASK:

Are these strips just as long as each other?

Cut one of the strips and combine them as shown on the right in the diagram. Tell the students that you have a rabbit that is going to move along the two paper paths.

ASK:

Would the rabbit make just as many hops on each path or would it make more or fewer hops on one of the paths?
Why do you think so?

If the children think the uncut paper is longer, they do not conserve length and will have difficulty understanding units and measurement.

Conservation of Length (Ages 7–8)

Draw the following diagrams of the snakes.

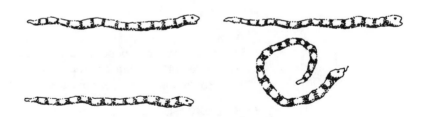

ASK:

What do you notice about the lengths of the snakes on the left?
In the diagram on the right, is the coiled snake longer, shorter, or the same length as the other snake?

Take a rope and lay it out flat. Then twirl it.

ASK:

Is the rope now longer, shorter, or the same length as when it was straight?

DISCUSSION:

Ask students to measure the rope. But even if they measure it and do not conserve length, they will still think the curled rope is shorter.

Conservation of Area (Ages 7–8)

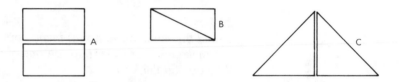

Cut a piece of paper into two rectangles (A).

ASK:

Do these two pieces of paper cover the same amount of table?

Cut another piece of paper of the same size diagonally as shown in B and arrange as shown in C.

ASK:

Do the cut pieces of paper in C cover as much as the paper in A?
Why do you think your answer is correct?
How could you prove your answer is right?

DISCUSSION:

If the students suggest that C covers as much as A, this indicates they conserve area. They should then suggest that if the two pieces of paper were combined together as in A, they would be the same. This indicates that they are capable of *reversing* and establishing *logical necessity*. This also means that they reason; since nothing has been taken away, the paper covers as much. Reversibility and logical necessity are intrinsically involved in conservation tasks.

Ascending a Class Hierarchy (Ages 7–8)

Prepare 10 pictures of animals. Include some birds, fish, and mammals.

ASK:
Please group these animals any way you want
How did you group them? Why did you group them that way?
Which of these groups were fish?
Which of these groups were birds?
Which of these groups were mammals?
Is there some way we can place all of them in one group?
What would the group be? Why?
Are birds animals?
Are fish animals?
Are hairy animals (mammals) animals?

DISCUSSION:
If the children realize on their own that all of these things are animals and that the subgroups of birds, fish, and mammals can be grouped under animals, they are able to ascend a classification hierarchy.

Time—Understanding Sequence and Duration (Ages 7–8)

Time requires the coordination of motions. Set up the apparatus as shown in the diagram.

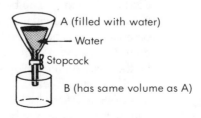

Give a sheet with several sketches of the apparatus to the children but show no water in either the top or bottom container. Have the children note, in the demonstration, the water level in A. Let a little water flow from A to B.

ASK:
Please draw where the water is now in A and B.

Repeat this six or seven times, varying the amount of water you let through the stopclock.

ASK:
Please number your drawings in order in the margin.

You determine whether the order is correct.

ASK:
Please cut off the numbers indicating the order.
Please cut the paper into strips so that each separate drawing is on its own strip.
Please shuffle these and then arrange them in their proper order.
When water A was at (pick a certain level), where was B?
Which drawing did you make at B that equals the one in A?
Did the time it took for the water to leave A equal the time it took to fill B?
Does the liquid take as much time to go from this level of A (point to one level change) as it does to go from here to here in B?

DISCUSSION:
Time is a relatively complex thing for primary school children to learn. To comprehend it, they have to understand that motion is involved with time. They also have to understand that in time, things follow a sequence, have a duration, occur in a succession, and are simultaneous. When water goes from A to B, all of these things occur.

To read time on a clock, children, furthermore, must be able to order, know numbers, and know what units are. They also must understand that they may be repetitive and follow in succession in a linear as well as a circular manner as in seconds, minutes, and hours on a clock. Teachers may be fooled into thinking some young children understand time if they can read a digital clock. This may not be the case. All the children may be doing is mouthing a sequence of numbers without really understanding their relationship to the duration of time. After all, 4:30 has quite a different meaning from 430, although the same numbers are used.

Spatial Relations (Ages 7–8)

Ask the children to draw a mountain and place trees on it.

DISCUSSION:

If they have good spatial relations, they will draw the trees perpendicular to the mountain.

Constructing a Set Containing a Single Element (Ages 7–9)

Show six triangles. Let five triangles be all red and the sixth one yellow. On the back of the yellow one, make an X. Show the children both sides of the triangles. Then place all of the triangles color side up with no markings.

ASK:

Which one of these objects is entirely different from the others?
What makes it different?
How could we group all of these objects?

DISCUSSION:

If students can identify the triangle with the X on the back as being different, they are able to establish a set as having a single element.

Making All-and-Some Relationships: Realize that Some Objects (Those in the Subset) Are Also Included in the Group Referring to All of Them (the Set) (Ages 7–9)

Cut triangular, circular, and rectangular shapes out of the colored paper.

ASK:

Are all of the squares red?
What color are all of the circles?
What color are the triangles?
Are all of the triangles red triangles?

Invite the students to group all of the triangles together.

ASK:

Are all of these things triangles?
Are some of these triangles green?
Are all of these triangles green?

DISCUSSION:

Some children in this age group have difficulty differentiating between *some* and *all* because they do not class-include well. The advent of this ability indicates that the children are beginning to develop the class-inclusion operation. They still may not, however, understand that all dogs are also animals.

Reordering (Ages 8–10)

Cut ten straws so they vary from short to tall. Prepare ten pictures of trees ordered in a similar way.
Ask the children to order the straws from short to tall and place the trees in the opposite order (tall to short next to them). One study found that only about 10 percent of second graders could do this.

DISCUSSION:

Reordering means to be able to order in different ways, foward as well as backward. This activity requires children to order in each way as well as to do one-to-one correspondence. For example, for every large tree, there is a small straw.

Spatial Reasoning (Ages 8–10)

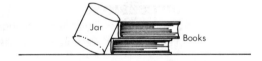

Show a tipped bottle and tell the children the bottle is supposed to be one-half filled with water.

ASK:

Please draw how you think the water will look in the jar.

After they have finished their drawing, take a bottle and fill it one-half full of water. Have them check their drawings with what they saw.

DISCUSSION:

Children do not have a good concept of coordinates. Therefore, they will draw the water oriented to the sides or bottom of the jar rather than to the table it is sitting on.

Unit Repetition or Iteration (Ages 7–10)

In this exercise, students measure a large area by using a small unit over and over again. Cut a rectangle as shown in A. Then cut a triangle as shown with one side 2 cm long.

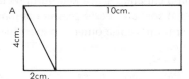

ASK:

How would you use triangle B to determine the area in A?
Why do you think your response is correct?

DISCUSSION:

If students achieve the task, this shows they can use units to determine area by superimposition. In this case, they superimpose the small triangle on the rectangle and then total the number of triangles used to state the area in triangles. More advanced students may be able to determine the area mathematically.

Ordering by Weight (Ages 9–10)

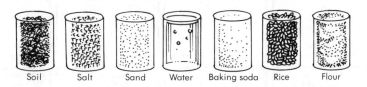

Try to obtain several (six or more) different pieces of metal of the same volume or take medicine vials or empty 35 mm film containers of the same volume and fill them with different kinds of materials, for example, salt, sand, soil, water, baking soda, rice, flour, and so on.

ASK:

Please place these things in order by weight.

Later have them weigh the objects and order them.

ASK:

How good were your estimations?

DISCUSSION:

Children may have difficulty doing this for as long as two years after they are able to order by length or height.

Concept of a Null Class (Ages 9–11)

Cut 12 triangular, circular, and rectangular shapes from colored paper. Draw and paste pictures of plants, animals, or houses on 9 of them. Leave the other 3 papers blank.

ASK:

Please group these things any way you wish.

They should now place them in only two groups: blank and nonblank.

DISCUSSION:

Children up to age 11 have difficulty realizing the existence of a null set. This may be attributed to their concrete thinking; a null set requires abstract reasoning.

Descending a Classification Hierarchy (Ages 9–11)

Insure that the students know the characteristics of mammals. Prepare ten pictures of mammals, birds, and other animals. Include several dogs as well as other mammals and ducks as well as other birds.

ASK:

Please group these animals any way you like. What groups did
*   you get?*
How many mammals did you get?
How many birds did you get?
Is there any way you can divide your mammal group? Why?
Is there any way you can change your bird group?
What group of animals do dogs belong to?
What group of animals do ducks belong to?

What group do mammals belong to?
What group do birds belong to?

Ask the students to mix all of the pictures again, make a few groups, and use these groups to try to make more subgroups.

ASK:
How did you group your animals?
Why did you group them that way?

DISCUSSION:
If students go from animals to mammals and birds and then to dogs and ducks, they have indicated they can descend a classification hierarchy.

Conservation of Weight (Ages 9–12)

Obtain some clay. Have students prepare two round balls that weigh the same. They can check their weight by using a balance.

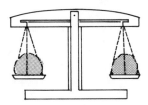

ASK:
Please make one of your clay balls into a hamburger shape.
Will your clay now weigh more, less, or the same amount as before?
How could you tell?

Have the students weigh their clay and find out.

ASK:
What did you find out?
Why do you think it weighs the same?
Is there some rule you can give about changing things and their weight?

DISCUSSION:
If they state that spreading things out changes the thickness but also increases the area covered, and that there is no loss in weight, they are giving a compensation type of justification. This means that the weight of the increased area compensates for the loss in weight in the

thick area. If they state that when you roll the ball up again, it will weigh the same, they are demonstrating reversibility. This means they can reverse their thought processes. Both reversibility and compensatory reasoning characterize concrete-operational thought.

Conservation of Displacement Volume (Ages 11 and older)

Obtain a graduate or use a jar. Fill it three-fourths full of water. Take a cube of clay and wrap a string around it so it can be lowered into the water. Place a rubber band around the graduate to estimate where the water will be when the clay is lowered into it. Lower the clay very slowly.

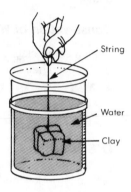

ASK:

How good was your estimate?

Move your rubber band so the top of it marks where the water is. Now take your clay out of the water. Cut it in half. Tie each half with string. Estimate where you think the water will be now when you lower these two halves into the water. Use a marking pencil to mark where you think it will be. Do not move your rubber band. Lower your two pieces of clay into the water slowly.

ASK:

What did you discover?
Can you give a rule for what you discovered?

DISCUSSION:

If the children explain that the volume of the two halves of clay is the same as the whole piece and that they displace the same amount of water, they are conserving displacement volume. It is the volume here, and what it displaces, that is important and not the weight.

Law of Buoyancy—Flotation (Ages 11 and older)

An object will float if its weight is less than that of an equal volume of water. The object will float above the water line when its weight displaces an equal amount of weight of water.

Tell the students that 1 ml of pure water weighs 1 gram. Have them make a small clay boat or make one out of a small milk carton and weigh the boat. Tell the students you have a rectangular barge that weighs 500 grams and has a volume of 1000 ml.

ASK:

How much water would it displace?
How far would it sink into the water? Why?

DISCUSSION:

If they suggest that it would sink about halfway in the water, they probably understand the concept of buoyancy and flotation. A further check would be to give them problems where odd numbers of weights and volumes are used for the barge. They should then estimate how many grams and milliliters of water their boat will displace. Have them obtain a large graduate or calibrated beaker and fill it three-fourths full with water, determine the amount of water in the container, and then place the boat in it.

ASK:

How far does the ship sink in the water?
Add a 10-gram weight and determine how high the water moves.

ASK:

How high would it move with a 20-gram weight? Why?

Conservation of Internal Volume (Ages 10–12)

Present students with 27 small cubes arranged to form a large cube. Tell the students that each cube represents a hollow room and all of the cubes have open doors between them. Inside the hollow rooms there is a butterfly that flies from room to room. These rooms can be rearranged by the owner since they are modules.

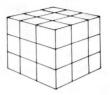

One day the owner has to move the modules to a different lot. She has to arrange the modules in a different way.

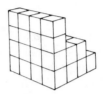

ASK:
Is there just as much, more, or less space inside now for the butterfly to fly? Why?
How would you prove it?
How could you use mathematics to prove it?

If they indicate that no rooms have been taken away or added, therefore, there is the same amount of interior, they are using logical necessity to justify their answer. A more sophisticated response showing higher cognitive abilities would be to demonstrate that the number of rooms is the same.

Spatial Relations (Ages 11–12)

The child realizes that the angle at which light or an object hits a surface or another object will be reflected at the same angle. In scientific terms: the angle of incidence equals the angle of reflection.

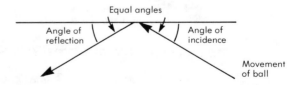

Give students a marble or ping-pong ball. Invite them to hit it against a wall.

ASK:

What kind of rule can you discover about how the ball bounces back?

DISCUSSION:

If they come up with an explanation that the ball seems to bounce from the wall as it goes in, they probably understand the rule.

Continuous Divisibility (Related to Concept of Infinity) (Ages 11–12)

Ask the students to divide a circle through its center as many times as possible and see if they keep at it for a while.

ASK:

How long could you keep on dividing the circle?

DISCUSSION:

If they come up with the idea that this could go on and on and on, they have grasped the basic concept of infinity and realize that some things, as in nature, can be continually divided, for example, the measurement of temperature, time, motion, and change. Consider whether the students understand the continuous possibility of divisibility.

ASK:

How long could you go on dividing a rod or line?

Spatial Relations (Ages 11 and older)

Show one surface of a cube.

ASK:

How many edges can't you see?

DISCUSSION:

Most students have difficulty perceiving the object from different viewpoints. Many adults have difficulty with this problem, too, and suggest numbers other than eight.

List of Appendices

APPENDIX A   Science Supplies, Equipment, and Materials Obtainable from Community Sources

This is only a partial list of places in the community that are possible sources of items for a science program in the elementary school. Other sources that should not be overlooked are local factories, the janitor of the school, the school cafeteria, radio and television repair shops, florists' shops, the other teachers in the school, the junior and senior high school science teachers, and so on. The materials are there; it just takes a little looking.

There are times, though, when in spite of the most careful searching, certain pieces of equipment or supplies are not obtainable from local sources; there are also many things that schools should buy from scientific supply houses. A partial list of some of the selected, reliable, scientific supply houses serving elementary schools is given in appendix C.

Dime Store or
Department Store
balloons
balls
candles
compasses (magnetic)
cotton (absorbent)
flashlights
food coloring
glues and paste
inks
magnifying glasses
marbles
mechanical toys
mirrors
mousetraps
paperbook matches
scissors
sponges
thermometers

Drugstore
adhesive tape
alcohol (rubbing)
bottles
cigar boxes
cold cream
corks
cotton
dilute acids, preferably
    1–5%
dilute H_2O_2 (1½%)
forceps

heat-resistant nursing bottles
limewater
medicine droppers
pipe cleaners
rubber stoppers
soda bicarbonate
spatulas
straws
sulfur
tincture of iodine, diluted to
    straw color

Electrical Appliance Shop
bell wire
burned-out fuses and light
    bulbs
dry cells
electric fans
electric hot plates
flashlights
flashlight bulbs
friction tape
magnets (from old
    appliances)
soldering iron

Fabric Shop
cardboard tubes
cheesecloth
flannel
knitting needles
leather
needles

netting
silk thread
spools
scraps of different kinds of
    materials

Farm or Dairy
birds' nests
bottles
clay
containers
gravel
hay or straw
humus
insects
leaves
lodestone
loam
rocks
sand
seeds

Fire Department
samples of material used to
    extinguish various types of
    fire
water pumping equipment

Garden Supply Store
bulbs (tulips, etc.)
fertilizers
flower pots
garden hose
garden twine

growing plants
labels
lime
seed catalogs
seeds
sprinkling cans
spray guns
trowels and other garden
   tools

Gas Station

ball bearings
cans
copper tubing
gears
gear transmissions
grease
inner tubes
jacks
maps
pulleys
tools
valves from tires
wheels

Grocery Store

ammonia
baking soda
borax
candles
cellophane
clothespins
cornstarch
corrugated cardboard boxes
fruits
paper bags
paraffin
plastic wrapping
salt
sponges
sugar
tinfoil
vegetables
vinegar

wax
waxed paper

Hardware Store

brace and bits
cement
chisels
clocks
dry-cell batteries
electric push buttons, lamps,
   and sockets
extension cords
files
flashlights
fruit jars
glass cutters
glass funnels
glass friction rods
glass tubing
hammers
hard rubber rods
insulated copper wire
lamp chimneys
metal and metal scraps
nails
nuts and bolts
paints and varnishes
plaster of paris
pulleys
sandpaper
saws
scales
scrap lumber
screening
screwdrivers
screws
steel wool
thermometers (indoor and
   outdoor)
3–6 volt toy electric motors
tin snips
turpentine
wheelbarrow
window glass (broken pieces
   will do)

wire
yardsticks

Machine Shop

ball bearings
iron filings
iron rods
magnets
nuts and bolts
screws
scrap metals
wire

Medical and Dental Offices and Hospitals

corks
flasks
funnels
glass tubing
hard lenses
litmus paper
microscopes
models, such as teeth
rubber sheeting
rubber tubing
rubber stoppers
test tubes
test tube holders
thermometers
tongue depressors

Music Shop

broken string and drum
   heads
musical instruments
pitch pipes
tuning forks

Pet Shop

air pumps
animal cages
aquariums
ant houses
cages

fish	*Restaurant, Diner, or Fast*	five-gallon cans (oil)
insects	*Food Outlet*	food coloring
nets (butterfly, fish, etc.)	bones (chicken, etc.)	gallon jars (wide-mouthed,
plastic tubing	bottles	pickles, mayonnaise, etc.)
strainers	cans (coffee, 5 gallons)	gallon jugs (vinegar)
terrariums	drums (ice cream)	pie tins

For additional sources of common, easily obtained supplies and apparatus suitable for your elementary school science program, see Alfred DeVito and Gerald H. Krockover, "Gear to Gather For the Well-Appointed Science Classroom," in NSTA *Directory of Science Education Suppliers* (Washington, DC: National Science Teachers Association, 1983), 11–12.

APPENDIX B   Free and Inexpensive Materials for Use in the Elementary Science Classroom*

1. **"Ad-vailables."** *Science and Children* magazine. The National Science Teachers Association, 1742 Connecticut Ave., NW, Washington, DC 20009. $20/8 issues.
   Regular column describes free or low cost supplementary materials, publications, and events of interest to elementary, middle, and junior high school science teachers.

2. **Educators Guide to Free Audio and Visual Materials.** James L. Berger and Walter A. Wittich, eds. Educators Progress Service, 214 Center St., Randolph, WI 53956. 1980. $13.50.
   Subject, title, and distributor are included in this annotated listing of videotapes, audiotapes, scripts, and audiodiscs. (Revised yearly.)

3. **Free Stuff for Kids.** Meadowbrook Press, 18318 Minnetonka Blvd., Deephaven, MN 55391.
   Materials on many topics, including science. Single copy free. (Revised yearly.)

4. **Consumer Information Catalog.** Consumer Information Center, Pueblo, CO 81009.
   Describes selected federal publications. Most are free or under $3. (Published quarterly.)

5. **Free for the Taking.** Joseph R. Cooke. Fleming H. Revell Co., 184 Central Ave., Old Tappan, NJ 07675. $7.95.
   Lists free materials on many science subjects.

6. **Educators Guide to Free Films.** John C. Diffor and Mary F. Horkheimer, eds. Educators Progress Service, 214 Center St., Randolph, WI 53956. $17.75.
   Describes films for educational and recreational use. Listed by subject, title, and distributor. (Revised yearly.)

7. **Educators Guide to Free Filmstrips.** John C. Diffor and Mary F. Horkheimer, eds. Educators Progress Service, 214 Center St., Randolph, WI 53956. $13.
   Comprehensive listing of filmstrips, slides, and transparencies. Listed by subject, title, and distributor. (Revised yearly.)

8. **Educational Media Yearbook.** Libraries Unlimited, Inc., P.O. Box 263, Littleton, CO 80160. $20.
   Contains a multimedia information section with an annotated listing of free materials. (Published alternate years.)

9. **FAA Film Catalog.** Federal Aviation Administration, 800 Independence Ave., SW, Washington, DC 20003. 1976.
   Lists over 75 films, filmstrips, and slides. Description, length, and date of film are included.

10. **Forest Service Films Available on Loan.** Contact your local U.S. Forest Service office. 1973.
    Provides a variety of color/sound films on many topics prepared by the U.S. Forest Service.

11. **Free and Inexpensive Learning Experiences.** 1220 Maple Ave., Los Angeles, CA 90015. $24 per year.
    Lists materials on a variety of topics including the environment and science.

12. **Free and Inexpensive Learning Materials.** Incentive Publications, P.O. Box 12522, Nashville, TN 37212. 1979. $4.95 plus $1 postage.
    Excellent coverage of free and inexpensive materials including science.

13. **Free! The Newsletter of Free Materials and Services.** Ken Haycock, ed. Dyad Services, London, Ontario, Canada. $10 per year.
    Annotated list of materials evaluated and recommended by teachers and librarians. (Bi-monthly.)

14. **Freebies: The Magazine with Something for Nothing.** P.O. Box 5797, Santa Barbara, CA 93108. $6/9 issues.
Contains information on how to utilize free and inexpensive materials and where to get them.

15. **Free Magazines for Teachers and Libraries.** Ken Haycock. Ontario Library Association, 2397 Bloor W. Toronto, Ontario, Canada. 1977.
International sources of free magazines indexed by subject and title.

16. **Index to Free Educational Materials/ Multimedia.** National Information Center for Educational Media, University of Southern California, Los Angeles, CA 90007. 1977. $26.50.
More than 20,000 titles indexed by subject and producer/distributor.

17. **Educators Index of Free Materials.** Linda Keenen and Wayne J. Krepel, eds. Educators Progress Service, 214 Center St., Randolph, WI 53956. 1980. $39.50.
Annotated listing of free materials including science topics. (Revised yearly.)

18. **Bibliography of Materials for Environmental Education.** Wisconsin Vocational Studies Center, University of Wisconsin, 1025 West Johnson St., Madison, WI 53706.
Bibliography of environmental education materials. Free loan materials included.

19. **"Materials/Information Center."** *Instructor* magazine, 757 Third Ave., New York, NY 10017. $16.
Lists catalogs and other resources offered by advertisers in the current issue.

20. **NWF Conservation Education Catalog.** National Wildlife Federation, 1412 Sixteenth St., NW, Washington, DC 20036. 1981. Free.
Lists materials available on conservation of natural resources.

21. **Free and Inexpensive Materials in Environmental Science and Related Disciplines.** Ann Hope Ruzow. Vance Bibliographies, P.O. Box 229, Monticello, IL 61856. 1978. $2.50.
Tabulates sources of materials in environmental sciences.

22. **Educators Guide to Free Science Materials.** Mary H. Saterstrom and John W. Renner, eds. Educators Progress Service, 214 Center St., Randolph, WI 53956. 1980. $15.50.
Annotated listing of audiovisual and science curriculum enrichment aids. (Revised yearly.)

23. **Science and Technology Programs.** Available from local Bell Telephone Company. 1980.
Lists free science films available from Bell Telephone Co.

24. **Selected U.S. Government Publications.** Superintendent of Documents, U.S. Government Printing Office, Washington, DC 20402.
Lists selected government publications, many of which apply to science. (Monthly.)

25. **Free Magazines for Libraries.** Adeline Mercer Smith. McFarland and Co., Inc., P.O. Box 611, Jefferson, NC 28640. 1980. $16.95.
Sources of free magazines, many of which deal with science subjects.

26. **Guide to Government Loan Films.** Daniel Sprecher, ed. Serina Press, 70 Kennedy St., Alexandria, VA 22305. 1978. $12.95.
Describes more than 3,000 16mm films available on loan in the U.S.

27. **Guide to Government Loan Films, Vol. 2.** Daniel Sprecher, ed. Serina Press, 70 Kennedy St., Alexandria, VA 22305. 1976. $9.95.
Lists films, filmstrips, and slides available on free loan from federal agencies.

28. **The Book of Free Books.** W. M. Tevarrow. Contemporary Books, Inc., 180

North Michigan Ave., Chicago, IL 60601. 1979.

Annotated selection of books on a variety of subjects including science. Book is out of print, but can be found in many university libraries.

---

*Note: Addresses (and prices) may change, so check sources in libraries or post offices for up-to-date information.

Source: Paula J. Zsiray and Stephen W. Zsiray, Jr., "Utilizing Free and Inexpensive Materials In The Science Classroom," *Science and Children,* 19, no. 5 (February 1982): 20–21.

APPENDIX C Selected Sources of Scientific Supplies, Models, Living Things, Kits, Computers, and Collections

Accept Science
P.O. Box 1444
Saginaw, MI 48605
(517) 799–8103

American Nuclear Products, Inc.
1232 E. Commercial
Springfield, MO 65803
(417) 869–4432

American Optical Instrument Div.
P.O. Box 123
Buffalo, NY 14240
(716) 891–3000

American Science Center/ Jerryco
601 Linden Pl.
Evanston, IL 60202
(312) 475–8440

Analytical Products, Inc.
P.O. Box 845
Belmont CA 94002
(415) 592–1400

Apple Computer, Inc.
20525 Mariani Ave.
Cupertino, CA 95014
(408) 996–1010

Bausch & Lomb
42 East Ave.
Rochester, NY 14603
(716) 338–6000

Bel-Art Products
6 Industrial Rd.
Pequannock, NJ 07440
(201) 694–0500

Carolina Biological Supply Co.
2700 York Road

Burlington, NC 27215
(919) 584–0381

Center for Multisensory Learning
Lawrence Hall of Science
University of California
Berkeley, CA 94720
(415) 642–8941

Central Scientific Co.
11222 Melrose Ave.
Franklin Park, IL 60131
(312) 451–0150

Chem Scientific, Inc.
67 Chapel St.
Newton, MA 02158
(617) 527–6626

Connecticut Valley Biological Supply Co., Inc.
82 Valley Rd.
Southampton, MA 01073
(413) 527–4030,
(800) 628–7748

Delta Education, Inc.
P.O. Box M
Nashua, NH 03061–6012
(800) 258–1302

Education Development Center
55 Chapel St.
Newton, MA 02160
(617) 969–7100

Educational Activities, Inc.
P.O. Box 392
Freeport, NY 11520
(800) 645–3739

Fisher Scientific Co., Educ. Div.
4901 W. Le Moyne Street

Chicago, IL 60651
(312) 378–7770;
(800) 621–4769

Frey Scientific Co.
905 Hickory Lane
Mansfield, OH 44905
(419) 589–9905

Hubbard Scientific
1946 Raymond Dr.
Northbrook, IL 60062
(800) 323–8368
(312) 272–7810

Ideal School Supply Co.
11000 S. Lavergne Avenue
Oak Lawn, IL 60453
(312) 415–0800

Lab-Aids, Inc.
P.O. Box 158
130 Wilbur Pl.
Bohemia, NY 11716
(516) 567–6120

LaPine Scientific Co.
6001 South Knox Avenue
Chicago, IL 60629–5496
(312) 735–4700

McKilligan Supply Corporation
435 Main Street
Johnson City, NY 13790
(607) 729–6511

NASCO
901 Janesville Avenue
Fort Atkinson, WI 53538
(414) 563–2446

Nasco West Inc.
P.O. Box 3837
Modesto, CA 95352
(209) 529–6957

Nova Scientific Corporation
P.O. Box 500
Burlington, NC 27215
(919) 229–0395;
(800) 334–1100

Sargent-Welch Scientific Co.
7300 N. Linder Avenue
Skokie, IL 60077
(312) 677–0600

Science Kit, Inc.
777 E. Park Drive
Tonawanda, NY 14150
(716) 874–6020

Turtox
5000 W. 128th Pl.
Chicago, IL 60658
(312) 371–5500

Ward's Natural Science Establishment, Inc.
P.O. Box 1712,
Rochester, NY 14603
(716) 467–8400

Wilkens-Anderson Co.
4525 W. Division St.
Chicago, IL 60651
(312) 384–4433

APPENDIX D   Noncommercial Sources and Containers for Living Things

Organisms	Noncommercial Source	Culture Containers
POND SNAILS	Fresh water ponds, creeks	Aquaria, large battery jars, gallon glass jars
LAND SNAILS	Mature hardwood forests: on rocks, fallen logs, damp foliage	Terraria, large battery jars
DAPHNIA	Freshwater ponds: at water's edge, and associated with algae	Gallon glass or plastic jars
ISOPODS AND CRICKETS	Under rocks, bricks, and boards that have lain on ground for some time; between grass and base of brick buildings.	Glass or plastic terraria, plastic sweater boxes (Provide vents in cover.)
MEALWORM BEETLES	Corn cribs, around granaries	Gallon glass jars with cheese cloth
FRUIT FLIES	Trap with bananas or apple slices. (Place fruit in a jar with a funnel for a top.)	Tall baby food jars, plastic vials (Punch hole in jar lids, cover with masking tape and then prick tiny holes in tape with a pin.)
WINGLESS PEA APHIDS*	Search on garden vegetables, e.g., English peas	On pea plants potted in plastic pots, milk cartons (Keep aphids in a large terrarium so they cannot wander to other plants in the school.)
GUPPIES	Obtain free from persons who raise guppies as a hobby. (They are usually glad to reduce population when they clean tanks.)	Aquaria, large battery jars
CHAMELEONS*	Dense foliage along river banks or railroad tracks (Catch with net or large tea strainer.)	Prepare cage from broken aquaria. (Broken glass can be replaced by taping cloth screening along sides.)
FROGS*	Along edges of ponds, ditches, creeks (Catch with large scoop net.)	Large plastic ice chest (Set near a sink so a constant water supply can be provided.)
CHLAMYDOMONAS AND EUGLENA	Freshwater pond	Gallon glass jars, aquaria, battery jars
ELODEA (ANARCHARIS)*	Ponds, creeks: usually along edge or in shallows	Aquaria, large battery jars
EELGRASS*	Wading zone of brackish water	Aquaria, large battery jars
DUCKWEED	Edge of ponds or fresh water swamps	Aquaria, large battery jars

APPENDIX D   Continued

Organisms	Noncommercial Source	Culture Containers
COLEUS AND GERANIUM	Persons who raise them (Start by rooting cuttings in 1 part sand, 1 part vermiculite, in plastic bags; keep moist.)	Clay pots, milk cartons, tin cans

*These species are difficult to obtain from their natural habitats. Unless you have a convenient source, it is better to buy them commercially. Try a local aquarium or pet shop.

Source: Carolyn H. Hampton and Carol D. Hampton, "The Establishment of a Life Science Center." Reproduced with permission by *Science and Children,* 15, no. 7 (April 1978): 9. Copyright 1978 by The National Science Teachers Association, 1742 Connecticut Avenue, N.W., Washington, DC, 20009.

For additional excellent articles on raising and using living things in elementary school classrooms, *see* Carolyn H. Hampton, et al., *Classroom Creature Culture: Algae to Anoles. A Collection from the Columns of Science and Children* (Washington, DC: National Science Teachers Association, 1986).

APPENDIX E   Food Requirements for Various Animals

Food and Water	Rabbits	Guinea Pigs	Hamsters	Mice	Rats
Daily					
pellets or grain	rabbit pellets: keep dish half full	corn, wheat, or oats	large dog pellets: one or two	canary seeds or oats	canary seeds or oats
green or leafy vegetables, lettuce, cabbage, and celery tops *or*	keep dish half full 4–5 leaves	2 leaves	1½ tablespoon 1 leaf	2 teaspoons ⅛–¼ leaf	3–4 teaspoons ¼ leaf
grass, plantain, lambs' quarters, clover, alfalfa *or*	2 handfuls	1 handful	½ handful	—	—
hay, if water is also given					
carrots	2 medium	1 medium			
Twice a week					
apple (medium)	½ apple	¼ apple	⅛ apple	½ core and seeds	1 core
iodized salt (if not contained in pellets)	or salt block	sprinkle over lettuce or greens			
corn, canned or fresh, once or twice a week	½ ear	¼ ear	1 tablespoon ⅓ ear	¼ tablespoon or end of ear	½ tablespoon or end of ear
water	should always be available		necessary only if lettuce or greens are not provided		

Food and Water	Water Turtles	Land Turtles	Small Turtles
Daily			
worms or night crawlers or	1 or 2	1 or 2	¼ inch of tiny earthworm
tubifex or blood worms and/or			enough to cover ½ area of a dime
raw chopped beef or meat and fish-flavored dog or cat food	½ teaspoon	½ teaspoon	
fresh fruit and vegetables		¼ leaf lettuce or 6–10 berries or 1–2 slices peach, apple, tomato, melon or 1 tablespoon corn, peas, beans	
dry ant eggs, insects, or other commercial turtle food			1 small pinch
water	¾ of container	always available at room temperature; should be ample for swimming and submersion large enough for shell	half to ¾ of container

APPENDIX E   Continued

Food and Water Plants (for Fish)	Goldfish	Guppies
Daily dry commercial food	1 small pinch	1 very small pinch; medium size food for adults; fine size food for babies
Twice a week shrimp—dry—or another kind of dry fish food	4 shrimp pellets or 1 small pinch	dry shrimp food or other dry food: 1 very small pinch
Two or three times a week tubifex worms	enough to cover ½ area of a dime	enough to cover ⅛ area of a dime
Add enough "conditioned" water to keep tank at required level	allow one gallon per inch of fish; add water of same temperature as that in tank —at least 65°F	all ¼–½ gallon per adult fish; add water of same temperature as that in tank —70°–80°F
Plants: cabomba, anarcharis, etc.	should always	be available

	Newts	Frogs
Daily small earthworms or mealworms	1–2 worms	2–3 worms
or tubifex worms	enough to cover ½ area of a dime	enough to cover ¾ area of a dime
or raw chopped beef	enough to cover a dime	enough to cover a dime
water	should always be available at same temperature as that in tank or at room temperature	

Source: Grace K. Pratt, *How to . . . Care for Living Things in the Classroom* (Washington, DC: National Science Teachers Association, 1965), 9.

APPENDIX F   Selected Professional References for the Teacher or School Library

Professional Books in Elementary School Science

Abruscato, Joseph. *Teaching Children Science.* Englewood Cliffs, NJ: Prentice-Hall, 1982.

_____, and Hassard, Jack. *Loving and Beyond: Science Teaching for the Humanistic Classroom.* Pacific Palisades, CA: Goodyear Publishing Co., 1976.

Baez, Albert V. *Innovations in Science Education—World-wide.* New York: UNESCO, 1976.

Blough, Glenn O., and Schwartz, Julius. *Elementary School Science and How to Teach It.* 7th ed. New York: Holt, Rinehart & Winston, 1984.

Butts, David P., and Hall, Gene E. *Children and Science: The Process of Teaching and Learning.* Englewood Cliffs, NJ: Prentice-Hall, 1975.

DeVito, Alfred, and Krockover, Gerald H. *Creative Sciencing: A Practical Approach* (vol. 1) and *Ideas and Activities* (vol. 2). Boston: Little, Brown and Co., 1980.

Edwards, Clifford H., and Fisher, Robert L. *Teaching Elementary School Science: A Competency-Based Approach.* New York: Praeger, 1977.

Esler, William K., and Esler, Mary K. *Teaching Elementary Science.* Belmont, CA: Wadsworth, 1984.

Friedl, Alfred E. *Teaching Science to Children: An Integrated Approach.* Westminster, MD: Random House, 1986.

Gabel, Dorothy. *Introductory Science Skills.* Prospect Heights, IL: Waveland Press, 1984.

Gega, Peter C. *Science in Elementary Education.* 5th ed. New York: John Wiley & Sons, 1986.

Good, Ronald G. *How Children Learn Science.* New York: Macmillan, 1977.

Haney, Richard E., and Sorenson, Juanita S. *Individually Guided Science.* Reading, MA: Addison-Wesley Publishing Co., 1977.

Harlen, Wynne. *Teaching and Learning Primary Science.* New York: Teachers College Press, 1985.

_____, ed. *Primary Science: Taking The Plunge.* London:Heinemann Educational Books, Ltd., 1986.

Henson, Kenneth T., and Janke, Delmar. *Elementary Science Methods.* New York: McGraw-Hill, 1984.

Hill, Katherine E. *Exploring the Natural World with Young Children.* New York: Harcourt Brace Jovanovich, 1976.

Holt, Bess-Gene. *Science with Young Children.* Washington, DC: National Association for the Education of Young Children, 1977.

Hounshell, Paul B., and Trollinges, Ira R. *Games for the Science Classroom.* Washington, DC: National Science Teachers Association, 1977.

Jacobson, Willard J., and Barry Begman, Abby. *Science for Children.* 2nd ed. Englewood Cliffs, NJ: Prentice-Hall, 1987.

Kauchak, Donald, and Eggen, Paul. *Exploring Science in Elementary Schools.* Chicago: Rand McNally, 1980.

Lerner, Marjorie E. *Readings in Science Education for the Elementary School.* New York: The Macmillan Co., 1985.

Lowery, Lawrence, and Verbeeck, Carol. *Explorations in Physical Science.* Belmont, CA: D. S. Lake Publishers, 1987.

McIntyre, Margaret. *Early Childhood and Science.* Washington, DC: National Science Teachers Association, 1984.

New UNESCO Source Book for Science Teaching. New York: UNESCO, 1975.

Peterson, Rita; Bowyer, Hane; Butts, David; and Bybee, Rodger. *Science and Society: A Sourcebook for Elementary and Junior High School Teachers.* Columbus, OH: Merrill, 1984.

Renner, John W., and Regan, William B. *Teaching Science in the Elementary School.* New York: Harper & Row, Publishers, 1973.

_____, and Stafford, Don G. *Teaching Science in the Elementary School,* 3rd ed. New York: Harper and Row, 1979.

Rowe, Mary Budd. *Teaching Science as Continuous Inquiry,* 2nd ed. New York: McGraw-Hill Book Co., 1978.

_____, and Marek, Edmund A. *The Learning Cycle and Elementary School Science Teaching.* Portsmouth, NH: Heinemann, 1988.

Sprung, Barbara, et al. *What Will Happen If . . . Young Children and the Scientific Mind.* New York: Educational Equity Concepts, Inc., 1986.

Tolman, Marvin N., and Morton, James O. *Science Curriculum Activities Library Series: Physical Science Activities for Grades 2–8, Earth Science Activities for Grades 2–8, Life Science Activities for Grades 2–8.* West Nyack, NY: Parker Publishing Co., Inc., 1986.

Trojcak, Doris. *Science With Children.* New York: McGraw-Hill, 1979.

Victor, Edward. *Science for the Elementary School.* 5th ed. New York: The Macmillan Co., 1980.

Wolfinger, Donna M. *Teaching Science in the Elementary School.* Boston: Little, Brown, 1984.

Science Education Periodicals for Teachers and Children

Children and teachers can keep abreast with the rapid development in research in science and science education by referring to the following periodicals. They provide the most information and are an invaluable supplement to science textbooks.

(T)—teacher oriented
(C)—child oriented

American Biology Teacher. The National Association of Biology Teachers, 19 S. Jackson St., Danville, IL 61832 (Monthly) (T)

American Forests. The American Forestry Association, 919 17th St., N.W., Washington, DC (Monthly) (T)

The American Journal of Physics. American Association of Physics Teachers, 57 E. 55th St., New York, NY 10022 (Monthly) (T)

The Aquarium. Innes Publishing Co., Philadelphia, PA 19107 (Monthly) (C&T)

Audubon Magazine. The National Audubon Society, 1130 Fifth Ave., New York, NY 10028 (Bimonthly) (C&T)

Biology & General Science Digest. W. M. Welch Co., 1515 Sedgwick St., Chicago, IL (Free) (T)

Chemistry. Science Service, 1719 16 St. N.W., Washington, DC 20009 (Monthly) (T)

Cornell Rural School Leaflets. New York State College of Agriculture, Ithaca, NY 14850 (Quarterly) (T)

Current Science and Aviation. American Education Publications, Education Center, Columbus, OH 43216 (Weekly during the school year) (C&T)

Geotimes. American Geological Institute, 1515 Massachusetts Ave, N.W., Washington, DC (Monthly) (T)

Grade Teacher. Educational Publishing Co. Darien, CT 06820 (Monthly Sept.–June) (T)

Journal of Chemical Education. Business and Publication Office, 20th & Northampton Sts., Easton, PA 18042 (Monthly) (T)

Journal of Research in Science Teaching. John Wiley & Sons, 605 Third Ave., New York, NY 10016 (T)

Junior Astronomer. Benjamin Adelman, 4211 Colie Dr., Silver Springs, MD 20906 (C&T)

Junior Natural History. American Museum of Natural History, New York, NY 10024 (Monthly) (C&T)

Monthly Evening Sky Map. Box 213, Clayton, MO 63105 (Monthly) (C&T)

My Weekly Reader. American Education Publications, Education Center, Columbus, OH 43216 (Weekly during the school year)

National Geographic. National Geographic Society, 1146 Sixteenth St., N.W., Washington, DC (Monthly) (C&T)

Natural History. American Museum of Natural History, 79th St. and Central Park West, New York, NY 10024 (Monthly) (C&T)

Nature Magazine. American Nature Association, 1214 15th St., N.W., Washington, DC (Monthly Oct. to May and bimonthly June to Sept.) (C&T)

Our Dumb Animals. Massachusetts Society for the Prevention of Cruelty to Animals, Boston, MA 02115 (Monthly) (C&T)

Outdoors Illustrated. National Audubon Society, 1000 Fifth Ave., New York, NY (Monthly) (C&T)

Physics and Chemistry Digest. W. M. Welch Co., 1515 Sedgwick St., Chicago, IL (Free) (T)

Physics Today. American Institute of Physics, 335 E. 45th St., New York, NY 10017 (Monthly) (T)

Popular Science Monthly. Popular Science Publishing Co., 335 Lexington Ave., New York, NY 10016 (Monthly) (C&T)

Readers Guide to Oceanography. Woods Hole Oceanographic Institute, Woods Hole, MA 02543 (Monthly) (T)

School Science and Mathematics. Central Association Science and Mathematics Teachers, P.O. Box 48, Oak Park, IL 60305 (Monthly 9 times a year) (T)

Science. American Association for the Advancement of Science, 1515 Massachusetts Ave., N.W., Washington, DC 20025 (T)

Science and Children. National Science Teachers Association, Washington, DC 20036 (Monthly 8 times a year) (C&T)

Science Digest. 959 8th Ave., New York, NY 10019 (Monthly) (T)

Science Education. Science Education Inc., C. M. Pruitt, University of Tampa, Tampa, FL 33606 (5 times yearly) (T)

Science Newsletter. Science Service, Inc., 1719 N. Street, N.W., Washington, DC 20036 (Weekly) (T)

Science Teacher. National Science Teachers Association, National Education Association, 1742 Connecticut Ave., N.W., Washington, DC 20036 (Monthly—Sept.–May) (T)

Science World. Scholastic Magazines, Inc., 50 W. 44 St., New York, NY 10036 (T&C)

Scientific American. 415 Madison Ave., New York, NY 10017 (Monthly) (T)

Scientific Monthly. The American Association for the Advancement of Science, 1515 Massachusetts Ave., Washington, DC 20005 (Monthly) (T)

Sky and Telescope. Sky Publishing Corp., Harvard College Observatory. Cambridge, MA 02138 (Monthly) (C&T)

Space Science. Benjamin Adelman, 4211 Colie Dr., Silver Springs, MD 20906 (Monthly—during school year) (Formerly *Junior Astronomer*) (C&T)

3-2-1 Contact. Children's Television Workshop, P.O. Box 2933, Boulder, CO 80322 (10 issues per year) (C&T)

Tomorrow's Scientists. National Science Teachers Association, Washington, DC 20036 (8 issues per year) (T)

UNESCO Courier. The UNESCO Publications Center, 801 3rd Ave., New York, NY 10022 (Monthly) (T)

Weatherwise. American Meteorological Society, 3 Joy St., Boston, MA 02108 (Monthly) (T)

APPENDIX G   Professional Societies for Science Teachers and Supervisors

American Association for the Advancement of Science
1515 Massachusetts Ave., N.W.
Washington, DC 20005

American Association of Physics Teachers
335 E. 45th St.
New York, NY 10017

American Chemical Society
Chemical Education Division
1155 Sixteenth St., N.W.
Washington, DC 20036

American Nature Study Society
(No permanent headquarters.
Current officers listed in *Nature Teaching Tips.*)

Association for Supervision and Curriculum Development
1201 Sixteenth St., N.W.
Washington, DC 20036

Central Association of Science and Mathematics Teachers
(No permanent headquarters.
Current officers listed in *School Science and Mathematics.*)

Council for Elementary Science International
1742 Connecticut Ave., N.W.
Washington, DC 20036

National Association of Biology Teachers
1420 N. Street, N.W.
Washington, DC 20005

National Association for Research in Science Teaching
(No permanent headquarters.)

National Association of Geology Teachers
(No permanent headquarters.
Current officers listed in *Journal of Geological Education.*)

National Science Teachers Association
1742 Connecticut Ave., N.W.
Washington, DC 20036

APPENDIX H   Some Safety Suggestions

1. Do not permit students to handle science supplies, chemicals, or equipment in the classroom until they have been given specific instructions in their use.

2. Instruct students to report immediately to the teacher:

   □ any equipment in the classroom that appears to be in an unusual or improper condition, or

   □ any chemical reactions that appear to be proceeding in an abnormal fashion, or

   □ any personal injury or damage to clothing caused by a science activity, no matter how trivial it may appear.

3. Prevent loose clothing and hair from coming into contact with any science supplies, chemicals, equipment, or sources of heat or flame.

4. Do not allow science materials, such as chemicals, to be transported through hallways by unsupervised students or during a time when students are moving in the hallways.

5. Instruct students in the proper use of sharp instruments such as pins, knives, and scissors before they use such objects.

6. Instruct students never to touch, taste, or inhale unknown chemicals directly.

7. Instruct students never to pour chemicals (reagents) back into stock bottles and never to exchange stoppers or caps on bottles.

8. Warn students of dangers in handling hot glassware or other equipment. Be sure proper devices for handling hot objects are available.

9. Check electrical wiring on science equipment for frayed insulation, exposed wires, and loose connections.

10. Instruct students in the proper use of eye-protection devices before they do activities in which there is a potential risk to eye safety.

11. Give appropriate, specific safety instructions prior to conducting any activity in which there is a potential risk to student safety and provide appropriate reminders during the activity.

12. Instruct students in the location and use of specialized safety equipment such as fire extinguishers, fire blankets, or eye baths when that equipment might be required by the science activity.

13. Instruct students in the proper care and handling of classroom pets, fish, plants, or other live organisms used as part of science activities.

14. Have sufficient lighting to ensure that activities can be conducted safely.

15. Ensure safe access to the facility, equipment, and materials for students with handicapping conditions. Consider:

    □ access to laboratories and equipment, placement of chemicals, distances required for reaching, and height and arrangement of tables.

    □ physical accessibility to equipment needed in cases of emergency.

16. Provide practice sessions for safety procedures.

Source: *Elementary Science Syllabus*, 49.